CISTERCIAN STUDIES SERIES: NUMBER TWO HUNDRED TWENTY-TWO

The Lives of Monastic Reformers, 1: Robert of La Chaise-Dieu and Stephen of Obazine

CISTERCIAN STUDIES SERIES: NUMBER TWO HUNDRED TWENTY-TWO

The Lives of Monastic Reformers, 1: Robert of La Chaise-Dieu and Stephen of Obazine

Introduced and translated by

Hugh Feiss, OSB
Maureen M. O'Brien
Ronald Pepin

Cistercian Publications
www.cistercianpublications.org

LITURGICAL PRESS
Collegeville, Minnesota
www.litpress.org

A Cistercian Publications title published by Liturgical Press

Cistercian Publications
Editorial Offices
Abbey of Gethsemani
3642 Monks Road
Trappist, Kentucky 40051
www.cistercianpublications.org

1 2 3 4 5 6 7 8 9

Library of Congress Cataloging-in-Publication Data

Robert of La Chaise-Dieu and Stephen of Obazine. / introduced and translated by Hugh Feiss, Maureen M. O'Brien, Ronald Pepin.

p. cm. — (The lives of monastic reformers ; 1) (Cistercian studies series ; no. 222)

ISBN 978-0-87907-322-0

1. Robert, de La Chaise-Dieu, Saint, d. 1067. 2. Stephen, of Obazine, Saint, ca. 1085–1159. 3. Benedictines—France—Auvergne—Biography. 4. Christian saints—France—Biography. I. Feiss, Hugh. II. O'Brien, Maureen M. III. Pepin, Ronald E.

BX4700.R54L58 2009
271'.102244—dc22

[B] 2009030364

To Vanessa, Bart, Julia and Andrew

Contents

Foreword ix

Abbreviations xiii

Map xv

The Life of Robert of La Chaise-Dieu 1

Introduction 3

Life 19

The Tripartite Life of Robert, Abbot of La Chaise-Dieu 61

Introduction 63

Life 71

The Life of Stephen of Obazine 103

Introduction 105

Life 129

Foreword

The ferment that brought diversity and vitality to the monastic life in the eleventh and twelfth centuries included not just Cluniacs, Cistercians and Carthusians, but a host of other movements and experiments following both the *Rule of Saint Benedict* and the *Rules* of Saint Augustine. This volume includes English translations of the lives of two of the initiators of new monastic families, Robert of La Chaise-Dieu (d. 1067) and Stephen of Obazine / Coyroux (d. 1159). Both of them are among the surprising number of monastic innovators who were active during the reformation and renaissance of the eleventh and twelfth century in what is today south-central France.

There were similarities in the lives of these two men and connections between their respective monastic families and with other movements of the time. Robert of La Chaise-Dieu was a canon who thought to become a monk at Cluny, but then became a hermit and finally the founder of a new Benedictine congregation. His biographer, Marbod of Rennes, wrote letters to Robert of Arbrissel (c. 1045–1116), the founder of Fontevrault, to one of his followers at Grandmont, and to Vitalis (c. 1050/60–1122), the founder in 1112/13 of Savigny, a reform center on the borders of Normandy, Brittany and Maine. Marbod also composed a life of Walter, who in 1032 introduced the *Rule of St. Augustine* into the community of canons regular at Lesterps in the diocese of Limoges. In 1114, Bishop Gerard of Sales (d. 1120) founded an abbey at Dalon, twenty miles northwest of Tulle; Dalon figures in Stephen of Obazine's life and death. At the time it was affiliated to the Cistercians in 1167,

Dalon had at least five daughter houses. Seguin (1078–1094), the third successor of Robert as abbot of La Chaise-Dieu, was instrumental in founding the Carthusians.

Stephen of Obazine probably received his elementary education at the Benedictine priory of Pleaux. Pleaux belonged to the abbey of Charroux, which was established near Poitiers in Carolingian times. In 989, Charroux was the site of the first 'Peace Council,' which tried to put an end to the pervasive violence of the time by inaugurating 'The Peace of God.' It was reformed in 1014 at the instigation of the duke of Aquitaine. Pleaux, which also was established in Carolingian times, was about fifty miles southwest of Clermont. Stephen then served as a parish priest, before becoming a hermit with his friend and fellow priest, Peter. Others joined them to form a community of hermits. Women joined them at nearby Coyroux. The twin communities of Obazine and Coyroux adopted the *Rule of Saint Benedict*.

The author of the *Life of Stephen of Obazine* had passed his youth in a monastery connected with La Chaise-Dieu, perhaps the priory of La Port-Dieu. After a brief sojourn in the world, this anonymous author, on the advice of Stephen, became a religious at Cîteaux. From there he went to Obazine, where he spent the rest of his life. The monastic congregations of Savigny and Obazine were incorporated into the Cistercian *ordo* at the General Chapter of 1147, the same chapter that refused to incorporate the monastic family of Gilbert of Sempringham.[1]

The *Lives* of these two reformer monks are revealing windows into the monastic ferment of the eleventh and twelfth centuries. They show us how even austere monasteries were deeply intertwined with the world around them. In Robert and Stephen we meet two men who were searching for a way of life that would bring them to God. Neither found what he was looking for in the existing forms of monastic life, and each of them pioneered a new, austere way of life which suited him and attracted many followers,

1. Gilbert (ca. 1083–1189) founded the only new medieval religious order to originate in England. While he was parish priest in Sempringham a group of women who wished to live for Christ in detachment from the world gathered around him. For them he created a monastery that became the motherhouse of a congregation of double monasteries.

so that, somewhat ironically, they became founders of monastic congregations which had much in common with existing monastic institutions.

The geographic and historical overlapping of La Chaise-Dieu and Obazine is mirrored in the overlapping efforts of the authors of these translations of their lives. Ronald Pepin translated the *Life of Stephen of Obazine*, and Hugh Feiss translated the *Life of Robert of La Chaise-Dieu* and the *Tripartite Life*. Hugh Feiss wrote the introduction to the *Life of Stephen of Obazine*; Hugh Feiss and Maureen O'Brien wrote the introductions to the *Life of Robert of Chaise-Dieu* and the *Tripartite Life*. All three have read the entire work and made suggestions that have been incorporated into the translations and introductions. Maureen O'Brien was instrumental in securing some of the sources. She did the final authorial editing before the manuscript was submitted to Fr. Mark Scott,OCSO, the editorial director of Cistercian Publications, who kindly guided us during the final stages of our work. Dr. E. Rozanne Elder originally commissioned the translations, and she also did some editorial work on the manuscript. Our thanks to both Dr. Elder and Fr. Mark.

Abbreviations

AA SS	*Acta sanctorum,* ed. Ioannes Bollandus, et. al. Antwerp, Bruxelles, Paris, 1643–1894.
AA SS OSB	*Acta Sanctorum Ordinis S. Benedicti*, ed. Lucas d'Achery et Iohannes Mabillon, 9 vols., 2nd ed., Venice, 1733–1740.
Abbaye	Bernadette Barrière, *L'abbaye cistercienne d'Obazine en bas-limousin: Les origins–le patrimonie.* Tulle, 1977.
Berman	Constance H. Berman, *Women and Monasticism in Medieval Europe: Sisters and Patrons of the Cistercian Reform*. TEAMS. Kalamazoo: Medieval Institute Publications, 2002.
Cartulaire	*Le cartulaire de l'abbaye cistercienne d'Obazine (xiie–xiiie siècle),* ed. Bernadette Barrière, Publications de l'Institut d'Études du Massif Central, 33. Clermont-Ferrand: Université de Clermont-Ferrand II, 1989.
CS	Cistercian Studies Series
CSEL	Corpus Scriptorum Ecclesiasticorum Latinorum
Degl'Innocenti	Marbodo di Rennes, *Vita beati Roberti*, ed. Antonella Degl'Innocenti. Florence: Giuti, 1995.
Dial.	Gregoire le Grand, *Dialogues*, 3 vols., ed. A. de Vogüé, SCh 251, 260, 265. Paris: Cerf, 1978–1980.
Gaussin	Pierre-Roger Gaussin, *L'abbaye de la Chaise-Dieu (1043–1518)*. Paris: Editions Cujas, 1962.

Genoux	Simon Genoux, *Histoire de l'abbaye de la Chaise-Dieu*. Paris, Bibliothèque Nationale, MS latin 12818.
Jaffé	*Registra pontificum romanorum*, ed. Philipp Jaffé. Graz: Akademsiche Drück-U. Verlaganstalt, 1956.
Liber	Bernard of La Chaise-Dieu, *Liber Tripartitus de miraculis sancti Roberti*, in AA SS OSB, tom. IX, 213–231.
Kardong	Terrence G. Kardong, translator. *Benedict's Rule.* Collegeville: Liturgical Press, 1996.
PG	J.-P. Migne, *Patrologiae cursus completus, series greca*, 162 volumes, Paris, 1857–1866.
PL	J.-P. Migne, *Patrologiae cursus completus, series latina*, 221 volumes, Paris, 1844–1864.
O'Brien	Maureen M. O'Brien, *Far From the Heart: The Social, Political, and Ecclesiastical Milieu of the Early Abbots of La Chaise-Dieu, 1052–1184*. Ph.D. diss., Western Michigan University, 2006.
RB	*Rule of Saint Benedict.*
SCh	Sources chrétiennes series. Paris: Editions du Cerf.
Vie	*Vie de Saint Étienne d'Obazine*, ed. Michel Aubrun, Publications de l'Institut d'Études du Massif Central, 6. Clermont-Ferrand: Institut d'Études du Massif Central, 1970.

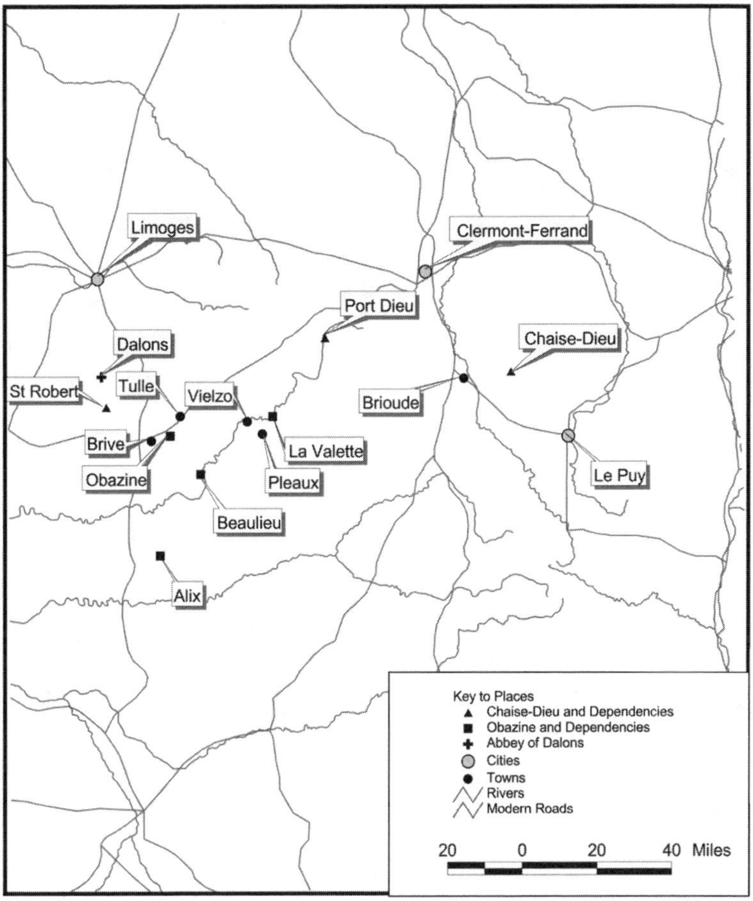
Limoges
Clermont-Ferrand
Port Dieu
Dalons
Chaise-Dieu
Tulle
St Robert
Vielzo
Brioude
Brive
La Valette
Obazine
Pleaux
Le Puy
Beaulieu
Alix
Key to Places
Chaise-Dieu and Dependencies
Obazine and Dependencies
Abbey of Dalons
Cities
Towns
Rivers
Modern Roads
20 0 20 40 Miles

The Life of Robert of La Chaise-Dieu

by

Marbod of Rennes

Introduction to
The Life of Robert of La Chaise-Dieu

FOUNDED IN 1043 by the Auvergnate noble Robert of Turlande, La Chaise-Dieu was declared 'the mirror of monastic perfection in our own times and an example,"[1] by Pope Lucius II in 1144. Pope Lucius was not the first pontiff to recognize this abbey's preeminence. Robert and his successors had all cultivated a close rapport with the bishops of Rome. During the abbacy of Seguin of Escotay (1078–1094), fourth abbot of La Chaise-Dieu, it became one of the foremost monastic centers of its time. This position was bolstered on 27 March, 1080, when Gregory VII issued a bull[2] that confirmed, among other privileges, the free possession of all the monastery's lawful goods and wealth and, in case of disputes, the right of appeal directly to the Holy See. In short, La Chaise-Dieu enjoyed privileges equal to those of the Burgundian abbey of Cluny. From that time onwards, the popes of the eleventh and twelfth centuries considered the Casadéen abbey a center of reform and so entrusted to its control other monasteries and priories. Little by little, with the increase of donations and with the general expansion of La Chaise-Dieu, the original standards of austerity and poverty declined and a powerful organization emerged.

Abbot Seguin, arguably the real founder of the Casadéen congregation, recognized what had happened and realized that he had to act to protect his community's interests. He was torn, however, because he also realized that his community was moving away from

1. Bull of Lucius II, dated 22 May 1144; *Gallia Christiana*, 2:334.

2. *Monumenta pontificia Arverniae*, ed. Chaix de Lavarene (Clermont-Ferrand, 1880) doc. XXVIII, 50–53.

its founder's ideals. Two possible courses of action were open to him: retreat or expansion. Abbot Seguin chose expansion. Despite the decline of the ideal of poverty, the monks strove to maintain a rigorous standard of asceticism and contemplation while at the same time expanding their congregation.

With the rapid success of Seguin's strategy and the expansion of La Chaise-Dieu, it was perhaps inevitable that the monks should start to draw some criticism of Robert's aim to combine contemplation with active service to those outside the monastery. Seguin was resolute in his desire to protect Robert's memory and to reaffirm the authentic monastic spirit of Robert's synthesis of contemplation with the practice of active charity. He evidently decided that the formulation of his monastery's defense required the assistance of a professional. Seguin sought out Marbod of Rennes, a professor of rhetoric, and commissioned a new *Life* of Robert. Behind his request was the desire not only to reassert the sanctity of the abbot-founder, but also to defend his memory. Marbod accepted the task and wrote Robert's *Life* in two books; over half of the second book was devoted to defending the saint.

The Author and His Book

Marbod of Rennes[3]

Marbod of Rennes (*c.* 1035–1123) was an important writer in his time. Born at Angers, he studied at the cathedral school there under Rainald (d. 1075), who was a student of Fulbert of Chartres (ca. 960–1028), an outstanding teacher and bishop. Around 1069, Marbod became master and chancellor, and later archdeacon, of Angers. In 1096 he was named bishop of Rennes. By then he was already a well-known author who had written a book on rhetoric, a lapidary, sacred and secular poetry, and some hagiographical works. He was thus a prolific and versatile writer. After his appointment as bishop, he continued to write, penning *The Book of Ten Chap-*

3. Much of what follows about Marbod is from Marbodo di Rennes, *Vita beati Roberti*, Antonella Degl'Innocenti, ed. (Florence: Giunti, 1995) vii–xxiii.

ters, letters, hagiography, and poetry.[4] His poetic themes include female beauty, love, and nature. In *The Book of Ten Chapters*, he is a moralist, inculcating serene and measured contempt of the world. Somewhat ashamed of some of his youthful writings, he now opts for more dignified meters and content. His reflections make use of pagan moralists who, while congruent with Christianity, are not Christian.

Marbod had been a bishop for almost thirty years when, in his late eighties, he retired to the monastery of Saint-Aubin where he died on 11 September 1123. A few of the letters that Marbod wrote while he was a bishop have survived. These include a letter of counsel to a monk named Agenorid, one to Vitalis of Savigny[5] recommending to him a young woman who wished to consecrate herself to God, and three letters to hermits, of which one is addressed to Robert of Arbrissel, the founder of the monastery and order of Fontevrault, and the other two to Ingilgerius, a disciple of Robert of Arbrissel.[6]

4. Most of the works of Marbod are found in PL 171: 1465–1780. Modern editions include Marbodi, *Liber decem capitulorum*, ed. R. Leotta (Rome, 1984); Marbode of Rennes, *De lapidibus*, ed. J. M. Riddle, tr. C. W. King (Wiesbaden, 1977); A. Degl'Innocenti, *L'opera agiografica di Maboda di Rennes* (Spoleto: Biblioteca di Medioevo Latino, 1990); Marbodi Redonensis Episcopi *Libellus de Ornamentis Verborum*, ed. William Carey (http://www.thelatinlibrary.com/marbodus.html).

5. Vitalis of Savigny was born in Tierceville (Normandy) about 1050/1060. He came from a family of modest means but was well educated. After his ordination to the priesthood, he became chaplain to Count Robert of Mortain. He abandoned his ecclesiastical career in 1095 and became a hermit in the border region between Normandy, Maine, and Brittany, where Robert of Arbrissel, Raoul of la Futaie, and Bernard of Tiron had also gone. Vitalis became the leader of a group of disciples and also travelled about preaching. After seventeen years of this life of solitude and preaching, in 1112/13 he founded the monastery of Savigny, which lay in the same region, adjoining the dioceses of Avranches, Le Mans, and Rennes. He served as abbot of Savigny for the last years of his life. Under his successor, Geoffrey (1122–1138), the congregation expanded. When, in 1147, it was incorporated into the Cistercians, the order had thirty-one abbeys, including more than a dozen in the British Isles, where King Stephen (who had been count of Mortain) was an important patron.

6. Robert of Arbrissel (c. 1045–1116) was born in the diocese of Rennes and educated in Paris. He became an advisor to Bishop Sylvester of Rennes. After Sylvester's death, Robert went to Angers for more schooling. Shortly after that, a conversion led him to the forest of Craon, where he founded a community of

In these last three letters Marbod criticizes three aspects of Robert's community: they accept women into their company (by so doing, Robert has forfeited his status as canon, his stability of place, and his pastoral authority over the brothers); although he is a canon and a priest, he dresses in rough clothes; and, finally, his sermons not only criticize the faults of the laity but also condemn those of the clergy, and so encourage clergy to abandon their posts to follow him. Marbod sees in Robert of Arbrissel a threat to the existing order of the Church. He calls on him to return to a more moderate, less idiosyncratic way of life. In his letters to Ingilgerius, Marbod criticizes the latter's community because it questions the validity of sacraments administered by unworthy priests and because they do not have a proper understanding of the Church's hierarchy. Marbod may not have been adverse to church reform, but his enthusiasm for it was certainly restrained.

While he was still at Angers, Marbod had written a *Life* of a local saint, the bishop Licinius, a contemporary of St. Gregory the Great (d. 604). He was, likewise, probably still in Angers when he wrote his five hagiographical poems. They praise Maurice and his companions in the Theban legion, who were martyred at Martigny near the Lake Geneva about 287; Lawrence, the deacon of Rome, who was martyred about 258; Felix and Adauctus, who were martyred under Diocletian; Thaïs, a Christian who became a prostitute and then converted at the urging of St. Paphnutius; and Maurilius, an early bishop of Angers. The subjects of his other prose lives are Magnobod, another bishop of Angers, the canon Walter of

regular canons. He left there to become a travelling preacher of conversion. His extreme asceticism and spirited preaching won many men and women over to him as followers. At Angers in 1096, he received a preaching mandate from Pope Urban II, who asked him, however, to moderate the tone of his preaching. In 1098 he settled his followers in Fontevrault in a forested area on the borders of the dioceses of Poitiers, Angers, and Tour. He established there two enclosures, one for men and one for women. He considered himself *magister*, not abbot. He turned over the leadership of the community to two noble widows, Hersende de Montsoreau, who was prioress, and Petronilla de Chemille, who was her assistant and successor. He continued his wandering life and founded more communities, also led by women. For the sources for the study of his life and work see, J. Dalarun, et. al., *The Two Lives of Robert of Arbrissel, Founder of Fontevrault. Legends, Writings, and Testimonies* (Turnhout: Brepols, 2006).

Lesterps,[7] and the subject of our study, Robert of La Chaise-Dieu. The last two lives were requested by the communities that each of them founded.

Marbod was not a particularly original hagiographer. He used and elaborated the hagiographical tradition and existing sources about the saints he wrote about. His five hagiographical poems were all based on pre-existing prose works. He seldom abbreviated; instead, he amplified his sources by adding introductions and dialogues. In his introductions, he said that in reworking the existing sources, he wished to eliminate prolixity and obscurity in favor of brevity and simplicity. The clergy of his area seem to have preferred to refurbish the cult of early saints rather than to promote the holiness of near-contemporaries.[8] Walter of Lesterps and Robert of La Chaise-Dieu were the only two recent saints Marbod wrote about.

The Life of Blessed Robert, Abbot[9]

Marbod's most important hagiographical work is his *Life of Blessed Robert, Abbot*. The first of its two books contains a prologue and an account of the life of the saint, which concludes with some miracles worked by Robert when he was still alive. The second book, written some time after the first, includes a prologue, a spirited defense of Robert's interweaving of action and contemplation, and then stories of the miracles he worked after his death. In writing his life of Robert, Marbod made use of a life of the saint no longer extant, whose author is identified in Bernard of La Chaise-Dieu's *The Tripartite Life of Robert, Abbot of La Chaise-Dieu* (1160) as Gerald of Laveine.[10]

7. Walter of Lesterps died in 1070. Marbod's life of Walter can be found in PL 171.1565–1576 and *Acta Sanctorum*, May 11, 2:701–06 (3rd ed. 699–704).

8. As will be seen below, similar sentiments created resistance to *The Life of Saint Stephen of Obazine*. The anonymous author of that life lamented that either because there were fewer saints or fewer authors not many saints' lives were being written at his time. He thought that people tended to prefer older lives of saints because they did not like the style of contemporary works or were suspicious about their purposes and veracity.

9. Degl'Innocenti, xxiii–lxiv.

10. Bernard of La Chaise-Dieu, *Liber tripartitus de miraculis sancti Roberti* in *AA SS OSB*, vol. 9:213–31.

When Robert died in 1067, Marbod was thirty-two years old and about to become master of the school of Angers. It seems unlikely that he would have had an opportunity to meet the subject of his later biography. It should not be surprising, however, that by 1096 he found Robert's life appealing; he would have appreciated Robert of La Chaise-Dieu's discretion and stability compared to Robert of Arbrissel's unruliness and rootlessness. There was a charisma about Robert of Turlande—better known as Robert of La Chaise-Dieu—that resonated with Marbod. In Book One of his *Vita Roberti*, Marbod excelled at giving meaning to Robert's raw experiences: he was educated by the canons of Saint-Julien of Brioude and served as a zealous and beloved priest; he then retired with two companions to a solitary place. There he dedicated himself to prayer, the poor, and teaching. Disciples flocked to the small community and Robert gathered them into a monastery under the *Rule of Saint Benedict*. This monastery, where he died in 1067, became the center of a network of monastic communities. Marbod's endeavor in the first book was one of inspiration, not scrutiny.

The second book of Marbod's *Vita Roberti* is dedicated to *Seguinus*, Seguin of Escotay, who was abbot of La Chaise-Dieu from 1078–1094. His abbacy ended two years before Marbod became a bishop. In Book Two Marbod defends Robert at length against detractors who criticized Robert for forsaking the higher, contemplative life of a hermit to devote himself to the active life of ministry to others outside the cloister, thereby—in their opinion—returning from a higher state to a lower state and so reversing the proper order. We are not told the identity of Robert's detractors. Sometimes Marbod refers to them in the plural; at other times he argues against a singular adversary. Marbod seems to enjoy the controversy; it offers him an occasion to use his rhetorical gifts. His passionate language surrounds the controversy with an aura of importance that it may not in fact have had. Nevertheless, Marbod had some reason to abandon his use of earlier sources and to devote some pages to writing this defense. What was at stake?[11]

Evagrius of Pontus (345–399), followed by John Cassian (*c.* 360–*c.* 435) who carried his ideas to the West, distinguished between two

11. In what follows, we somewhat modify Degl'Innocenti, xxvi–xxxviii.

successive stages in the life of the monk.[12] In the first stage, that of the practical or active life (*bios praktikos*; *vita activa*), the monk worked to achieve *apatheia* or purity of heart by quieting his mind and emotions. Crucial to the active life was the discernment of spirits or discretion, by which one identified good and bad impulses and developed tools to resist and tame the bad ones. Having once achieved inner peace, the monk could then devote himself to the contemplation of God. By the time of Saint Benedict (*c.* 480–550), who was heir to the traditions of eastern monasticism and recommended the works of Cassian,[13] discretion meant not just the capacity to discriminate wisely, but also the result of that capacity, moderation.[14] The *Rule of Saint Benedict* may, however, manifest the impress of the early distinction between the practical and contemplative lives when it provides for those who wish and are ready for a more advanced form of life to pass from the community governed by his 'little rule for beginners' to the single combat of the eremitical life.[15] By contrast, according to the *Life* of Saint Benedict in Book Two of the *Dialogues* attributed to Gregory the Great, Benedict began as a hermit, and then after several unsuccessful attempts, interspersed with times of solitude, founded a community. Over the next few centuries, the active and contemplative 'lives' became more specifically associated in western monasticism with the twofold command of love of God and love of neighbor. The active life came to mean service of neighbor in activities like preaching, pastoring, and the corporal works of mercy. The contemplative life was the life of prayer, including not just solitary contemplation but also, and principally, liturgical prayer. Both distinctions—the earlier one between an ascetical life aimed at self-mastery and a

12. See, for example, Evagrius Ponticus, *The Praktikos and Chapters On Prayers*, translated by John Eudes Bamberger, CS 4 (Spencer-Kalamazoo: Cistercian Publications, 1981); and Bernard McGinn, *The Foundations of Mysticism* (New York: Crossroad, 1991) 149–152; John Cassian, *Conferences*, 1.1–10, translated by Boniface Ramsey, Ancient Christian Writers 57 (New York: Paulist, 1997) 41–48; McGinn, *Foundations*, 219–221.

13. RB 73: 5; Kardong, 603, 608, 612–614.

14. RB 64: 18–19, Kardong, 526-527, 536. See also RB 25: 5; 31: 12; 41: 5, 9; 48: 9; Kardong, 263–264, 333, 335, 389.

15. RB 1: 3–5.

contemplative concentration on God, and the later one between works of service and ministry to others on the one hand and praise and contemplation of God on the other—were and are somewhat artificial. The desert monks who went to uninhabited places to pray were famous for their hospitality.[16] They were sought out as spiritual guides, just as Cassian had sought Evagrius.[17] Gregory the Great, a very major exponent of the second distinction, which interprets the active life as service to others, taught that the life of every Christian necessarily combines action and contemplation. His *Pastoral Rule*[18] influenced Marbod's defense of Robert.[19]

Carolingian monasteries were centers of culture and administration as well as of prayer. Nevertheless, there was a tendency then, as there is still today, to harden the distinction between the 'active life' of service and the call to contemplative prayer. Religious groups used the distinction to identify themselves and distinguish their way of life from other ways. It was widely assumed that contemplation was a higher form of endeavor than the works of the active life, so various groups identified themselves as 'contemplative' in contrast to other groups whom they regarded as more 'active'. There were practical consequences. For one thing, there was prestige attached to being more contemplative. Secondly, there arose a principle that a person could transfer from a lower (more active) state of life to a higher (more contemplative) state. In the burgeoning diversity of forms of monastic life in eleventh and twelfth centuries, this principle had frequent applications, as Christians seeking, as Benedict had, for a setting suited to their aspirations attempted to move from one form of religious life to another.

Many of the founders of new religious communities during the reformation and renaissance of the eleventh and twelfth centuries began their quest for God as hermits. Like Robert and his compan-

16. Lucien Regnault, *The Day-to-Day Life of the Desert Fathers in Fourth-Century Egypt* (Petersham, MA: St. Bede's, 1999) 139–149; William Harmless, *Desert Christians* (New York: Oxford, 2004) 176–177, 204–205, 280–281; Kardong, 431–432.

17. Columba Stewart, *Cassian the Monk*, Oxford Studies in Historical Theology (New York: Oxford, 1998) 11–12.

18. St. Gregory the Great, *Pastoral Care*, tr. Henry Davis (Westminster, MD: Newman, 1950); see especially 1. 5, 29–31.

19. Cuthbert Butler, *Western Mysticism* (New York: Dutton, 1924) 213–241.

ions, and like Stephen of Obazine, they frequently combined their lives of solitude with service to the poor and religious instruction for their neighbors. Some, like Robert of Arbrissel, were not so much dwellers in solitude as wandering preachers with no place to lay their heads. These solitaries, like the desert monks of old and like Saint Benedict of the *Dialogues*, often attracted disciples who wished to live with them. Marbod tells us that, after being prevented from going to Cluny (1.6.2–6), Robert of La Chaise-Dieu deliberately sought two companions to withdraw with him into solitude so that there, committed to God alone, they could follow the canonical hours of the Divine Office (1.6.7–8). When others subsequently joined them, Robert of La Chaise-Dieu, like other charismatic hermits, needed to organize his disciples into a community. He elected to adopt the *Rule of Saint Benedict* and took all the steps necessary to become a community recognized by the local bishop and later by the pope.

Marbod does not tell us who Robert's critics were. Antontella degl'Innocenti, who skilfully edited Marbod's *Life of Robert*, thinks the critics may have been monks of the Cluniac observance. Cluny, founded in 910, was a dominant force in eleventh-century monasticism, and there were Cluniac monasteries in the Auvergne, the area of La Chaise-Dieu. The Cluniac observance gave pride of place to liturgical prayer, which, by their reckoning, was an essential part of the contemplative life. In fact, their monasteries were often centers of charitable activities, and many Cluniacs lived as hermits or in small cells.[20] Some of Robert's Cluniac neighbors may, however, have resented his new version of monastic life which was different from their own and was drawing off both recruits and donations. By the time of Seguin's abbacy, as we have seen, La Chaise-Dieu was an important monastic center with the same papal privileges as Cluny itself and a growing congregation of affiliated monasteries. Perhaps, too, the austere living of Robert's community was

20. Ivan Gobry, *L'Europa di Cluny*, tr. Annamaria Sanfelice di Monteforte (Roma: Città Nuova, 1999) 148, 171, 436; Edwin Mullins, *Cluny: In Search of God's Lost Empire* (New York: Blue Bridge, 2006) 140–141; Colin Morris, *The Papal Monarchy: The Western Church from 1050 to 1250* (New York: Oxford, 1989) 68–69; Irven M. Resnick, "Peter Damian on Cluny, Liturgy and Penance," *Journal of Religious History* 15 (1988): 61–75.

seen as a reproach to the power and affluence of the Cluniacs. Another possibility is that the critics were canons who resented Robert's going over to the *Rule of Saint Benedict*. Their complaint would be that Robert had been a canon, then he became a hermit because he wanted to live for God alone, but now he was a monk doing many of the pastoral and charitable activities he had done as a canon, while claiming to be leading the contemplative life. The opponents' actual criticisms may have been fairly muted without the rhetorical fireworks that Marbod puts in their mouths. Nevertheless, Seguin and the monks of La Chaise-Dieu—who found themselves in the difficult position of administering an order after the initial passion of its founder had worn off—may have felt they needed answering.

That Marbod was no champion of radical innovation in monasticism is evident from his letters to Robert of Arbrissel and Ingilgerius. Nevertheless, by the time Marbod wrote his *Life of Robert of La Chaise-Dieu*, Robert's foundation was an established, recognized, and stable community that Marbod could approve. Marbod's answer to those who criticized Robert for having embraced a contemplative life only to return to an active ministry moves the argument from the level of rigid, abstract distinctions. He argued that the love of neighbor that takes the form of active service when the opportunity that presents itself is not incompatible with the love of God. In fact, one cannot love God without loving one's neighbor. He cites many biblical examples (2.6.2). Jesus and the apostles alternated prayer and acts of service to others. Robert's choices did not therefore represent a new rule of holiness. He was following in the footsteps of the saints of old. Marbod thought that Robert of Arbrissel lacked discretion, the mother of the virtues.[21] Robert of La Chaise-Dieu, by contrast, manifested the discretion that the *Rule of Saint Benedict* required of the abbot and adapted himself to the needs of each of his monks (1.5.4–5). In his discretion, he was like the saints of old (2.6.2). His discretion charted a course embracing both action and contemplation (2.5.9).

21. *Ep* 6; PL 171.1486.

Marbod as Author

Marbod was a former teacher and the author of a book on rhetoric. In the *Life of Robert* he employs many literary commonplaces, especially in the dedications at the beginning of both books. The *Life* has a good many biblical allusions, though Marbod does not quote the Scriptures often. There are a few allusions to classical authors, but they are not frequent or emphasized. He cites the *Mathesis* of Firmicius Maternus,[22] and most of Chapter Six of Book Two parallels Gregory the Great's *Pastoral Rule*, II.5. Marbod does not emphasize the miraculous in Book One; it contains only seven miracles. He recognizes that the faith of the simple (1.20.1) needs to be bolstered by exterior signs (1.19.2). Even wicked people can perform miracles, but only saints achieve constancy or perseverance (1.20.2). He has Robert deliver to his first followers a lengthy exhortation on perseverance, and in subsequent chapters shows how Robert helped them grow in constancy.

The apologetic nature of Book 2 requires Marbod to devote more space to miracles. In their telling, he shows his skills as a storyteller. In a series of short sketches he indicates where the petitioners were from, what the nature of their disease was, the pain it caused the sufferers and their families and friends, and why their recourse to Robert's tomb. Then Marbod tells of their climactic cure and their joy at the favor granted. In each miracle the faith of the petitioners and the merits of Robert combine to bring exorcism and healing.

Marbod, a churchman, emphasized Robert's insertion into the life and structure of the Church. Robert was educated by a community of canons in Brioude and grew up to be a canon and priest there (1.3.1). He was, in fact, a model priest. He went to Rome to seek divine help in discerning God's will for him (1.6.9). He sought an abandoned parochial church as his new home precisely in order to avoid conflicts with existing churches (1.7.5). Robert and his companions obtained the site lawfully from two brothers, both of them men of the church, one an abbot, the other a canon (1.11.2).

22. About 335, Julius Firmicius Maternus wrote a handbook on astrology called the *Mathesis*. He converted to Christianity a decade later and wrote *De errore profanarum religionum*.

Before building a monastery he obtained the permission of Bishop Rencon of Clermont (1.17.5) and then obtained the approval of Henry I of France and Pope Leo IX (1.17.1–3). He became the first abbot of La Chaise-Dieu with the blessing of the bishop (2.18.4). At the end of Book Two, the archbishop of the province of Embrun[23] endorses the miracles worked at Robert's tomb (2.17).

If Robert is shown as being on good terms with the hierarchy of the Church on earth, he is also devoted to the saints in heaven. Robert's veneration of Mary is referred to several times (1.7.6; 1.19.8; 2.9.2–7; 2.17.8). Devotion to the saints (of whom Robert now is one), their power, their protection, and their example are also recurrent themes (1.4.7; 1.10.8; 1.15.2, 6).

Robert of Turlande and La Chaise-Dieu in Context

Since neither cartulary nor customary survives from La Chaise-Dieu, Marbod's *Life* is the primary source of information about Robert and the founding of La Chaise-Dieu. Here we will try to situate Marbod's story in a wider context of Robert's time, the eleventh-century, and his place, the Auvergne.

Robert lived at a time when Europe was expanding economically and demographically. However, the Auvergne where he was born and lived was remote from the control of any king or great lord. Political control there was in the hands of a powerful and fractious local aristocracy. To protect themselves and their flocks, bishops there convoked councils that promoted the 'Peace of God,' which sought to limit the frequency and damage of wars.[24] This was the setting for Marbod's story.

Marbod's says that Robert was born into a noble family in the Upper Auvergne at the beginning of the eleventh-century. When he was about seven or eight years of age, his parents placed him in the care of the canons at Saint-Julien of Brioude. There, according to Marbod, Robert grew in devotion both to God and to the poor.

23. Lantelmus, who was archbishop in 1080.

24. *The Peace of God: Social Violence and Religious Response in France around the Year 1000*, ed. Thomas Head and Richard Landes (Ithaca: Cornell University Press, 1992).

When he decided to go to Cluny to dedicate himself completely to God, the people at Brioude were devastated, so Robert returned there for a time. He then went on a pilgrimage to Rome to pray to the saints for guidance.

Robert subsequently decided to find a solitary place where he could live a regular, canonical life with several like-minded people. He was joined by Stephen, one of his father's former soldiers. Later, Stephen invited a former companion named Dalmatius to join them. Looking for a place where they might settle, Stephen set out to the shrine of Notre-Dame of Le Puy-en-Velay. On the way he found an abandoned church that suited their needs. There the three men settled in a small hut, where they divided up the chores. They ate moderately, and what they did not eat they gave to the poor. Robert preached to the local inhabitants. He drew additional followers from among soldiers and clergy. Then, around 1050, with the consent of Rencon, bishop of Clermont, they built a monastery which they called *Casa Dei* (House of God). They adopted the *Rule of Saint Benedict*, and their undertaking was confirmed by King Henry I of France and Pope Leo IX. According to Marbod, the community grew to three hundred members, and Robert restored almost fifty abandoned churches.

Robert's Family

Marbod suggests that Robert was descended from the house of Aurillac. Gerald of Aurillac (855–909) was the premier saint of the region.[25] However, Marcellin Boudet, through detailed study of regional cartularies from Conches, Saint-Flour, Brioude, and Sauxillanges, determined that on his father's side Robert descended from the Turlande, who were lesser nobility in the Auvergne. The Turlande were benefactors of Conques and Saint-Flour. Robert's uncle was Odilo of Mercoeur (962–1049), who had been a canon at Brioude, and later became abbot of Cluny (994–1049). After Robert entered the canonical community at Brioude, Gerald II of

25. *St. Odo of Cluny. Being the Life of Odo of Cluny by John of Salerno and the Life of St. Gerald of Aurillac by St. Odo*, ed. Gerard Sitwell (New York: Sheed and Ward, 1958).

Turlande gave the community of Saint-Julien a farmhouse to help support his 'brother Robert'.[26]

That Robert initially chose to go to distant Cluny, rather than to Conches or Saint-Flour, with both of which his family had connections, may be explained by his uncle's position as abbot of the great Burgundian abbey. Whether Robert reached Cluny is not known. If he did, he may have found that the demanding liturgical life conflicted with his concern for the poor. In any case, neither Marbod nor Robert criticizes Cluny. Shortly afterward, Robert went on pilgrimage to Italy and may there have come into contact with hermits. In any case, it was to the eremitical life that Robert turned.

Stephen of Chaliers, and probably Dalmatius, Robert's other initial companion, had been in the service of Robert's father and brother. The land the three of them decided to settle on probably belonged to the castle of Beaumont; it was held by two brothers, Rostaing and Albert: the former was a canon of Notre-Dame of Le-Puy-en-Velay, and the latter, abbot of the Benedictine monastery of Saint-Pierre-La-Tour.

At their hermitage, Robert and his companions followed a strict regimen of prayer, fasting, and work. However, Robert never forgot the needs of the poor. He was pulled simultaneously toward solitary prayer and toward helping those in need. Living among people in a backwoods of Christendom, Robert had to forego the strictly contemplative life for a state that was more natural for him, that of the monk-apostle.

In 1046, within six years of his pilgrimage to Rome, Robert began building a monastery. Between 1050 and his death on 17 April 1067, Robert worked tirelessly within the Massif Central, most notably in the diocese of Clermont, to restore old churches and to establish new ones. Many of these churches became small priories, usually with only a couple of monks who took care of one of more churches. Most of these new foundations, including a monastery for women,[27] were located in the high Livradois.

26. Marcellin Boudet, 'Saint Robert de Turland, fondateur de La Chaise-Dieu,' *Bulletin Historique et Scientifique de L'Auvergne* (1906) 68; *Cartulaire de Brioude*, ed. H. Doniol (1863) charter 67.

27. Raoul of Lugeac donated the church of Saint-Andrew of Comps to La Chaise-Dieu around 1050. There, sometime between 1052 and 1058, the wife and

Geoffroy, prior of Vigeois in the Limousin, wrote: 'In this century three men made themselves famous by their holiness: the first was Odilo, abbot of Cluny [Robert's uncle], the other Gautier of Lesterps [in the Limousin], and finally, Robert, who built La Chaise-Dieu.'[28] Robert may have had occasion to meet Geoffroy, because Robert visited the Limousin while establishing La Chaise-Dieu's most significant dependent house, Le Port-Dieu. This foundation was made possible by the donation of Raoul 'Passereau' whose benefactions also underlay the later priories of Chapelle-Saint-Robert in the diocese of Limoges and Saint-Christophe-Cambres in the diocese of Agen.[29] Other magnates supported Robert's foundations in and beyond the Massif Central. At the time of his death, the Casadéen network included seven major priories, six cells, and the monastery for women at Comps. As for smaller priories, there were twenty-seven in the Livradois, five in the remainder of the Auvergne, one in the Limousin, one in Agenais, one in Lyon, and one in Vivaris.[30]

The concentration of the abbey's expansion in the Livradois is not surprising. This was a marginalized area untouched by the economic and political growth, and the stability taking root in the north. There were no great lords in the area. With the help of his uncle, Bishop Rencon, Robert networked well with the secular and ecclesiastical aristocracy of the area. To this area Robert and his monks brought a spiritual renewal through their devotion to the life of prayer, and they devoted themselves not just to prayer, but also to the service of the poor.

Conclusion

Robert of La Chaise-Dieu remains a significant figure in the history of the monastic and ecclesiastical renewal of the eleventh

---

daughter of Gausbert of Breuil entered the community, and Robert established a monastery for women. *Gallia Christiana*, II, Instr. col. 107.

28. Geoffroy de Vigeois, *Chronicon Lemovicense*, in P. Labbe, *Nova bibliotheca manuscriptorum librorum*, vol. 2 (1657) 284.

29. *AA SS* April 3:330. Raoul wrote the life of Adelelmus, after the former abbot of La Chaise-Dieu's death in 1097 (*AA SS* January 3:671).

30. Gaussin, *L'Abbaye*, 115.

century, foremost as the founder of La Chaise-Dieu, but also as a reformer who attempted to integrate the active life (love of neighbor) and the contemplative life (love of God). For the monks of La Chaise-Dieu, some thirty years had passed since their founder's death, and his memory and spiritual legacy were coming under attack just as the abbey was beginning to experience remarkable success. The monks of La Chaise-Dieu were resolute in their desire to protect their founder's memory and to reaffirm the viability of their monastery's spiritual reforms, namely the reconciliation of the active life with the contemplative through the practice of charity. To do this, the monks commissioned Marbod of Rennes to write a new *Vita* for the abbey's founder. The criticisms leveled against Robert's spiritual ideals and choices struck at the core of issues already on Marbod's mind. For Marbod, monastic reform had to be tempered by discretion and stability, both of which he deemed lacking in Robert of Arbrissel, while Robert of La Chaise-Dieu's foundation had become a renowned and stable community on behalf of which the master rhetorician could mount an enthusiastic defense.

The Life of Robert of La Chaise-Dieu

Prologue to the Life of the Blessed Abbot Robert

(1) With the help of God, we are going to try to narrate simply and briefly the life of Blessed Robert which, we think, one of his disciples told truthfully but in a difficult and wordy style.[1] A brief telling will ward off fatigue and a simple style will allow for easy understanding. We do this not because we disdain that author's skill, but because we hold in highest esteem the religion and authority of those who had good reason to enjoin this undertaking.[2] (2) Because the deeds of the saints are put in written form in order to move all readers or hearers to imitate them, the writer must be especially careful that, in so far as possible, what aims at the utility of all exceeds the capacity of none. (3) Otherwise, the whole undertaking will fall short of its proper aim, if those to whom the beauty of the material is inviting are excluded by the useless difficulty of the text, and those who do have access to the text are tired out by excess wordiness. (4) For this reason there is no point to using unusual or foreign language or to extending the discourse with various applications. (5) Nor should one be afraid that the poverty of the style will swallow the richness of the subject matter. Rather, it is to be hoped that in such a noble cause, after every

1. Marbod is referring to a now-lost life of Robert by Gerald of Laveine, who was Robert's disciple and assistant. Bernard of La Chaise-Dieu, who in 1160 wrote *The Tripartite Life of Robert, Abbot of La Chaise-Dieu (Liber tripartitus de miraculis s. Roberti)*, says there that after writing his life of Robert, Gerald went to Rome and informed the pope of Robert's deeds and holiness. Bernard also reports that the pope then granted the monasteries of the order of La Chaise-Dieu the right to celebrate the day of Robert's death as a solemn feast.

2. Marbod is evidently referring to the monks of La Chaise-Dieu. The reference to 'those who enjoin this undertaking,' like the preceding references to *brevitas* and *simplicitas* and other elements in the rest of this prologue and in the prologue to Book 2 (2.1), are literary devices common in medieval Latin literature.

veil has been removed, the dignity of the subject will be its own safeguard, and the limitations of the poor language will be enriched by the greatness of the material. (6) So, we solicit both the good will and the attention of the reader, so that our reward will be all the greater, when with God's help our efforts please so many more. (7) It will benefit those whom it pleases, but it will also please us very much that it benefits them. Thus, our effort becomes the cause of another's progress, and the progress of another the cause of our reward. (8) We will try in every way with all our strength to please, taking care, as we said, to be brief, not in order to remove anything necessary, but to avoid what is unnecessary; taking care to be accessible, not to diminish the dignity of the material, but to promote ease in understanding. (9) If the careful style displeases readers a little, let them at least be pleased by the eager devotion of the writer, the truth of the account, the fresh recollection of the saint's holiness. (10) For while in any circumstance the recollection of deeds done well is pleasing to the faithful, the hearer is deeply moved when contemporary evidence, placed before his eyes, removes suspicion of falsity. Now, because enough has been said about this, let us come to the story.

The Life of Blessed Robert, Confessor of Christ and Abbot

2. (1) Robert was born a free person of Christian parents in the Auvergne. His mother was Ringarde, and his father, Gerald, who, it is thought, was descended from the line of Blessed Gerald of Aurillac.[3] (2) From his earliest days, certain signs showed that he would be a servant of God. It seems right to insert them in this story. (3) When his mother was pregnant with him, she went toward a certain town[4] because she felt his birth was imminent. By God's providence she had to give birth in a solitary place. (4) The child was going to be a lover of solitude. He was going to think that this life, into which he was then born, is a road, not a homeland. (5) He

3. Marbod seems to be mistaken in thinking that Robert was a descendant of Gerald of Aurillac.

4. An eighteenth-century historian of La Chaise-Dieu identified the town as Reilhac, which was about 30 kilometers south of Brioude.

was taken from there with his mother to the town. As was customary, he was given to a certain woman to be nursed. But when she offered him her breast, he refused to taste, not because he did not like the smell of the milk, but because he felt distaste for the sin of the nurse. (6) This was clear immediately when he happily sucked the breasts of his mother, but when the other woman's breast was offered again to tempt him, he rejected it. (7) That woman was a prostitute, and so when he refused her milk he condemned her sin. He did not know what he was condemning, but the power of God works even in those who are unaware.

3. (1) Divine mercy grew with the infant.[5] When he had grown to be a boy he was sent for instruction to the village of Brioude to the church of the martyr Julian. There he became a cleric and found admittance among the canons. Then as time went on, he proceeded through the ecclesiastical orders to the priesthood. (2) Thus, he spent his youth in such a way that he safely evaded the evils with which that tender age is generally affected through a person's own wickedness or someone else's. From the beginning he meditated on innocence and filled the pure vessel[6] of his heart with the fresh perfume of virtues. Forestalled by God's sweet blessings,[7] he could admit no bitter vices. (3) Already full of faith[8] in eternal realities and despising all temporal things, he put all his hope in the Lord.[9] Although he was still small, he loved the Lord with no small affection. He often spent whole nights weeping and keeping vigil in church. Those who found him were surprised that the watchmen were unaware of him. (4) He prayed and read very often, so that alternately he commended God to himself and himself to God.[10] (5) He pursued humility and obedience, so that he dealt with men in such a way that he incurred no offense against God. (6) He attended the poor and afflicted with heartfelt mercy. He

5. This phrase is an adaptation of Jb 31:18: 'for from my infancy, mercy grew with me. . . .'

6. Prv 25:4.

7. Ps 20:4. (Psalms are cited according to the Vulgate numbering.)

8. Acts 6:5; 11:24.

9. Ps 72:28; 77:7.

10. On this theme see Jean Leclercq, *"Etudes sur le vocabulaire monastique du moyen âge," Studia Anselmiana* 48 (Rome: 1961): 131–32.

helped those whom he could and showed compassion to all. (7) More than once he touched and washed with his own hands[11] the bodies of the sick that were full of sores that filled others with repugnance. He calmly accepted exterior uncleanliness while he kept his mind on interior gain. As a result, it was believed that by the loving touch of his hands illness could be banished.

4. (1) This boyhood was followed by a young adulthood, when he used his increased means and strength in the service of God. During that passionate time of life many people's chastity suffers enticing shipwrecks, as their minds are buffeted by the wind of new impulses. He wisely had anticipated this and imbibed such a love of chastity that no unclean thought could trouble his heart nurtured with virtue. (3) He added virtue to virtue and indefatigably constructed a tower[12] whose foundations he had established in his boyhood. (4) The trees that he had planted in his heart grew and bore fruit unto eternal life.[13] From day to day divine grace shone more clearly in him, and now many were moved by his word and example[14] to live better lives. (5) He fasted willingly and prayed, and as much as he could he distributed open-handedly to the poor. He built an almshouse in the village so that by ministering to the sick there he could exercise vigorously as if in a training gym for sanctity. (6) It is certain that after he had given everything to the poor, he often added his cape and cloak for them to use. He clearly saw Christ in the poor, and thinking little of his own nakedness, he strove to cover theirs. (7) In the same way, Martin once divided his cloak with a poor person and so deserved to see Christ covered with the same garment. Although I dare not compare Robert with Martin, I do not hesitate to compare the one event to the other.[15]

11. 1 Jn 1:1.

12. Is 5:2; Mk 12:1.

13. Mk 4:20.

14. 'Word' and 'example' are found conjoined at 1.10(3) and 1.18(7) also. See Caroline Walker Bynum, *Docere verbo et exemplo: An Aspect of Twelfth-Century Spirituality*, Harvard Theological Studies 31 (Missoula: Scholars Press, 1979).

15. Supicius Severus, *Life of Saint Martin*, in *The Western Fathers*, F. R. Hoare, tr. (New York: Sheed and Ward, 1954) 14–15.

5. (1) Meanwhile, he exercised his priesthood vigorously. He attended the regular hours in the church and offered sacrifices to God frequently for the salvation of the Christian people. He embraced that whole people in magnanimous love as though they were a single individual. (2) He invited sinners to penitence, sometimes striking them with fear of punishments, and at other times presenting them with joyful rewards. He taught that no one, if he were contrite and genuinely converted, should despair of pardon. (3) Above all he promised the support of his prayers and in this way he kept winning over many. When his voice was silent, his life spoke, although when he spoke, he was silent about his life. For although he displayed the form of right living in himself, he did not in any way put himself on display. (4) His moral integrity was evident on his countenance, and his bearing and clothing bespoke the modesty of his mind. He was friendly to everyone, even though he offered to each the feeling proper to his or her state in life, age and manner of life. (5) With this discretion,[16] he prudently provided for the salvation of all, so that, as if nearer and more familiar to all, he might persuade them, since he had transformed the personalities of each individual into his own. Although he was ahead of all in the worthiness of his life, he wanted himself thought of as inferior to all. (6) In the midst of all this he was on fire with love of contemplation. He always wished to add better to good, and best to better. He had had a passing taste of how sweet the Lord is[17] and with every fiber of his heart he wished to occupy himself with God alone,[18] so that he might drink deeply from a sweetness he had only just tasted.

6. (1) Therefore, he decided to move to a new place and, having left everything, follow Christ. (2) Moved by its fame for holiness and discipline, he chose the monastery of Cluny. (3) He undertook the journey accompanied by only one companion, who shared his

16. Discretion was a very important idea in the monastic tradition. It was used with reference to 'discernment of spirits,' discernment between good and evil, and moderation, the outcome of such discernment. See A. Cabassut, *Dictionnaire de Spiritualité* (Paris: 1937–1995) 3:1311–1330. Marbod uses the term again in 2.6(2).

17. Ps 33:9.

18. *Vacare soli Dei* was used to describe a life devoted to prayer, and hence the calling of a hermit.

journey, but not his plans. He did so because he feared that, as in fact happened, he would be restrained from what he was undertaking if he departed openly. (4) For who would want to lose one who had been a protector of all and had often supplied the needs of so many: (5) sight for the blind, a healthy foot for the lame, clothes for the naked, food for the hungry, a man and father for orphans and widows, an open door for the confined, a roof for pilgrims, medicine for the sick, burial for the dead?[19] (6) When it was learned that he was leaving secretly (his family, surprised that their lord was leaving alone and silently, had quickly disclosed the fact), everybody, concerned about the public well-being, immediately went after the fugitive, took hold of him, and led him back. (7) The holy man was embarrassed. He was not more sorry that his plan had been impeded than that it had been revealed. His mental distress made him sick. (8) When he had begun to get better, he understood that he had been recalled from the place he intended to go by the will of God, because he might be able to do more good elsewhere. So he experimented to see if he could achieve what he wanted among his own people. (9) But when no one of his acquaintances acceded to his salutary admonitions, he set out for Rome, irrevocably committed to his purpose. He wanted the intercession of the apostles asking God to grant him the counsel he desired. (10) What he wanted was this, that, removed from the company of people, he might be able to build a monastery in a solitary place, where professed to God alone, he could live the canonical life in the religious habit with two or three others. (11) Having returned from Rome, he awaited steadfast in faith for what he had asked.[20] He was delayed for a while, and I think that the delay increased his desire.

7. (1) Meanwhile, a soldier, who had been moved to compunction by God's inspiration, came to the man of God to seek his counsel about how, by worthy satisfaction, he could eliminate the burden of his sins, which was tormenting his conscience. There was nothing so arduous that he would not undergo it in order to recover the grace of God. (2) He received from the saint the advice to leave everything and transfer to the army of Christ. He told the saint that he would

19. This list of good works draws on Tb 1:20, Is 61:1 and Mt 25:35-36.
20. Jas 1:6.

do that most willingly, if he could do it with him. At that the man full of God[21] understood that this was the man destined by God to be his companion and the servant of his will.[22] (3) He was very happy and opened to him the whole of his secret desire. He promised to be his companion and made a pact with him. Then he sent the man away happy, giving him the task of seeking a place suitable for their enterprise and if possible admitting a third companion. (4) He indicated a suitable place would be a small, parochial church in an isolated place, even if deserted and abandoned, where they could acquire food by the labor of their hands or from the roots of plants. I think he wanted a parochial church, because if they built a new oratory in an unfamiliar place, they might seem to do injury to existing establishments. (5) It would not be right that what they aimed to acquire solely for the sake of heavenly reward be shadowed by any hint of earthly greed. (6) The soldier was now full of faith and perseverance. So that God's mercy might prosper his undertaking, he decided to go to the shrine of the Blessed Virgin at Le Puy.[23] He knew that nothing would be more helpful to him in attaining his petition than the intercession of Mary with her Son. (7) While he was still hurrying on his way there, God saw to it that he found what he sought, an old church surrounded by a vast solitude which fulfilled all his requirements.[24] (8) His holy desire had been heard before his prayers, and through the merits of the saint the desired effect preceded the servant's petition. (9) He continued on toward his destination, so that he could offer thanks instead of petitions. However, he also added petitions that by divine mercy God might complete what God had begun in them. He returned to his teacher and reported what he had done. He described the solitude of the

21. The expression 'man (full) of God' derives from the biblical books of Kings and was used of Saint Martin and Saint Benedict in the influential biographies of the two saints by Sulpicius Serverus and Gregory the Great respectively. Marbod uses it often of Robert in book 1.7(1), 8(4), 15(11), 16(1).

22. Later [1.11(4)] Marbod will identify this first disciple as Stephen.

23. Le Puy-en-Velay is located in the Auvergne about one hundred km from Clermont-Ferrand. There the cathedral of Notre-Dame possessed some relics of the Blessed Virgin and was a pilgrimage site.

24. This church, the site of the future monastery of La Chaise-Dieu, was located in the forest of Livradois near the headwaters of two streams, the Dore and the Senouire. It is about forty km from Brioude and Le Puy.

place and other inconveniences convenient for living austerely. The man of God was pleased. He gave thanks and urged the brother to accomplish his remaining tasks diligently and vigorously.

8. (1) One of their aims was still unfulfilled. They wished to find a third companion for their great undertaking. For a third person serves as a link of charity between two, and it seemed that united in this number they would more fittingly serve God, triune and one. (2) In a short time what was missing presented itself, as divine grace furthered the effort of the soldier. When he returned to his people and, it is said, thought about acquiring a companion, he made no effort to keep from his countenance the changed disposition of his mind. He was asked by a certain soldier who was an acquaintance of his why he seemed unusually preoccupied. He said: 'I would tell you if I knew you would faithfully keep the secret.' (3) The man quickly gave the assurance that was asked of him, and then listened to what he had asked to hear. While he was listening, he conceived a great love of virtue. Moved by the example of his comrade, he felt a great desire to be included in a project of such great perfection. (4) Then he asked with humble entreaties that he, a sinner, be introduced to the man of God and that he not be considered unworthy of sharing in their laudable undertaking. (5) He offered himself not as a colleague, but as a servant. He promised on his faith never to depart from the course that he had professed. Thus the first soldier, having gained a second, returned rejoicing with his companion to his teacher.

9. (1) Robert rejoiced over the spiritual success and commended to God in prayer the fruits of the seeds that he had sown.[25] He addressed the recruits to the divine army:[26] 'My sons, I am very happy with your eager devotion. Conscious of my own weakness, I wish to have you as comrades and supporters on the way of God, which He tells us is very narrow and difficult.[27] (2) However, I know we should be very fearful lest we rashly enlist in this most demanding army, thinking only of the rewards. (3) What is praiseworthy is not

25. Mk 4:1–20.

26. Marbod favors the traditional metaphor which sees the monastic calling as service in the army of Christ: 1.9(2), 10(2), 11(8-14).

27. Mt 7:14.

to make a good beginning, but to finish. The former sometimes happens by impulse; the latter always happens because of virtue. For this reason, not to propose the highest summits is allowed because of human frailty, but to fail at what one has promised is condemnable and a diabolical transgression. (4) Keep a diligent watch, therefore, and again and again ponder interiorly, lest, while you strive for the summit of perfection, you become for yourselves the cause of greater damnation, which God forbid. As far as possible, think about all the good things you aim to do without, and their opposites, the many and great injuries to which you expose yourselves by taking leave of the world. Hunger, thirst, cold, nakedness, sleepless watches, work, contempt, slander—whatever people flee, you seek. Be careful lest when these things come along you flee yourselves.' (7) He said such things not to deter them from their salutary undertaking, but to forearm them against whatever was to come and so to make them strong enough to bear those things because they would be prepared for any kind of temptation.

10. (1) For their part, they were not budged from their proposal; rather they were all the more stirred by the words of the holy man. They promised, with the help of Christ, not to be broken by any adversities, nor to be moved by the recollection of any pleasures. (2) It sufficed for them that they had had enough experience of the difficult paths of sin, and they realized that they had worn themselves out to no purpose. Now, they wished to fight for Christ. One cannot serve him without a reward, since not to serve sin is itself a great reward. (3) Moreover, God had fully provided for their weakness and ignorance by giving them a teacher whose word could instruct them and whose example could strengthen them. (4) He knew how to suggest what should be done and to do the things suggested. So they were going to stay with him and serve him devoutly in all things. (5) In response, the holy man, attributing everything to God and nothing to himself, said: 'God is able to make firm the wavering and instruct the ignorant. (6) In no way should those whom the supreme power protects fear the assaults of an opposing force. Without doubt God protects you who serve God, for God is accustomed to protect those who do not serve so that they may come to serve him. (7) So, if you have decided to cling firmly to God, you will have me as comrade and servant, who will,

I hope, be both useful and devoted. (8) Beware of the inconstancy of the human mind. Now, if it is not a burden, go to the church to beg God with the intercession of the martyr Julian[28] that he may provide whatever will be most useful.' They went into the church; they prostrated in prayer; and they returned more steadfast.

11. (1) He had examined their faith sufficiently, and the time had come to depart. Only this remained: that the place granted them by God would also be handed over by the earthly lords. (2) Robert took one of the two and went to Le Puy. There stayed two noble brothers. Both of them were canons, and one was an abbot. One's name was Albert; the other's was Rostagnus.[29] The abbot Albert was later a monk and disciple of the blessed man himself. (3) From them he easily obtained what he asked, for they necessarily knew of his reputation for sanctity because the places were close together. (4) When everything had been prepared in the way decided, on the appointed day he sought the hermitage with two disciples, of whom the first was called Stephen, the other Dalmatius.[30] (5) They found thorns and brambles, horror and solitude,[31] in short, a place lacking in all good things, except that it was good for them to lack all good things. (6) They believed that the further they were from men, the closer they were to God, and the more temporal goods they lacked, the more eternal goods they would receive. (7) The coarseness of their neighbors increased the difficulties of the place; the savagery of their behavior resembled that of wild beasts. They abused and threatened God's servants, whom they should have supported. They thought them mad to have begun, without resources, to live in a sterile place that they could not bear even if they had brought supplies with them. (8) It is no wonder that they who had undertaken

28. The church of Brioude was dedicated to St. Julian and contained his tomb. According to tradition, he was the tribune of a Roman legion that converted to the faith and took refuge at Brioude, where they were martyred in 304.

29. Rostagnus was a canon of Le Puy and Albert was abbot of Saint-Pierre-la-Tour.

30. According to the tradition at La Chaise-Dieu they arrived at the site on December 28, 1043.

31. See John Cassian, *Conferences* 24.2, E. Pichery, ed., *SCh* 64 (Paris: Cerf, 1959) 3:173; trans. Boniface Ramsey, *Conferences*, Ancient Christian Writers 57 (New York: Newman, 1997) 827.

a struggle against the devil were now attacked by his members. (9) I think that how many troubles they suffered and bore may be told better by silence than speaking. For silence can indicate much or all, when words express only a part. (10) However, they resisted by suffering adversities, and they conquered those attacking them by not fighting back. (11) The third fortified the minds of the other two, as a veteran in an army strengthens new recruits, teaching them that if they overcame the first attacks of the enemy, they would conquer later ones more easily. For, as fear grows in the conquered, so the confidence of the victor is increased. (12) Thus he not only made them victors in the present, but also made them more ready for future combat. (13) He told them that if later a more vehement temptation oppressed them, it would be all the more base if those who conquered in the first engagement fell in the second, for the battles they had experienced had made them more astute and their victories had made them stronger. (14) In this way the man expert in the arms of the spirit strengthened the less astute and weaker spirits of his comrades-in-arms. Like an artisan, he developed in them patience in toil by using the hope of later victories to win earlier battles and the memory of battles won to gain subsequent victories. (15) But he also instructed them from sacred authorities that 'they should choose rather to be afflicted' a little 'with the people of God than to have the pleasure of temporal sin,'[32] for eternal damnation follows the latter, and eternal happiness the former. (16) So they kept their eyes on the reward, gazing on Jesus, the author and perfecter of the faith, who for the sake of the joy that lay ahead bore the cross, despising its shame.[33] (17) With these and similar measures he restored the sometimes flagging spirits of his companions, while he was not worn down by the common work nor his proper task of brotherly solicitude. After a short time, he had rendered them so constant and perfect, that they not only suffered all sorts of vexations happily, but also prayed for their persecutors.

12. (1) They made a little hut next to the church; it was of branches and leaves, I believe. They divided the household tasks among them, so that they worked with their hands to provide food, while he spent

32. Heb 11:25.
33. Heb 12:2.

his time in reading and prayers. (2) They labored by using their hands; he worked by genuflecting often. Their physical exertion produced sweat; his compunction of heart bathed him in tears. Their breaks from work restored them from fatigue; his reading refreshed him from languor. (3) What each did profited all, but what the third worked profited more than the other two. He brought God to them through teaching based on reading; he brought them to God through insistent prayer. Thus, since he sowed his spiritual seeds in them, it was not so great a matter whether he reaped their physical sowing.[34] (4) Meanwhile, in the oratory that they had restored, they offered common prayers at specified hours of the day and night. (5) They took the sparse and dry food together with thanksgiving; the greater part of it was kept for the poor and pilgrims,[35] in case any should turn aside to the place. (6) It was their custom that if they had anything, they gave it to anyone who asked.[36] Thus, the blessed man instructed his comrades to give increasingly and completely, without thinking about the morrow.[37]

13. (1) One day, when the brothers had gone out to work while he stayed alone in the church, where it was his custom to offer daily and unceasing tears and prayers, he heard the voice of someone asking alms. (2) He rose quickly, went to the hut, and gave all that he found. All that was there was a piece of bread that was left over from yesterday's supper. However, it would have sufficed for another meal for all three of them, because their eating was not much different from fasting. (3) When they came back from work, there was no food. Dalmatius bore this with ill grace. The holy man quickly checked his complaining by citing the words of Christ: 'do not be concerned about yourselves, saying what will we eat or what will we drink. For your Father knows that you need these things'.[38] (4) What happened immediately confirmed this saying, and a miracle revealed the doubting brother's lack of perfection. (5) Abbot Albert, who, as was noted above, had let them have the place, knew that the infertility of their

34. 1 Cor 9:11.
35. Lv 19:10; 23:22.
36. Lk 6:30.
37. Mt 6:34.
38. Lk 12:22 and Mt 6:31.

solitary place was an added burden upon the voluntary poverty of the holy men. He sent to them with his blessing three pack animals loaded with bread and wine. (6) The messengers presented two of them to the blessed man, but said that the third had died during the journey in a very peculiar way. It was no less strong than the other two, and previously it had not given any signs of weakness. (7) At this, the holy man gave thanks. Because his way of speaking was always plain and edifying, he turned to the brothers with a cheerful countenance and said: 'Let our beloved brother, Dalmatius, learn never again to hesitate in his faith in Christ. Our faith is recompensed by this present reward, while he finds that for his murmuring he has been inflicted with a small but clear punishment that is sufficient for his correction. (8) Let him know that his part has remained behind. It has not been taken away, but delayed. So that he will not waver in his faith, what is lacking will be restored. What a great thing is faith that even beasts of burden sense its absence!'

14. (1) Making frequent use of these and similar talks, he not only instructed his comrades, but also softened the earlier ferocity of the inhabitants, so that gradually eliminating their brutish habits, he was making men out of wild beasts. This was a greater miracle than if, as fables tell, human bodies were transformed into wild animals. (2) He raised up the eyes of their minds to recognize the creator of all. Enumerating the labors and dangers of earthly life, he easily convinced them that apart from the creator there is no peace for souls. (3) Thus, it happened that some soldiers abandoned their military life to become members in his holy band and dedicated themselves to serve Christ there in perpetuity. Moreover, some of the clerical order, instructed by his teaching, preferred the solitary and poor life to the comforts of their home. (4) As the number of his disciples grew so did their religious observance, which was elicited not only by the strict discipline, but also by the perfection of charity. (5) To what was required of all communally, each added something on his own.[39] There occurred in that poor little flock of Christ a marvelous exchange of holiness, since each added to his own virtues whatever he saw was imitable in another. (6) Since

39. RB 49.5-6; Kardong, 402.

poverty sufficed for those who for the sake of Christ had nothing, only lack of holiness bothered them. Crass love of money usually causes the greedy to place little value on whatever they have acquired, since they long only for the things they wish to acquire. Here, however, there was at work a most noble love of justice and, if one may speak that way, a religious avarice. (7) The flag-bearer and teacher of great perfection guided them in this quest, for he forgot the things that were left behind and stretched toward the things ahead, and so followed the way to his destination as the Apostle had done,[40] until he reached his goal. His disciples' pursuit was sustained by his example.

15. (1) The fame of their holy way of life moved their neighbors near and far to praise God. (2) To the merit of their lives was joined such a power of miracles that no one in those places doubted that the holy man had clearly merited from God the grace of healing.[41] To safeguard his humility, he so exercised his healing ministry for those who asked in faith that he attributed God's benefits not to his own merits but to those of the holy martyrs, Agricola and Vitalis, in whose church he was serving.[42] (3) However, the demons were not silent about his merits when they were driven from the bodies of possessed people at his command. (4) Through the faith of her friends, a demoniac woman, the wife of a peasant, was brought to him for healing. (5) She had barely entered the church where the saint was praying, when the enemy who possessed her rebelled and began to hurl threats and insults at him from his horrible sounding mouth: 'Robert, Robert of La Chaise-Dieu, why do you, a stranger, try to force us from our residence? (6) Instead we will shortly disturb you and yours, adding a fire to the unbearable torments that they suffer here. Nor will your colleagues, Agricola of Bologna, Symphorian of Autun, Marcel of Die, Privatus of Mende, and Julian of Brioude, whom you are preparing to enlist to fight against us, be of any use to you.' (7) The devil foresaw that a place called by the new name of La Chaise-Dieu would be founded there and that

40. Phil 3:13-14.

41. 1 Cor 12:28.

42. The church that Robert and his companions restored was dedicated to the Bolognese martyrs, Agricola and Vitalis.

the relics of the saints whose names he recited would be brought there. While he unwillingly prophesied future good things, he lied about the harmful things that he wanted to happen. (8) The only thing he predicted willingly about the future was that the site was going to be burned up in a fire. Even in this the good he did by his prediction outweighed the harm he later did by causing it. By his prediction, he fortified the patience of the saints; by afflicting them, he tested their patience.[43] (9) Meanwhile, the woman, wildly running and jumping through the church, suddenly turned toward the altar as though she were going to put her hand on the sacred objects. (10) The holy man, saddened by the unhappy woman's madness, prayed for a while, then proceeded toward her, struck her lightly with the rod he was holding, and reproved her severely. Then he turned to the demon and said: 'In the name of the Lord, I command you, get out, give glory to God, and once you are expelled never again come back'. (11) The woman fell down when he said this, and exhausted at the enemy's departure she immediately fell asleep. She woke up after a little while with her mind healthy but her body still fatigued. She asked that some bread be brought to her. She eagerly took the bread blessed by the man of God, and thus healed she returned home. She lived for a long time afterward and was a model of lively virtue.

16. (1) On another occasion, a peasant named Constantius, who dwelt near St. Victor,[44] was so filled with a demon that, sparing no one, he attacked himself with his teeth. He proclaimed openly that the only thing he feared was the presence of the man of God. His relations wrapped his whole body with chains and transported him like a dead man on a bier. They presented him, terrified and unwilling, to the saint. (2) He prayed over him, raised his eyes and mind to heaven, and adjured the enemy in God's name, ordering him to depart. (3) The adversarial spirits knew the power of his words and that it was impossible to disobey what he had ordered. (4) So, at the first sound of his commanding voice, the frightened adversary

43. Rv 13:10.

44. Marbod may be referring to St-Victor-sur-Arlanc, which lay a few kilometers from La Chaise-Dieu.

was compelled to leave the captive vessel,[45] and so he did the only thing he could and left him tired and disturbed. (5) The man was restored after a little while. When he had taken the blessed bread that the saint brought him, he went home healthy and happy.

17. (1) The spreading fame of these events brought forth many from their homes. A mixed crowd of noble and ordinary people came together to see the new example of ancient virtue. (2) He received them very courteously and kindly. Although in that solitary place he did not have enough bodily food for such crowds, he put before all of them the word of God. In this way it was as if he nourished the souls of believers with bread and fishes and various delicious dishes. (3) All were amazed at the modesty of his countenance and the spiritual eloquence of his speech that was accommodated to each person. With them he changed the minds of some, so that they immediately spurned the pleasures of the present life and burned with love for nothing except future happiness. (4) When many pledged to serve Christ only under his leadership, and the multitude of those asking to do so was large, both the desolation of the place and the variety of interests seemed to make it impossible for so many to dwell there together. Out of necessity, a new plan was formulated, for even difficulties serve divine providence. A monastery was built there, in which, as in the Lord's sheepfold, those whom God had gathered could dwell with one mind under the discipline of a monastic rule.[46] The devotion of many faithful paved the way for building it; they eagerly and voluntarily provided estates and money for this purpose. (5) The servant of God saw this divinely prepared opportunity for so much good; he rightly knew that it would be at the peril of his soul if out of concern for his own quiet he turned his back on the salvation of so many. Taking counsel on the matter with his brothers, and with the advice and consent of Rencon, of happy memory, the Bishop of Auvergne,[47] he set himself to this laborious effort and, to everyone's great joy and with the support of all, began to build

45. 1 Mc 2:9.

46. According to *The Tripartite Life*, the community now accepted the *Rule of Saint Benedict*.

47. Again according to *The Tripartite Life*, Rencon, bishop of Clermont (1028–1052), was Robert's uncle.

a monastery near the place where he had first dwelt. (6) Previously he had desired a solitary life with few companions and commanded that no money or possessions be accepted from anyone. However, when he had received these things, and ever more extensive gifts from God's abounding generosity followed, he did not want to seem ungrateful for the heavenly benefactions. With the offerings that the faithful brought either spontaneously or at his exhortation, he successfully completed the work he had begun.[48]

18. (1) At that time, Henry was the ruler of France, and Leo IX occupied the Apostolic See.[49] (2) The bishop mentioned above went to the pope, and the holy man to the king of France. Each sought to enhance the stability of the new foundation with the sanction of higher authority and fitting privileges. (3) Each obtained what he sought. The king not only confirmed the grant of whatever had been given to the monastery or would be conferred in the future, but also honored La Chaise-Dieu and the holy man with royal gifts. The pope, who had heard of the man of God's reputation for holiness, confirmed his project with apostolic decrees and commanded him, despite his unwillingness and resistance, to preside over his brothers.[50] (4) So it happened, when the monastery had been dedicated with great rejoicing by all, the blessed man, compelled by the requests of his brothers and the authority of his bishop, accepted with a blessing the monastic habit and the role of superior. (5) Otherwise, he thought it was safer to be ruled than to rule, and to give an account of his own life only, rather than of the lives of many.[51] By the grace of God, he was capable of either, since in neither would he have presumed on his own strength. (6) After he accepted the task of ruling, the spiritual results of his labor testified to the extent of the ready vigilance he showed toward those subject to him, while frequent signs manifested how the simplicity of his mind shown before God. (7) He gained the souls of a large multitude of secular people by the

48. The monastery's construction probably was completed about 1050.

49. Henry I (1031–1060) and Leo IX (1049–1054).

50. On September 20, 1052, at Vitry-aux-Loges, Henry issued a charter of protection for La Chaise-Dieu. Pope Leo IX issued a charter on May 2, 1052, assuring La Chaise-Dieu of his protection.

51. See Rom 14:12 and RB 2.34; 64.7.

word of his preaching, the example of his life, and the intercession of his prayers. From among them he gained about three hundred monks. He restored about fifty churches to the service of God after they had long lain desolate. Most of all, he transmitted his own form of simplicity and charity to his disciples, and he left to the place that he had founded a most precious gift, the legacy of his holiness.

19. (1) We will tell about a few of his miracles, with that faith with which those who said they saw them handed them on to us. For the rest, his whole life on earth was a kind of great miracle. (2) If some people are more easily taken with exterior signs, not because such signs are great, but because such people are less endowed and usually more moved to wonder through the physical senses, there is no dearth of the kind of material which will serve usefully for such people. (3) A soldier named Bernard from Montgacon[52] had been suffering continually for three years from a kidney ailment which doctors call nefritis. Robert cured him of his bodily ailment by sprinkling holy water on him and praying over him. Later, when the soldier had become a monk, Robert also dedicated him to the army of Christ. (4) There was another man who suffered from dropsy (a disease that involves internal accumulation of water because of unhealthy blood); because the natural sources of his bodily heat were flooded, he was liable to be suddenly overwhelmed by the quantity of superfluous liquid. Robert restored him to health by the laying on of his sacred hands. (5) He cured by the same power, through the imposition of his hand combined with prayer, a demoniac boy, who was unable to walk or speak. He was the son of a certain farmer who is said to have lived below Chaumont.[53] In doing so he worked a threefold miracle in the same person, restoring speech to one who was mute, the capacity to walk to a cripple, freedom to a captive. (6) Another time a demoniac was brought to him, to whom he offered blessed bread at the door of the church; the devil, unable to bear such power of faith, departed from the man with a horrible shriek and unbearable odor and left him healthy. (7) A woman, who had lost all use of her limbs, attended the sacred mysteries while he

52. Montgacon was near the river Allier, about 20 kilometers north of Clermont-Ferrand.

53. Probably Chaumont-le-Bourg, 20 kilometers north of La Chaise-Dieu.

celebrated mass. She was carried there not by her own feet, but by the hands of others. She was quickly restored to health when with faith she listened to his voice proclaiming to the people the praises of [Mary], the ever virgin on her feast of the Annunciation. (8) The effect of such power was not hidden from those in attendance, for the noise emitted by the shaking of her nerves, like the crashing down of a roof, filled those present with instant panic.

20. (1) It is enough to have remembered briefly these few examples from among the miracles of this holy man, so that the steadfastness of the more advanced is not taxed and the faith of the simple is strengthened. (2) For quite apart from the mention of those deeds of power which in legal processes are called common places because they do not always happen to the good and sometimes even happen to the wicked, just the very constancy of the life of the saints serves the wise for faith and example, for only a good person could achieve it. (3) What could ever be more noteworthy than a miracle, if not to keep the mind's intention firmly focused amid the variety of worldly things? (4) By God's gift, this blessed man kept his mind so fixed that no change of season, place, time or fortune could budge him from his sacred commitment. (5) One thing he had asked from the Lord, this he sought, to dwell eternally in the house of the Lord.[54] In the light of this intention, he judged as nothing the pleasure and hardship of the present life. (6) It came to pass that after a brief period of labor (everything which passes away is short) he gained the prize of eternal life[55] and happily exchanged earthly things for heavenly ones. (7) It is believed that he foresaw the day of his death. He called the brothers together, spoke to exhort them with divine warnings, kissed each one, and said goodbye. Then he turned to God and commended himself and them in prayer, and full of days died in Christ. He was buried on April 24th in the new La Chaise-Dieu, which he had built, in the reign of our Lord Jesus Christ.[56]

54. Ps 26:4.

55. Phil 3:14.

56. According to the tradition handed on by Bernard in *The Tripartite Life*, Robert died on April 17, 1067 and was buried on April 24. Liturgical manuscripts and printed martyrologies of the sixteenth and seventeenth centuries assign his feast to April 24. Later martyrologies assign it to April 17.

Book II

1. (1) From Marbod, a sinner, to the lord abbot, Seguinus,[1] a man truly holy and most esteemed among the members of Christ.

I composed an earlier book in a simple style about the life of Blessed Robert. I hope I was as effective as I was willing. You, venerable sir, frequently ask or rather, under the guise of making a request, very strongly order and compel that I add to the earlier book the following work about his miracles according to the titles used by the first writer.[2] (2) The command of this new distinction honors my insignificance, but the assumption of the heavy labor burdens my weakness. (3) You would not have required the second work from me so insistently, if the first had displeased you, but on the other hand, what was pleasing could not be accomplished without effort and industry. But I am not so foolish that, if I do something good, I attribute it to my strength instead of to Him from whom all good things come. Nor am I so unfaithful that I have no hope of divine help in honorable and devout labors. (4) So, rather, I am pleased that that little work pleased you and the holy brothers, and I give thanks for the divine grace that made it pleasing. (5) I now approach what remains to be done, confident in the same divine aid, which is assured to me not by the presumption of my own merits, which are evil or non-existent, but by the intercession of the blessed patron, about whom I am speaking, and of your holiness. (6) If there is anything amiss, let it be attributed to me, and whatever is right let it be attributed to heavenly grace. I beg you, do not let the unworthiness of the writer be held against the dignity of the cause undertaken, since out of regard for their masters worth is often attributed to insignificant slaves. (7) The faithful reader should pay attention to what is said rather than to how it is said, since depending on the skill of the speaker, frequently true things are discussed briefly, and false things are treated at length.

1. Seguin of Escotay, *Seguinus*, was abbot of La Chaise-Dieu from 1078–1094.

2. Marbod did not compose the second book immediately after the first book but after an interval and at the urging of the abbot of La Chaise-Dieu. In fact, over a dozen manuscripts contain only Book I, whereas four manuscripts contain both books. The second book is meant to narrate Robert's miracles, his works of power (*virtutes*).

For healthy foods are served in earthen vessels, and lethal poison is sometimes mixed in gold cups.

2. (1) Before I tell of the miracles of the saint, it does not seem irrelevant to me to counter the blasphemies of some people on whose foreheads and in whose sacrilegious mouths one sees without any doubt the sign of the dragon and the beast.[3] (2) For it is written of him that 'he will open his mouth in blasphemies toward God, to blaspheme his name and his tabernacle and those who dwell in heaven.'[4] Thus, those who vainly try to slander this holy man surely show themselves to be of the number of that beast. (4) They say (I am not reluctant to explain, as before judges, their crafty and evil intent that must be refuted): 'This new holy man overturns for us the ancient order of holiness. (5) For while all the others, who with love faithfully maintain hope for higher things, arrange in their hearts ways of going higher and always undertake to go from the lower to the higher, only this man, although he had first put his foot on the summit, afterwards gradually slipped down to lower things. (6) Far from earthly and burdensome tumults, above the clouds on a high mountain, he undertook to gaze upon only divine and heavenly things with the peaceful gaze of his mind. Then, behold, little by little he turned away to active labor and human affairs, and finally to taking care of the dead. "He had begun a wine-jar, but he finished a water-pot."[5] (7) He altered the marriage customs and contrary to the ways of the fathers and the trustworthy report of the Old Testament, he merited the embraces of Rachel before the bedchamber of Leah. (8) Having experienced both, he preferred the beautiful face to the bleary-eyed one; then he repudiated the former to be united permanently with the latter. Or better, having experience of neither, he tried in vain for both and was repulsed as an unworthy suitor.[6] (9) In preferring Martha to Mary, he went

3. Rv 16:2; 20:4.

4. Rv 13:6.

5. This is an echo of Horace, *Ars Poetica* 21–22. It is cited by Jerome, *Epistle* 27.3 and by Hildebert of Lavardin, *Vita Hugonis Cluniacensis* (PL 171:859).

6. Gn 29:26–17. For Leah and Rachel, Martha and Mary, and the whole question of the relationship between action and contemplation, see Giles Constable, *Three Studies in Medieval Religious and Social Thought* (New York: Cambridge UP, 1995)

contrary to the judgment of Christ who declared that Mary chose the better part.[7] Thus, he blasphemed, if not by voice, then in deed, which is worse. (10) He stands convicted by his own words, for he affirmed that what he did afterward is reprehensible. For when he was going to seek a solitary place, he said to his disciples: "It is tolerable not to aspire to the highest because of human weakness, but to fall from one's promise because of diabolical sin is worthy of condemnation."[8] (11) Therefore, either one ought not to put faith in the writer or this man who is accused of transgression by his own words is regarded as holy not through his own merit but though another's error.' What slander, full of envious cunning and proud quarreling!

3. (1) Our saint does not depart from the way of the blessed even in this: he is the object of the curses and hatreds of the wicked for the sake of the name of Jesus Christ, indeed, for the name of Christ even if his detractors are assigned the same name. (2) If Robert had not served Christ in a singular way and his great reputation for sanctity had not spread through different regions, these sons of pride[9] certainly would not have considered him worthy of their slander. (3) Now, however, because they are not afraid to claim hypocritically for themselves praise for their religion, they think that whatever praise is accorded others damages their glory. (4) So it happens that they bring to bear all the force of their learning to destroy Robert's name, misusing spiritual weapons, that is, the divine authorities, against the spiritual servant of God. Christ has nurtured them as internal enemies in his very encampment. (5) So, the greatest of these, whom their mother pride begot from their father, the devil,[10] dared to reprove Martin because, when he had been scorched with flames and threatened with death, he had hesitatingly prayed for the protection of flight. (6) At Christ's command, Sulpicius then presented Martin's case, and in the judgment of the reader forced

1–141; and Giles Constable, *The Reformation of the Twelfh Century* (New York: Cambridge U P, 1996) 189–191.

7. Lk 10:42.

8. Above, 1.9(3).

9. 1 Mc 2:47.

10. Jn 8:44.

his adversaries into confused silence.[11] (7) Now Christ, making use of our lowliness, is also mighty enough to confound or instruct ignorant pride that vainly congratulates itself on its knowledge. (8) Come now, whoever you are, who are the bitter assailant of the new holiness and really hostile to the new man, you still sound the image of the old man with your voice and bear it in your mind. (9) Come now, I say, you noble of foggy diligence, indeed, you notable show-off, you claim you have sharp eyesight, but really you see like a mole. (10) You think that the ancient rule of holiness is that one first engage in active labor through which charity, out of solicitous compassion, supplies neighbors with what they need. Then, moving to higher things by ever new advances in virtue, one victoriously obtains the summit of contemplative sweetness, in which one enjoys the insatiable love of God alone. (11) When one has arrived there, it is judged wrong to be concerned about lesser things. What has been said in jest about someone can fittingly be said of this person also: he looks at the doors of heaven, caring no more about men. (12) Thus, like a new authority and expert you divide the two lives of the church, assigning each limits, and so, confused by a mental error, you claim they are not mixed, so that whoever once attains the higher is to be condemned if he returns to the lesser. So, one who has loved God fully cannot love his brother also.

4. (1) You introduce a new rule of cruelty in place of religion. Wordy Greece tells a more humane story. When Orestes and Pylades were fleeing from their homeland, a violent storm cast them on a foreign shore. They were captured and taken before the altar of Diana of Scythia, so that a solemn offering could be made with foreign blood to the cruel goddess. However, since there was a law that only one ought to die, they offered the barbarians a protracted and thoroughly pious spectacle of friendly rivalry, as each tried to save the other by dying for him.[12] (2) Now you, a devout worshipper of Christ, urge an act more savage than those idolatries. (3) Suppose a gentle

11. The reference is to Sulpicius Severus, *Epistula prima. Ad Eusebium*, ed. C. Halm, CSEL 1 (Vienna, 1867) 138–141, tr. Hoare, 48-51, which is the source of the phrases 'scorched by fire' (*adustus incendio*) and 'the protection of flight' (*fuge presidium*).

12. Cicero, *On Friendship* 7.24; Augustine, *Confessions*, 4.6.11, ed. Henry Chadwick (New York: Oxford, 1991) 59.

father, standing on the edge of a pit, called with gentle voice to his children long held captive in a deep and dark prison, and, having sent down a ladder, urged them to climb up the well-worn steps. Then, while the rest remained anxious and too disturbed to pay heed to their father, one who was more ready to take risks and had wider experience attempted the difficult climb. When he happily emerged at the top, he turned his back on his siblings who vainly begged for his brotherly help. He refused the easy task of leading them up the steps that he now knew well. He lied and said that he did so out of love for their father. Meanwhile, the father, having pity on their distress, did not cease to urge him with fatherly love to undertake the task. Does this son seem perfect to you? (4) Suppose someone saw his brother fighting to the death in an amphitheater with a very fierce gladiator whom he himself had already conquered and whose strategy he knew well. He was able to coach him, but he did not. Rather, undisturbed about his brother's danger and retired from the fray, he sat and watched with his father whose untimely kisses he wished to enjoy. Would such a person not be judged shameless and cruel by everyone including his own father, and, because of his neglect of his brother, a vile parricide? (5) 'But,' you will respond, 'the fiery love of God devours and consumes any care for mortal things.' If that is so, then a new and monstrous division has arisen in the realm of charity, and the two commandments on which the whole law and the prophet depends[13] have been rent by an internal sedition even worse than a civil war. As a result, the sacraments of the whole Christian faith collapse. (6) For, to sum up briefly, if the all-consuming love of God, in which the summit of contemplative life consists, devours and extinguishes brotherly love, which is the principal concern of the active life, then the former is itself extinguished and no trace of love remains. (7) 'For how can someone who does not love his brother whom he sees, love God whom he does not see.'[14] Similarly, 'If someone sees his brother in need and closes his heart to him, how can the love of God remain in him?'[15] Therefore, either loving God one will love one's neighbor also, or

13. Mt 22:40.
14. 1 Jn 4:20.
15. 1 Jn 3:17.

despising one's neighbor, one will have contempt for God as well. (8) Furthermore, those who love their brother with God will, according to their means, provide necessities to whoever is in need. They will certainly be devoting themselves to the active life, whether they do so by deed, or if they do not have anything, by volition only. (9) On the other hand, fraternal love will be useless or null, if the intention of the mind is not directed toward God. (10) We are forced by irrefutable reasoning to admit that, although the two lives are distinct from each other in their merits, they can be possessed by the same person and exercised alternately.[16] (11) When out of necessity they turn toward what is lesser, this is not a fall, but a descent; not transgression, but compassion. (12) So, it is apparent that to censure the holy man for transgression in this matter is an offense that deserves to be censured with more than words.

5. (1) Unless you were dreaming, it is amazing that you say he subverted the traditional order by trying unsuccessfully for the beauty of Rachel before the bed of Leah, as though he was an impudent suitor. (2) I think that the clear and orderly story of his deeds is not lost even on someone as blind as you, for it was not silent about his earlier acts of almsgiving. (3) Furthermore, your accusation that contrary to Christ's teaching he preferred Martha to Mary proves to be a frivolous and empty objection. (4) For if this is said with reference to the time sequence, which the stupidity of such a reckless slanderer would not hesitate to do, the calumny of that wagging tongue is self-condemned, for now you are accusing him of doing what a little before you accused him of not doing. (5) For above your charge was that he did not marry Leah before Rachel; now it is that he preferred Martha to Mary. (6) However, according to the mystic meaning, Leah and Martha are identical, as are Rachel and Mary.[17] One cannot put Martha ahead of Mary, if one has not put Leah ahead of Rachel. (7) If it is primacy in dignity that is at issue, then your accusation is patently groundless, because you

16. This seems to be the meaning of Marbod's *ab eodem tamen communiter lege queunt viceria possideri.*

17. For the traditional identification of Leah and Martha with the active life, and Rachel and Mary with the contemplative life, see Giles Constable, *Three Studies* (1995) 1–141.

are making assertions about a judgment passed on someone else's mind of which you have no knowledge. (8) From the words and deeds of the holy man it can be seen that he truly put Mary before Martha in dignity when he ministered to the brothers because of love of God. In this compassion he was no backsliding violator of a demanding promise, but rather a most devout imitator of all the elect and of their head himself. This is the rule of holiness, whether ancient, modern or future: until the end of time the ready devotion of the servants of Christ does not cease to run with ready step on well-marked stages of virtue within the boundaries of both the active and contemplative lives.

6. (1) We think that we have said enough against the things which are said by those who judge that it is wrong to mix the active life with the contemplative life, in order to heap calumnies on blessed Robert, whose sanctity they envy. (2) However, we wish to illustrate our position from a different angle using sacred witnesses, so that no one may scorn us for preferring human reason to the authority of the Scriptures. We do not think it is irrelevant to the intent of this work if for the current edification of readers we show that the servant of God was conformed to the ancient saints in this act of virtuous discernment. (3) When Jacob, the patriarch, rested his tired head on a mystic rock while he slept, he saw the Lord resting on a ladder. Not only were angels ascending the ladder through divine contemplation; they were also descending out of compassion for humanity.[18] (4) This very patriarch experienced this same mystery in his marriage, for, after the embraces of his more beautiful wife, he often had intercourse with his more fertile spouse. (5) If those who in their temerity are envious had paid attention to this, they would have realized that the divine narrative gives no support to their foolish calumny. For what else does the most holy page of the Older Scripture and of the New Testament teach? (6) Let us say a few words about each. Did not Abraham, the father of faith, Isaac

18. Gn 28:12–13. This passage and those which follow show points of contact with Gregory the Great's *Pastoral Rule* 2.5, *Regula pastoralis*, ed. F. Rommel, SCh 381 (Paris: Cerf, 1992) 196–203.

the son of the promise,[19] Jacob the one chosen by spiritual grace,[20] who especially manifest the mystery of the blessed Trinity in themselves, often speak with God but nevertheless managed their family affairs. (7) This alteration is especially obvious in Jacob, who when he had seen God face to face—for which reason he called the place Phanuel—immediately, because of the demands of the journey, returned to organize his family, dividing his servants and wives with his children and flocks into groups.[21] (8) So, too, Moses the lawgiver, after staying alone with the Lord on the mount, went back repeatedly to the people entrusted to him. He did not always dwell in the hidden place of the divine tent, but went outside to decide the contentious cases of litigants,[22] which generally was no easy task. (9) Another example that seems not irrelevant to our understanding of the matter is that of Axa. Seated upon an ass, he asked from his father both the upper and the lower water sources, neither without the other.[23] (10) In the same way, the apostles of Christ, Peter and John, 'ascended to the temple for the ninth hour of prayer'.[24] This number stands for the summit of angelic contemplation. Then, as soon as they went out, they bestowed benefits on those who asked in Christ's name. (11) Next, there is Paul, pre-eminent among the teachers. He was rapt into paradise,[25] and more than once with the heightened vision of his mind investigated the secrets of the third heaven.[26] Afterwards, he adapted himself to human measure, even the measure of carnal men, in his benevolent compassion allowing some pleasure even to the incontinent. (12) He said, 'Because of fornication, let each man have his wife, and let each woman have her own husband. And let a husband render his debt to his wife, and likewise the wife to her husband.'[27] (13) Notice what perfect

19. Gal 4:28.

20. Rom 11:5.

21. Gn 32:30; 33:1-2.

22. Lv 24:10–11.

23. Jos 15:18–19; cf. Jgs 1:14–15. This story is not found in Gregory's *Pastoral Rule*.

24. Acts 3:1, followed by their cures of the sick in Acts 3.2–10.

25. 1 Cor 12:4.

26. 1 Cor 3:1.

27. 1 Cor 7:2-3.

charity does and imitate it! The one who was just privy to heaven's secrets becomes master of the private bedchamber. (14) Moreover, concerned about the collections that were made for the saints,[28] he diligently exhorts the Corinthians to prepare the promised gift. (15) Thus, through the fullness of twofold charity, he was at the top and the bottom, in heaven and on earth, in mental ecstasy for God, prudent for us.[29] None of Christ's other disciples deviated from this rule of holiness. (16) But to give the details proper to every example pertaining to this subject is both very long and not very necessary. Of himself, Jesus Christ, the Son of God, is sufficient example for us, for of his fullness all have received,[30] and his whole life on earth stands as a lesson on how to live. (17) Jesus now 'ascends the mountain to pray alone',[31] now comes to the disciples, whom he sees working on the water.[32] Now he speaks the word of God to the crowds; now he grants gifts of health. (18) When he was transfigured on the mountain, Jesus showed his glory to a few.[33] After he returned to the crowds, in the presence of many he paid heed to the misery of a father asking on behalf of his son.[34] (19) Sometimes he exulted in the Holy Spirit and gave praise to the Lord of heaven and earth.[35] At another time he was deeply moved and wept at the death of his friend.[36] (20) He taught by word what he showed by example when he urged us not only to pray to the Father behind closed doors,[37] but also to give visible aid to the brother who asks it.[38] (21) The contemplative church recommends the same in Song of Songs, when she voices her regret at being compelled to leave her bed of internal quiet for the external care and office of preaching that she had formerly exercised and to which her spouse calls her back. (22) She says: 'I am sleeping, but my heart keeps

28. 1 Cor 16:1.
29. 2 Cor 5:13.
30. Jo 1:16.
31. Mt 14:23.
32. Mt 14:24-25.
33. Mt 17:1-13.
34. Mt 17:14-17.
35. Lk 10:21.
36. Jo 11:33-35.
37. Mt 6:6.
38. Lk 11:15ff.

vigil. The voice of my beloved knocking on the door: My sister, my friend, my dove, my immaculate one, for my head is covered with frost and the locks of my hair with drops of dew. (23) I have taken off my tunic; how shall I put it on? I have washed my feet, how will I make them dirty? (24) My beloved puts his hand through the opening, and my stomach trembles at his touch. I have risen to open to my beloved.'[39] (25) I think from all this it is sufficiently established and evident that it is not only licit but necessary for contemplatives to move toward action often, nor does their previous merit suffer any detriment because, if they are deprived within of sterile beauty, they are compensated exteriorly by bleary-eyed fecundity. (26) Because the demonstration of this fact is so obvious that I have run out of time rather than examples, the things I have said are all the more sufficient, and the things omitted are missed all the less. (27) So, because truth has rebutted falsity and charity has instructed envy, silenced are 'the deceitful lips which speak ill against the just in pride and disdain'.[40] (28) In fact, since I intend to edify rather than to vanquish, let envy yield to charity, and let the impiety of wicked blasphemy make amends to the esteemed herald of truthful confession, so that we may together proclaim the merits of the blessed man in a spirit of love and peace.

7. (1) The miracles for which, through God's grace, the tomb of his sacred body is renowned, are for doubters certain proofs of his merits. (2) Therefore, in the continuation of this book let these be our answer to those who are unbelieving or ill-disposed, if any such remain from among those whom we opposed above in the measure that the Lord gave us. Thus, as the Apostle testifies 'tongues are a sign not for believers, but for unbelievers,'[41] so on the contrary, let signs be a tongue not for believers, but for unbelievers.

8. (1) On the very day that the body of the blessed man lay ready for burial,[42] while the others were occupied with the holy funeral

39. Sg 5:2-4.

40. Ps 30:19.

41. 1 Cor 14:22.

42. April 24, 1067. Bernard, *The Tripartite Life*, says this disciple's name was Radulf.

rites, one of his earliest disciples went apart by himself, since he suffered his sudden loss more deeply because of his long association with him. (2) Worn out and upset by his prolonged mourning, he had sat down, since as happens drowsiness followed upon sadness. (3) And behold, the light of his mind was divinely opened and he beheld a fiery ball come down from heaven and stop over the place where the saint's body lay; everything near it was brightly illumined by its radiant splendor. (4) When he was astonished and struck with dread at this terrible vision, there appeared a woman of incalculable beauty surrounded by the heavenly hosts and matching by her own splendor the brightness of the earlier light. By her majestic face and bearing she was clearly a queen. (5) She stood on the fiery ball above the bier. She stretched out her hand and took the right hand of the dead man, and urged him with her gentle voice to get up and ascend with her. (6) With their hands joined, they traveled straight to heaven with the light accompanying them. At the moment they seemed to reach the borders of the heavens, an immense right arm reached down and they were received into the open heaven. (7) There is no doubt that this was the mother of the Lord who led the soul devoted to her into the joys of heaven, after he had rightly discharged the tasks of the present life. There Christ received him.

9. (1) After Christ, it was to her allegiance that the holy man especially bound himself. While he was living in the flesh he loved her spiritually with such an intense affection that even when he was busy with something else, he could not restrain himself from her praises, and even when he was asleep he was awake to her memory.[43] (2) He bore the image of Christ and Mary deep within his heart. He cherished this as a unique and sweet treasure lodged in his joyful mind. (3) He had bound on his heart this pair of pearls that were of unequal but inestimable value. At every hour he recalled them before the eyes of his secret love with an insatiable desire. (4) Christ and Mary, chastity and mercy, remained ever on his lips. With delight he varied her titles, calling Mary the gate of heaven, the star of the sea, the sanctuary of the Holy Spirit, the refuge of the miser-

43. The Latin text, '*ad eius memoriam, etiam dormiens, animo vigilaret*,' might also mean 'even while he slept his mind kept vigil at her altar.'

able, the rose of modesty, the lily of chastity, the jewel of virginity. (5) It was his opinion that anyone who wished to receive the grace of Christ should first approach Mary, as a second mediatrix between God and human beings, for her Son had delegated to her a bountiful share in the work of reconciliation, so that he might commend to the Father those whom his own mother had commended to him.[44] (6) The devotion of his disciples demonstrates and expresses the fervor of their master still today. According to the tradition they received from him, in the monastery of La Chaise-Dieu they still joyfully celebrate together for the glorious Virgin the praises of the daily office. (7) Hence, there can be no doubt that his blessed soul in particular has been led into heavenly joy by her whom, save God, he strove to serve before all others. (8) The vision just mentioned is not lacking the authority of the whole Trinity: the fire signified the ardor of the Holy spirit; the right hand, the strength of the Son; and the beauty of heaven, the majesty of the Father.

10. Likewise, a certain man who lived in the region of Velay[45] was afflicted for two straight years with a quartan fever. (2) He had spent a long time going around to the sanctuaries and gravesites of the saints because he wished to beg for health. But all his effort was in vain as he added the trouble of this unseasonable effort to his dangerous illness. (3) He was unsuccessful not through some failure in his faith or a want of power in the saints, but so that he might be saved by God through the merits of blessed Robert, as the sequel made clear. (4) For, drawn by the news of Robert's holy death that had spread everywhere, he was led in haste amid large crowds to the site of the saint's body on the very day of his burial. He prostrated himself on the ground and pleaded for a cure for a long time with unwavering confidence that he would be granted health. While he was praying, a heavenly sleep came upon him and he slept peacefully. In the meantime, by the mysterious working of divine love, through the merits of the blessed man the passages of his veins were warmed, the baneful power of the sluggish cold began to dissolve, his pores opened, and all at once feverish sweats

44. Marbod here adopts the language of I Ti 2:5: '*unus et mediator Dei et hominum.*'

45. Velay was a region of the Massif Central whose capital was Le Puy.

poured from his whole body. (5) The sleeping man's nature, now freed from its burden, sensed the cure. When he awoke, suddenly freed from every malady without the discomfort of a medical cure, the man saw that he was changed and thought he had risen. (6) The thanks he offered to God for the health he had received and the shouts he addressed to Robert reflected his great joy, which can only be calculated by comparing that joy with his earlier misery. (7) As someone who has evaded a greater danger rejoices more, so the one who rejoices more offers greater thanks.

11. (1) News of this great act of power was quickly spread throughout the neighboring territories by the voices of those who had seen it and by those who believed their reports. Led by this news, crowds of the sick and infirm followed various paths to the sacred tomb of the blessed man, as if to a copious and only recently reported free clinic for dispensing cures to all those who were sick. (2) Among these was a poor old man. It was his misfortune that to his double burden of old age and poverty had been added the worst and most difficult burden of blindness. His worried wife brought him to the tomb of the confessor. (3) There that blind man spent three days. Having fixed the eyes of his mind on Christ with indefatigable zeal, he frequently repeated the name of Robert, whose patronage he trusted. Never for a moment did he cease from his praying. His wife who was, it seemed, offended by the insistent loquacity of the man, said: (4) 'At least stop bothering the people who are present here, even if you do not fear offending the one who rests here. (5) You do not think that the saint will hear you unless you shout excessively. While you ask for your lost sight, you are distressing the hearing of the one whom you are assaulting. You do not deserve to receive what you are praying for, when you who are blind importune him as though he were deaf. Instead, wait a while in silence, and pour forth prayers in the secret chamber of your heart.' (6) He was indignant and horrified to hear what she said, so he thought that this was not the simple talk of a woman, but the deceptive hissing of the devil. (7) He said: 'Woman, stop! Stop your stupid talking, and cover your wicked blasphemy with a semblance of faith. (8) Do you think that the ears of the saints are sensitive, and so they are worn out with excessive shouting? (9) In fact, the saints, instructed by Christ's divine teaching, ultimately

give to the one who keeps knocking doggedly what they do not give to the one who asks many times in a friendly way.'[46] (10) He immediately turned back to the saint and began to shout out his holy name ever more insistently. In this he imitated the blind man in the gospel who was aroused to even greater intensity in his prayers by the crowd that scolded him to be quiet.[47] (11) The loving-kindness of the priest[48] was moved immediately to ask from God the power of restoring sight to the blind man, but when He deferred giving what he asked, he tested the faith of the petitioner and also made the favor more cherished because it was more desired. (12) When the man persisted in his prayers, a hidden power produced a visible effect. The dense cloud of darkness began to be drawn away, and his blindness began to appear to the eyes of the onlookers as already far away, although they did not yet see the light, as when someone stretches a curtain in front of those looking at the light.[49] (13) The man immediately put his hands on his fluttering eyes and, surprisingly touching nothing, he wiped away whatever was causing the obstruction. (14) A wonderful light lit up his long dead eyes and immediately rendered brighter the whole substance of his illuminated body. (15) A joy beyond bounds burst the silence, and he, the most fitting person to preach about the new miracle that had occurred in him, instantly began to shout thanks mixed with praises throughout the whole basilica.

12. (1) Who of those present at that time and place could silence the praises of God? Who did not sing the merits of blessed Robert? (2) The power of the saint was indubitable in the face of public proof, since the blind man could give specific names to the various things brought to him as tests of his vision without being led into error by differences of color or form. (3) Here, if it can, let vicious envy find grounds for slander, and let him in his leisure try to concoct

46. Lk 11:8.

47. Mk 10:46–49.

48. The word 'priest' here evidently refers to Robert. This is the only place in Marbod's *Life of Robert* where this title is used of him. Robert was a priest; cf. 1.3(1).

49. The passage, 'and his blindness . . . looking at the light' is obscure. It has been the subject of several emendations, but the meaning remains elusive.

something to distort what in the end he cannot deny. (4) When he finds out that all his efforts fail in spite of exhausting effort, then, refuted, let him finally come to his senses with greater shame. Since he disdains to believe us, let him believe for himself, and following the example of that crazy prophet dismount from his jackass,[50] that is, from his own stupidity. (5) Perhaps he contends that the whole of this event of miraculous power is to be ascribed not to the merits of the holy man, but to the faith of the petitioner. (6) However, the faith of the petitioner was this: that he could obtain his lost sight through the prayers of Robert; that is why he frequently called out Robert's name. (7) Therefore, either he received what he asked through the merits of the same saint, or the faith with which he asked contributed nothing to his gaining his request. (8) Often before this, with Christian faith he had prayed for his lost sight at the tombs of other saints, but nevertheless he had never merited to be heard. (9) Finally, if the granting of favors were to be imputed completely to the faith of the petitioners, no graces would be attributed to Christ, who often granted various favors and cures to those who were burdened. He was not silent regarding the merit of faith, saying: 'your faith has made you well'.[51] That is, your faith has obtained the healing for which it asked, not by giving me the power, but by meriting from me the grace. (10) Hence, the faith of the one asking cancels out neither the power of the one granting nor the merit of the patron.

13. (1) Here is another evident proof of extraordinary holiness. A certain wretched woman from the Limousin[52] had been devastated for about twenty years by frequent incursions of an evil spirit. Finally, some faithful people brought her to the tomb of the blessed man. (2) The wicked force did not trouble her continuously as usually happens, but tormented her in a worse way intermittently, like chronic disease. (3) When she had been placed before the site of his holy body, with everyone else who was there, she

50. Nm 22:22ff.

51. Mk 10:52; Lk 18:42. In 2.10(2) Marbod presented another miracle in which other saints had failed to answer the petitioner's prayers.

52. The Limousin is the area around Limoges on the west side of the Massif Central.

waited in suspense, like a criminal waiting for a merciful judge to pronounce a sentence of absolution. Suddenly, she began to be convulsed throughout her whole body as if now her tormented countenance were gazing upon a dreaded death. (4) The wicked spirit trembled violently, unable to stand the presence of some invisible majesty. As if terrified by some unforeseen attack, it was hurrying to escape from her body which it had wickedly invaded. Since every exit was blocked, it ran around frantically banging into the walls of its prison. (5) The assailant was retained for a while, so that a penalty could be exacted from him, and also so that the public manifestation of the magnitude of the horrible affliction might commend the miracle of purification which was soon to take place. (6) So, when in that wretched state she had for some time presented the heart-rending spectacle of her affliction to the onlookers, the woman suddenly cried out and with often repeated shouts began to invoke the help of St. Robert. (7) Meanwhile, the custodian of the church took some holy water and sprinkled it into the mouth of the shouting woman. As though a shower had been sent down from heaven, this instantly restrained all the fire of her raging passion. (8) How wonderful are the merits of the devout confessor, who could rout the power of the enemy even through the offices of a humble minister. (9) This is certainly an indication of outstanding power, which could not come forth from just any saint at any time. (10) Christ empowered his apostles that they might command evil spirits in his name.[53] The apostles did so very often themselves, but seldom through others under their command.[54] (11) It is believed that the great and wondrous Elisha did this long ago, when the corpse of a man rose to life at the touch of his sacred bones.[55] (12) However, the servant sent ahead with his staff was not able to raise the dead son of the great woman at his command, not because he lacked confidence in the merits of such a great prophet, but because such an overflowing of grace is not always conferred even on the perfect. On the other hand, there is no room for doubt that those to whom it is sometimes conferred are indeed perfect.

53. Mt 10:1; Mk 6:7; Lk 9:1–2.

54. Cf. Acts 8:7.

55. 4 Kgs 13:21.

(13) The woman collapsed on the pavement and lay senseless for some time, so that it seemed clear to all that she was dead. (14) It was no great matter for the saint to raise the dead woman by his lively merits, if the situation were as it seemed. (15) When after a while her senses or her soul, whichever it was, returned, she opened her eyes and sat up quietly as Tabitha had done long ago.[56] She gave all the thanks she could to the servant of God, Robert, for having received back health of mind and body. (16) Then those who had been present and were struck with awe, when they experienced the outcome and saw so great and obvious a miracle, sounded together the praises of God with devout cries. (17) But the woman, having returned cured to her native place, carried with her the evidence of the wondrous power that she had experienced.

14. (1) Likewise a certain man who lived in the region of Forez,[57] pouring out devout prayers, carried his son to the tomb of the holy man in hopes of obtaining a cure for him. The son had suffered a long time from a contraction of his nerves, so that he seemed not so much to walk as to crawl. He stayed there a week, beseeching with tears and prayers in faithful anticipation of an act of divine mercy. (2) Then one day, while the brothers were celebrating mass, the boy began to be both agitated by sudden nervous movements and prompted by impulses of his nature coming back to life, as he tried to stretch out his limbs which had been so long inert. (3) He hesitatingly tried to move, and behold with a kind of rush the nerves of the skin were stretched noisily, so that now, even if he had tried, he could not have stopped. (4) Without doubt a heavenly force broke the confining chains of his nature too long held captive, and what took place was beyond human power. (5) The crippled man immediately stood up on feet long unused and was forced to take some first, unsteady steps. (3) Those who were watching ran to him weeping for joy, and supporting him on all sides with their hands, with praises they led him upright to the altar. (7) Everybody felt the joy that such an obvious manifestation of the divine presence deserved. (8) But above all their clamor the voice of the father resounded with the most festive rejoicing, for, since he had

56. Acts 9:40.

57. The Forez is in the extreme eastern part of the Auvergne.

greater cause to rejoice, he had more reason to shout. (9) When he returned to his own people with his son who now had steady feet and was no longer crippled, he spread the news of the great miracle in his own region.

15. (1) A noble knight from the town called Céreix[58] had a daughter who labored under the heavy burden of a double disgrace: her face was horribly disfigured with swelling, and she had been afflicted in both eyes for a long time. (2) After a while the father, who was deeply saddened by his daughter's afflictions, decided to direct her to the tomb of the holy man, where it was widely reported that many received health. (3) The blind woman, her face deformed with hideous tumors, was led to the saint. After a little while, she returned with her sight again and her face restored to its original beauty. (4) What happened was this. While she besought God with incessant prayers, to which the pain of her contrite heart urged her, and while she repeatedly called on the name and merits of blessed Robert, one of the brothers who served as guardian of the sanctuary, gathering from the face of the passionately gesturing girl the sentiments inspiring her supplication, paid attention to her cries. Moved with love he groaned and with the speed of love quickly took some wine which had washed the body of the saint and with it sprinkled the whole face of the trembling girl. (5) When she felt the beneficial drops of the sacred liquid, she entreated that this procedure be repeated for her often. When this had been done for several days, the woman became completely healthy. (6) She returned home with her face beaming; she was no longer ashamed to be seen nor did she need to envy those who looked at her. (7) Her father rejoiced when he saw his daughter healed, as did her family and neighbors. The entire town rejoiced together praising God in shared prayers. There was no dearth of praise for blessed Robert, who in his usual way took up the cause of the poor girl as her strong champion.

16. (1) There is a well-known town that its inhabitants called Monistrol.[59] There dwelt there a knight who had a daughter. She was

58. Céreix is about 15 kilometers from Le Puy.

59. Monistrol-sur-Loire is about 45 kilometers from Le Puy. See the reference to the Loire in 2.6(11).

troubled in wretched ways by a savage spirit. (2) She not only gave evidence of insanity by terrible shouting and horrible gestures and filthy language, but she also lunged to bite whomever she could. She did not even spare herself, if there was no opportunity for attacking others. (3) She did not even recognize her father, except when, at the urging of the hidden enemy, she attacked him with greater insults than she did other people. (4) But the more she inflicted insults on him, the more deeply he was moved with fatherly love for his poor girl. (5) The unhappy man saw himself being punished in the body of his daughter, and so in some way was tormented with even greater anguish. (6) Since he was of sound mind, he felt what he lamented, whereas in her case madness absorbed the feeling of grief. (7) She remained secure behind her fierce glances and the cruel stare of her crazed eyes. The sorrow of her grieving father made his pale cheeks and eyes overflowing with tears a sight worthy of compassion. (8) Her terrible gaping, her slobbering mouth, the tortured contortions of her twisted neck, and the frightful tangle of her uncombed hair, and whatever else was visible in the pitiable body of the senseless woman, the loving compassion of her father transferred it all to himself. (9) Moreover, since there was no apparent way for a cure, despair for her health further increased his desperate sorrow. While he was tossed on such waves of sorrow, suddenly a fresh wind of salutary advice blew up from his friends. It directed him to take the girl to the tomb of the holy man, who never disappointed the faith of those who invoked him with a just request. (10) He was immediately lifted up in the certain hope that this was the only way of reaching the shore, that is, the health of his daughter. He prepared his servants and a maid servant and whatever else seemed needed, and ordered that the girl be placed on a cart and led quickly to the saint, but with her limbs secured, so she could not leap out and wound those she met, as was her wont. (11) The Loire River crossed the middle of the route they were taking. Even sane heads feared its swift currents. (12) There the bound girl began to improve and to call to her companions with a calm look and gentle words. (13) This cure, which was the result of virtue rather than of nature, occurred at a place where her fragile nature easily could have been utterly terrified. 'Why,' she asked, 'have you wrapped me in a shroud like a dead woman.

Let me loose, for I am tired; you wouldn't want to coerce a harmless woman any longer.' (14) Having been let loose right away, she remained at peace during the rest of the journey. When she was led to the holy tomb, as to a place of judgment, the one who had lain hidden could not be quiet. (15) A violent convulsion passed through the limbs which were to be healed of their missing sinews. The malignant pestilence began to shake her teeth and to convulse her and then to torment in every way the body it was about to lose. (16) Three days later, the expelled deceiver took all the causes of her misfortune with him. Gradually her restored nature returned to a state of perfect health. After a little while she returned hail and hearty to her father's house, amazed at her own strength. We leave to the reader to imagine what joy and what prayers she caused. I would think that not even strangers, moved by simple affection for the misery of this poor woman who shared their nature, could refrain from praising God. (18) How much more did her father's love exult, urged on by personal as well as shared affection. Fittingly, all extolled with many praises the holy confessor of the Lord by whose glorious merits such great miracles were granted by God. (19) So no one will have any doubts, it seems desirable to recite at this point a final episode.

17. (1) The fame of such works of power spread through the Maritime Alps and aroused the hearts and tongues of peoples in praise of Saint Robert. The archbishop of that province, a man whose way of life accorded with the dignity of his office,[60] judged it unsuitable for the weighty pontifical office to put faith right away in the vain outcries of the fickle crowd. He decreed that there be an examination to determine what was collective error and what was public merit. (2) While the blessed man lived, he had been long acquainted with him and closely united with him in the love of the same endeavors. (3) When all the arrangements required for the journey had been made, he set out, not with the skeptical aim of a tempter, but with a zeal for showing the truth. (4) So, like the queen of the South, he came with his retinue to the place in order to

60. Bernard's *Tripartite Life* identifies him as the archbishop of Embrun. It was probably Lantelmus, who held that office from 1080.

investigate. She had probed the wisdom of Solomon; he was probing his power.[61] (5) He was received hospitably, as was fitting; and so, when the time seemed right he asked leave to enter the monastery. (6) What he asked was quickly granted, and when the doors of the sanctuary had been closed, he remained inside alone. (7) There he poured himself out completely in prayers as he lay prostrate at the tomb of St. Robert. He dissolved in tears because of the fiery intensity of his love. From the bottom of his heart he called on the true light,[62] that He deign to reveal to him clearly whether truly and without any shadow of doubt the divine power had granted to the blessed man a grace of miracles so great that it was unusual in recent centuries. (8) Turning to the saint, he said many things, as his soul suggested to him, bringing forth one prayer after the other. He did not cease calling on the Virgin Mother, nor did he omit the angelic spirits. (9) While he added prayers to prayers, the divine response was speedily apparent. It came not in the elementary sounds of words, but in the clear evidence of deeds. (10) A crowd, which by God's will had gathered from all over, accompanied with their communal prayers the body of a girl, long completely crippled, who was brought to the tomb of the saint as she had asked. (11) The gates were opened to those who knocked[63] and the accompanying crowd followed inside. Scarcely had the girl been let down onto the pavement when her knotted muscles loosed, the skin of her knees split, and she rose to her feet and walked around the whole basilica, glad to take the first steps made possible by this new gift. (12) The people raised their voices to heaven, and everywhere there sounded a tumultuous clamor. (13) The astonished bishop stood on one side, freed of his earlier doubts not only by the joint testimony of many but also by the credence he gave to his own eyes. (13) He acknowledged silently the grace for which he had asked and was amazed that he had been heard so quickly. (14) However, lest any occasion for base suspicion remain, there soon came the confirmation of a second miracle, so that the legal number of witnesses would not be lacking. (15) For the joyous uproar of the previous miracles had

61. Mt 12:14; Lk 11:31.
62. 1 Jo 2:8.
63. Lk 11:10.

barely subsided when a boy blind from birth, accompanied by a large crowd, was brought in, and turned the minds and voices of all who were present toward him. (16) He was quickly placed at the tomb, and all the people prayed for him. Immediately the darkness was expelled, and an unfamiliar light penetrated his awe-struck eyes. (17). Once more there arose joyous and thankful shouts. The bishop was amazed at the repeated miracle, whose specific nature seemed to allude to his own earlier blindness of mind. (18) The blindness corresponded to the doubter, and the illumination reflected faith. There was no place left for doubt and in the face of such evidence no Thomas could hesitate any longer.[64] (19) Faith, now advanced and strengthened, took voice and sounded in the ears of all, and profession of the truth resounded. (20) He said, 'I see here more than I have heard, and what is reported is less than the truth'. So the happy prelate returned home, taking back with him the riches of a precious testimony and giving glory to the God of heaven, who lives and reigns forever. Amen.

64. Jo 20:24ff.

The Tripartite Life of Robert, Abbot of La Chaise-Dieu

by

Bernard of La Chaise-Dieu

Introduction to *The Tripartite Life*

The Miracles of Robert and The Miracle of La Chaise-Dieu

Bernard of La Chaise-Dieu's *Tripartite Life of Robert of La Chaise-Dieu,* to which we now turn, fills in the story of Robert's life and death, tells of further miracles worked through his intercession after his death, and extends the story of the order's expansion another fifty years beyond the death of Abbot Seguin in 1094. In his brief prologue, Bernard spells out the aim and scope of his book. He wrote it in 1160. His subject matter is the miracles connected with St. Robert, whom he describes as his father and nurturer. He wants to tell of miracles omitted by others who wanted to keep their narratives brief. He divides his book into three parts, because Robert began with two companions in the name of the Trinity. The first part tells of miracles that God worked through Robert during Robert's lifetime. The second part describes miracles God worked after Robert's death in order to show that Robert was alive in heaven. In the final part, Bernard narrates meritorious deeds of the abbots of La Chaise-Dieu who succeeded Robert and of certain brothers renowned for signs and wonders, who lived under these abbots. Of some of these signs and wonders Bernard was himself an eyewitness.

Bernard adds some details of Robert's life that were not supplied by Marbod's *Vita*. Robert had been the treasurer at St. Julian in Brioude. He and his two companions went to their hermitage (*vastam eremum*) on the feast of the Holy Innocents (1.1). He consecrated the main altar of the church La Chaise-Dieu to divine charity (1.14). Robert retained the three lessons used by canons on the vigils of

Easter and Pentecost. When, after his death, the brethren wanted to replace them with the twelve lessons of the monastic office, they were divinely prevented from doing so (3.4).

Themes

Angels appear twice in the early chapters about Robert's earthly life. So diverse were the backgrounds and aspirations of the disciples who flocked to him that it seemed that they could not live together. While they were discussing how to find God's will for their common life, a stranger appeared at the door of the monastery. He presented a book to the porter and asked him to take it to the assembled community. Then, the stranger disappeared. The book was a copy of the *Rule of Saint Benedict*. The community took this as a clear sign that they should adopt Benedict's *Rule* (1.1). Another time, Robert was traveling across a field and met a stranger who asked for a coat to protect him from the cold. Robert took off his and gave it to him. The stranger, who was an angel, said that Robert would be blessed forever (1.4).

Robert and his hagiographer, Bernard, insist that monks should not be anxious about the morrow. This is emphasized on occasions when they were called upon to share their meager rations with those in greater need. Robert urged them to trust in the Lord, 'give and it shall be given to you' (1.5). On his deathbed Robert urged the community to practice charity, which is the principal name of God. They were to be generous to all, rich, poor and strangers (1.14; cf. 2.7).

The Feast of the Assumption was the occasion for several stories about Robert. His uncle, Rencon, bishop of Clermont, had decreed that the abbot and some of his monks should be feted by the canons of Clermont on the Feast of the Assumption (1.2). On one occasion, when he went to the priory of St. Mary at Fournoli to celebrate the Feast of the Assumption, the Blessed Virgin, 'Our Lady, the Queen of Heaven and earth,' appeared to him (1.6). Many of Bernard's stories are connected with Easter and Pentecost (1.12-13; 3.4, 5, 9, 12, 15).

Bernard arranges his stories so that the miracles that Robert worked while he was on earth parallel those of Christ. Robert cured lepers (1.2), drove out demons (1.10), healed the deaf and mute (1.7), and healed a woman's son (1.9). Robert's miraculous detection of the deadly eels (1.3) suggests Saint Benedict's detection and disposing of poisoned bread,[1] and both this miracle involving a crow and the story of a self-replenishing food container (1.8) are reminiscent of Elijah (1 Kg 17:4-16).

Bernard is careful to emphasize that when Robert worked a miracle, this occurred because God's power was at work through him (1.2; 1.7; 2.4). In one peculiar story, about a miracle that has no obvious religious or humanitarian purpose, Robert's gloves hang on a sunbeam. The onlookers saw this as an example of the 'wonders God works through his saints' (1.11).

A number of Robert's miracles occur away from La Chaise-Dieu. He seems to have visited regularly the houses of the Casadean family (1.3, 7, 9, 10, 11) and bishops in the region as well (1.2, 5).

Half of Part One, which is the biographical part, is devoted to Robert's death. On Palm Sunday a divine voice told him where his grave would be (1.2). During Holy Week he attended all the liturgical services. On Holy Saturday he had finished the services and begun the customary baptism of the children of the nobility. He took sick and was taken to bed. On Easter he celebrated Mass before returning to his bed (1.13). His staff, the symbol of his pastoral charge, he turned over to Christ and Mary (1.16). Having said farewell to his assembled community he died on the Wednesday after the octave of Easter, just as he and his companions had entered their hermitage on Christmas (1.18). He was buried eight days after the Octave of Easter. A great crowd of every sort of people came to his funeral. Repeating what Marbod's *Life of Robert* (2.8) relates, Bernard writes that one of his long-time disciples saw the Blessed Virgin come down over Robert's body. After his burial Robert's body was exhumed because he had appeared to some disciples and complained that a rock was crushing his face. His body was washed, his clothing saved as relics, and he was then reburied (2.3).

These appearances of the Blessed Virgin and of Robert are the first of the many miracles worked through or in connection with Robert after his death (2.4). Gerald Laveine described the life and miracles of Robert in a no longer extant book which he

1. *Dial.* 2.8.2–3, SCh 260:160–163.

presented to the pope, who authorized that Robert be included among the confessor saints and his feast day be celebrated (2.6). The archbishop of Embrun, who had known Robert, came to investigate the miracles worked at his grave and went away convinced (2.5). Through Robert's intervention, an eagle delivered a fish to the priory at Allanche on his feast day (2.7). Childless couples who put their trust in him were granted offspring (2.12).

These miracles brought so much fame and so many people to the monastery that the monks could neither lament their sins nor reverently carry on the divine services. They had to ask Robert to stop the tide of petitioners (2.8). One might surmise that Bernard wrote this to explain why in his time there were fewer miracles or why by then petitioners for Robert's intercession were welcomed with little enthusiasm. In what is perhaps another example of politically motivated narration, Bernard is careful to refer to many of the dependencies of the monastery (e.g., 2.2). These were part of the blessings which God bestowed on the monastery in response to Robert's charity (1.4[14]). Although Robert was ready to help anyone who asked him he also punished those who did not respect him. Aldebert, the bishop of Agen, fell unconscious after he spoke disparagingly of Robert at a synod (2.13). When a woman defiantly continued her spinning on Robert's feast day, her scarf and hair caught on fire (2.14). When a haughty knight rode his horse up some stairs into the monastery precincts, his beautiful horse was killed (2.16).

Raymond IV, count of St. Giles and later Count of Toulouse, did homage at Robert's tomb and asked the saint to restore his inheritance to him. His wish was almost immediately granted (2.10). When Raymond went on the crusade he took with him a cup that had been Robert's and Arbert, the prior of the Casadean monastery of Privezac. When Tripoli was captured, Raymond had Arbert appointed bishop there. After Raymond's death, the bishop had the cup and other riches sent back to La Chaise-Dieu (2.11).

The Abbots of La Chaise-Dieu to 1157[2]

The final part of the *Tripartite Life* tells of the period between Robert's death (1067) and the time when Bernard wrote his book (1160). Robert designated his first successor, Durand, who seems to have been a priest of the diocese of Clermont before he joined La Chaise-Dieu. Durand authorized Gerald of Laveine's now lost *Vita* of Robert and obtained the papal decree (1070) inscribing Robert among the saints (2.6). He secured a papal confirmation of the monastery's possessions and privileges and consolidated lay support, particularly that of Robert II, Count of Auvergne (1064–1096) (3.1–2).[3] At the invitation of Duke William VIII of Aquitaine (1058–1086), Durand founded Sainte-Gemme in the Saintonge.[4] In 1076 the reforming legate, Bishop Hugh of Die, appointed Durand bishop of Clermont (3.3). Durand resigned as abbot in 1078. He died after preparing the way for the visit of Pope Urban II to the council of Clermont in 1095.[5]

Adelelmus (d. 1097) succeeded Durand as abbot, but ruled only briefly in 1078 and then attempted to return to a more contemplative life. He then went to Spain and with the patronage of King Alfonso VI of Léon-Castille established Casadean monasteries there.[6]

2. Pierre-Roger Gaussin (1922–1999) has done the most extensive research on the history of La Chaise-Dieu. A good introduction to each of the abbots mentioned below can be found in his *L'Abbaye de la Chaise-Dieu (1043–1518)* (Paris: Éditions Cujas, 1962) 92–162. For a recent study of La Chaise-Dieu and its first abbots see Maureen M. O'Brien, "Far From the Heart: The Social, Political, and Ecclesiastical Milieu of the Early Abbots of La Chaise-Dieu, 1052–1184" (Ph.D. diss., Western Michigan University, 2006).

3. *Gallia Christiana*, II, Instr. col. 107. Dom Simon Genoux, *Histoire de l'abbaye de la Chaise-Dieu*, in *Librorum Monasterii S. Roberti Casae Dei catalogo inscriptus* (Paris, Bibliothèque Nationale, ms. latin, 12818) 272. See Gaussin, 124. See also, Etienne Baluze, *Histoire généalogique de la Maison d'Auvergne*, vol. 1 (Paris: A. Dezallier, 1708) 51. For Pope Alexander II's confirmation, see Jaffé, 4720; and *Monumenta pontificia Arverniae*, no. XXIII, 45.

4. André Baudrit, *Sainte-Gemme, histoire locale, église, prieuré* (Saint-Ouen-en-Brie: La Lucarne Ovale, 1996) 229–230.

5. Hugh of Flavigny, *Chronica*, in *Monumenta Germaniae Historiae*, vol. 8, 474; O'Brien, 67–89.

6. For the *vita* of Adelelmus, see "Altera S. Adelelmi Vita," in *España Sagrada*, ed. H. Flórez, vol. 27 (Madrid: M. F. Rodriguez, 1747–): 832–841, and 841–866. See also, F. Javier Peña Pérez, *El Monasterio de San Juan de Burgos, 1091–1436: dinámica*

Seguin (1078–1094) succeeded Adelelmus as abbot. 'During his time, the monastery's reputation for religious observance and its possessions expanded greatly'(3.5). Seguin was born at Escotay, thirty miles northeast of La Chaise-Dieu and joined the chapter of Saint-Jean at Lyon (3.5).[7] There he became acquainted with Hugh of Die, with whom he collaborated as abbot. Count Raymond IV was very devoted to Robert and supportive of La Chaise-Dieu during Seguin's abbacy.[8] From Pope Gregory VII Seguin secured papal support against interference from the canons of Clermont, and Gregory submitted to him the abbey of Saint Peter of Frassinoro in Modena. With Bishop Hugh of Chateauneuf he had an important part in the founding of the Carthusians.[9] Under Seguin, La Chaise-Dieu assumed stewardship of many monasteries and churches, and monks of La Chaise-Dieu were sent as reforming abbots to other communities. Seguin commissioned Marbod's *Vita* of Robert; Marbod dedicated the second book to Seguin. Seguin died at the dependent priory of Vignonet in 1094 (3.8).[10]

After the period of rapid growth under Abbot Seguin, which brought La Chaise-Dieu to an eminent place in the European church, Pons of Tournon (1094–1102) became abbot. Bernard describes him as 'a man of great discretion and piety' (3.9). He had come to the abbey as a child oblate.[11] Upon his election he traveled to Rome to seek papal confirmation of the abbey's goods and privileges. Pons traveled back to France with Urban II, who went to La Chaise-Dieu to bless the abbey church.[12] Pons was elected bishop of Le Puy in 1102 and died in 1112 (3.9).[13]

---

de un modelo cultural feudal (Burgos: Ediciones J.M. Garrido Garrido, 1989); O'Brien, 112–118.

7. Hugh of Flavigny, *Chronica*, 443.

8. For Count Raymond, see John Hugh Hill and Laurita Lyttleton Hill, *Raymond IV de Saint-Gilles* (Toulouse: Édouard Privat, 1959).

9. *Tablettes Historiques de Velay*, vol. 8 (Le Puy: Th. Bérard, Libraire, 1878) 14–15. See Bernard Bligny, *L'Eglise et les ordres religieux dans le Royaume de Bourgogne aux XIe et XIIe siècles* (Paris: Presses universitaires de France, 1960) 259.

10. O'Brien, 99–125.

11. See Gaussin, 139.

12. Jaffé, 5571.

13. O'Brien, 126–143.

Pons was succeeded by Aimeric (1102–1111), who then was appointed bishop of Clermont and held that office until 1150 (3.10). Under his successor, Stephen of Mercoeur (1111–1146), La Chaise-Dieu's 'reputation for religious life, and the monastery's possessions increased far and wide' (3.11). Stephen's prominent family had placed him in the abbey as a child oblate. Pope Eugene III, just before Stephen's death, issued a bull confirming the abbey's possessions and listing twenty-six dependencies.[14]

The list expanded during Stephen's tenure. Stephen was succeeded by Jordan of Montboissier (1146–1157), the brother of Peter the Venerable of Cluny.[15] Bernard lists a chapter on him in the table of contents to book three of the *Tripartite Life*, but he seems never to have written the chapter.[16]

Bernard was writing during the abbacy of Pons of Beaudiner (1157–1168), who had been a child oblate.[17] In 1168, after a decade of abbatial service during a time of growing political unrest, Pons left on pilgrimage to Palestine. He didn't actually resign, but his intent seems to have been to become a hermit in the Holy Land. He died at his retreat there on 30 April 1168. He was the last abbot of La Chaise-Dieu to be considered a saint.

Conclusion

From the perspective of a century, Bernard looked back on his spiritual father's life and death. He saw that the project that Robert launched at La Chaise-Dieu had grown and spread from the Auvergne to other parts of France and to Italy and Spain. He celebrated a series of highly effective abbots of a community and congregation that had done much to revitalize the church. By the time Bernard wrote, La Chaise-Dieu had reached its apogee. There

14. *Monumenta pontificia Arverniae*, no. CXXX, 207.

15. In his critical edition of the letters of Peter the Venerable, Giles Constable traces the earliest origins of this famous monk. See *The Letters of Peter the Venerable*, vol. 2 (Cambridge: Harvard University Press, 1967) 233–246.

16. O'Brien, 145–208.

17. François Gardon, *Histoire de l'Abbaye de la Chaize-Dieu* (1912; Marseille: Laffitte Reprints, 1981) 58–59.

were fewer miracles by his time, but Robert's greatest miracle was his home and his theme: the community.

Reflecting on a visit he made to La Chaise-Dieu almost a century ago, Hilaire Belloc wrote, 'I could wish to return in a hundred or two hundred years and see whether my guess that the great place should come into use again, had proved true or false; for certainly it bears the air of a foundation intended to endure, and to be restored to life.'[18]

18. Hilaire Belloc, *Towns of Destiny* (New York: Robert McBride, 1927) 233. Today, there is again a religious community at La Chaise-Dieu: http://www.abbaye-chaise-dieu.com.

The Tripartite Life of Robert, Abbot of La Chaise-Dieu

Preface

The august miracles of Christ, the eternal king, by which He deigns to declare continually in His saints the ineffable glory of His majesty, should be stored in our memories. As He is confessed and praised, they should be announced to the whole world. For this reason, since everyone should endeavor to do this, not unfittingly I have taken care to write down in three parts the welcome and admirable miracles of Blessed Robert, the confessor, my father and nurturer. God's grace wished these to be spread abroad widely, not only in the neighboring regions of Gaul, but also in foreign countries. With the help of God, I've reported these, which others, for the sake of brevity, omitted when they treated his deeds. I have learned these things from those who shared his life, or from those who testified to what they had seen, and even from what I myself have been able to grasp truly by sight or listening. I've omitted everything found in the life written of Lord Stephen,[1] his disciple, and what is in the acts of the distinguished fathers who founded St. Gemme's in the Saintonge.[2]

1. Stephen was Robert's first disciple. There is considerable information about him in Marbod's life of Robert. This paragraph seems to indicate that Stephen was the object of a life also. One possible interpretation of 3.8 below is that Bernard wrote a *vita* of Stephen.

2. At this point AA SS OSB 9:215 refers to a passage quoted from the cartulary of the monastery of St. Gemme by the authors of a history of the counts of Poitiers. The fragment was cited in the introduction above. William VIII, count of Poitiers and duke of Aquitaine, in 1074, invited Casadean monks into his lands to establish a community at Sainte-Gemme.

The first section contains the wonders that God arranged to shine forth through the blessed man while he was still alive. The second section includes those by which the Supreme Rewarder bore witness that after Robert finished the course of the present life he lived on in heaven. Finally, the third section contains the merits and names of those who succeeded him in the pastoral rule of the monastery of La Chaise-Dieu up to the present time, 1160 AD, and of those of their subjects who were renowned for signs and miracles. As one of three companions[3] he chose the service of the Supreme King in His threefold Name, and rewarded by that same God, One-and-Three, he is finally in glory, and so it seemed good to me to divide the book containing this small work into three sections and call it Tripartite. So much for that. Now let us come to what we have proposed.

Chapters of Part One

1 The Rule of Blessed Benedict, abbot, is brought by an angel.
2 Cleansing a leper.
3 Divinely given knowledge about some eels.
4 The holy man clothes a pilgrim angel.
5 A time when he was not solicitous about the morrow.
6 A time when Blessed Mary appeared to the holy man.
7 The healing of a man who was deaf and mute.
8 A small container of rations that was enough for many people for a year.
9 A knight and the cure of a matron's son.
10 A devil lying in wait for a woman.
11 Gloves supported by a sunbeam.
12 The place of his burial divinely indicated beforehand.
13 Though he was sick, he did not cease celebrating Mass.
14 Commendation of charity.
15 The season, hour and day when he crossed over from this light.
16 How he commended his pastoral care to Christ and His Mother.

3. The obvious meaning of *cum tribus sociis* would be 'with three companions', but see 1.18 below, where Robert is said to have had two companions.

17 How he died.
18 The time and date when he sought the hermitage and entered heaven.

1.1 The Rule of Blessed Benedict, abbot, brought by an angel.

A very distinguished man, named Robert, the treasurer of St. Julian in Brioude, left all worldly cares behind. After Christmas, on the day of the Holy Innocents,[4] with two companions he entered a desolate wilderness. After he had persisted in his holy resolve for a long time, and the reputation of his religious group had attracted many right-living people from far and wide, they determined to serve Christ there under his leadership. He yielded to their wishes, and a large multitude of clerics and former soldiers enlisted in his holy encampment. The number of disciples and the observance of religion increased. The desolation of the place and the diversity of their zealous intentions seemed to preclude these many people living together. Some sought to take up an eremitical life; others, a cenobitic one; still others, a canonial life. One day they were all having a discussion so that the divine clemency would show them to which of these forms of religious life they should be subject. A pilgrim, distinguished in countenance and clothes, handed a book to the porter of the monastery, saying, 'Take this book to the brothers gathered in chapter; they need it very much.' Very quickly he took the book to the brothers. They opened the book and saw that it was the *Rule of Saint Benedict*. They were amazed at this and gave thanks for this heavenly arrangement. They all gratefully accepted the monastic way of life. They did so all the more devoutly because they realized that it was divinely appointed. Because he did not want the pilgrim to leave unrewarded, the porter looked for him, but couldn't find him. He sent messengers, who diligently inquired, but they could not find him or anyone who had seen him. Evidently this was something divine, not human.

1.2 The cleansing of a leper.

Blessed Robert, now clothed as a monk, accepted the office of superior. One time, on the Assumption of the Blessed Virgin, he

4. In 1043, as a note in AA SS OSB 9:214 observes.

was present in the refectory of the canons of Clermont, in accord with an arrangement established with Bishop Rencon, his uncle.[5] This prelate, with all the canons, had decreed that on the Feast of the Assumption, reverently celebrated by the abbot himself, both Robert and all who succeeded him as abbot of La Chaise-Dieu, with six companions who were monks and seven servants, would be served at the head table in the refectory with the canons. An ample piece of meat was served. All the canons asked him to eat heartily of it for God's charity and the love of the Virgin. He saw that he was in a position where he could not decline without calling attention to himself. As he put a small bit in his mouth, he gave all the rest of the portion to a leper shaking his rattle at the door. The server said, 'It is going well for you, Peter (that was the name of the leper, the son of the canons' cook) for Dom Robert, abbot of La Chaise-Dieu has visited you with a very great gift.' So, the sick man, rejoicing and exultant, after his hunger was satisfied, wiped his face and his whole, ulcerous body. He said, 'God, who has deigned to visit me through blessed Robert in order to feed me, will through his merits look with mercy on my leprosy and heal it.' Wondrously, he immediately sensed that his illness was completely cured. He beheld the form and comeliness of his body and skin. And so on the octave of that Feast of the Assumption of our blessed and glorious Lady, he was led into the church, completely cured, while everyone praised God.

1.3 Divinely given knowledge about some eels.

Similarly, when Robert, the servant of the Lord, was at Saint Germain[6] during Lent, the prior of the monastery was having some eels, which he had found in the market, prepared for the meal. The

5. King Henry I's charter of 1052 required: 1) the bishop of Clermont ratify abbatial elections; and 2) the abbot of La Chaise-Dieu, with two or three monks, go to the cathedral in Clermont each year on the feast of the Assumption to celebrate the solemnity with the canons and to donate to them three pounds of incense (*Privilegium Henrici I Francorum regis pro Casae-Dei Monasterio* in PL 151:1031–32).

6. AA SS OSB 9:215 indicates that this seems to be the village of Saint-Germain, which is about twelve miles from La Chaise-Dieu. Robert established a priory there.

man of God came out of the evening office and entered the kitchen. He said to the cook, 'Throw those eels into the trash and be sure that no one eats them.' When he had done this, he returned to the church. When the divine praises were finished, the procurator of the house heard what had happened. He said to the blessed man, 'Lord, father, what will I do now, since I don't have the eels which I was glad to buy, and I cannot find anything to put before you to eat?' To him the man of the Lord answered, 'Don't be sad about this, son, because the servants of God ought not be sickened by bad food.' A few days later, a merchant, the owner of those eels, was found dead. His killer, who had stolen and sold the eels, was apprehended and hung on a gallows. O how great is God's mercy, which imbued the holy man with the spirit of prophecy and showed to future generations how great was his merit!

1.4 The holy man clothes a pilgrim angel.

One day while the servant of God, Robert, was traveling, he entered a wide, flat place. His companions had gone ahead a little way. He met a pilgrim of venerable appearance, who asked what he could give him since he was suffering from the cold, for he had nothing with him but a single garment. Robert took off his cloak[7] and gave it to the needy person. He accepted it gladly, and spoke these words to the man of God, 'Robert, Robert, know that you are blessed and more than blessed now and so you will be forever.' Robert's companions were waiting for him. Noticing that he was very affected by the cold north wind, they could not fail to know what he had done, even though the poor man who had accepted the gift never appeared in the open. The blessed man is regarded as blessed with blessings upon blessings, more each day, and his name has been proclaimed gloriously from sea to sea.

1.5 A time when he was not solicitous about the morrow.

The holy man had to go to the archbishop of Vienne on business. When the provisions that he and his companions needed on their journey had almost run out, the brothers did not take it lightly. He

7. *pelliciam*, a fur-lined cape.

said to them, 'You must not forget the saying of the Lord, who said, "Give, and it will be given to you"' (Lk 6:38). The archbishop supplied the man of God and his company magnificently. When Robert had finished the business for which he had come, the archbishop honored them with great generosity. And so when the holy man returned to his companions,[8] he said, 'Brothers, do not doubt any longer about God's overflowing goodness.'

1.6 A time when blessed Mary appeared to the holy man.

One time he decided to celebrate the Assumption of the Blessed Virgin Mary with the community at Fournols.[9] When a place had been prepared for him next to the altar, he wanted to remain there alone in vigil and prayer. When much of the night had passed, Gerald, his chaplain, was still in a corner of the church. At that point he heard the voices of two people speaking together near the altar. He stood astonished and amazed for a while. When the holy day dawned, this Gerald, because he was close to Robert, asked him privately, 'Lord, if it pleases Your Paternity, I want to be told plainly what and with whom you were speaking during the night of the holy feast.' He replied, 'Brother Gerald, why do you ask what it doesn't profit you to know? Nevertheless, you can know that Our Lady of heaven and Queen of all the earth deigned to appear to me. It is not helpful for me to say what she wished to reveal, nor is it helpful for you or any mortal to hear it at the present time.' From this one can gather how great and abundant is God's sweetness that He wishes to keep hidden for those who fear him. To those who have the charity that, when perfect, casts out fear, he makes known the sweetness of some of his secrets.

8. *ad sua*.

9. According to a note in AA SS OSB 9:218, this priory of La Chaise-Dieu, dedicated to the Blessed Virgin, was located in the diocese of Clermont about twelve miles from the abbey. Fournols was amongst the first churches given to La Chaise-Dieu by Bishop Rencon of Clermont, Robert's uncle (Genoux, *Histoire de l'abbaye de la Chaise-Dieu*, Paris, Bibliothèque Nationale, MS. latin 12818, 42).

1.7 The healing of a man who was deaf and mute.

This same blessed man, Robert, once went to the church of St. Desiderius, which was erected near the castle of Bocenelle.[10] He met a deaf and mute young man, whom he knew; he was the nephew of the priest of that church. He said to him, 'Where is the priest, your uncle?' The mute youth immediately responded, 'Lord father, he is out, but he will come soon.' When the priest heard that the abbot had come, he went to meet him as quickly as possible. When he saw his nephew rejoicing and jumping up and down for joy, speaking and hearing, he was unbelievably happy. The servant of God wanted this to be credited not to himself, but to Blessed Desiderius and to the young man's faith.

1.8 A small container of rations that was enough for many people for a year.

Again, the holy man went to his monastery at Luzillat. The community there was long wearied by the troublesome and clamoring voices of creditors of the brother who was in charge of the place. Robert called the brother and commanded him to quiet these clamors. His reply was 'Lord, I don't have anything with which to pay them back, except these rations, which are in this jar. They are scarcely enough for us for a month.' The man of the Lord said to him, 'Give out the little bit that you have and don't stop trusting in the goodness of our Lord.' So the brother began to pay off the creditors, and, miraculously, when all had been paid off, the container remained full. It proved sufficient for all their needs for a whole year. Thus, the servant of God wished to render to each what was his, knowing for sure that nothing is lacking to those who fear God' (Sir 40:26).[11]

10. According to AA SS OSB 9:217, this priory, and the one at Luzillat mentioned in the next paragraph, were located in the diocese of Clermont. The first church is probably Saint-Dier near Boissonnelle, entrusted to La Chaise-Dieu, as was Luzillat mentioned in the next paragraph, by Robert's uncle, Bishop Rencon of Clermont (Genoux, 42).

11. This story parallels the story in 2 Kgs 4:1–7 about Elisha and the widow whose jug of oil filled up miraculously.

1.9 A knight, and the cure of a matron's son.

There was a castle in the Auvergne, called Brosada,[12] which the man of the Lord frequently visited. There the head of the household prepared a chair, table and bed for him. The man was bothered by a serious physical ailment. The son of a matron was also suffering from a grave malady. Both hurried to the man of God with steps of faith. The man drank dust from the chair and table of the man of God; she laid her son on the bed of Christ's servant.[13] Both immediately received the gift of health that they desired. It was therefore clear to all how powerful is the faith that thus supplied to believers what they desired.

1.10 A demon lying in wait for a woman.

At the monastery called Port-Dieu,[14] a certain woman was collecting oil on Sunday. The man of God was passing by the monastery and saw a demon next to her urging her to this task. Because of this, the holy man groaned and said, 'What a horrible companion this woman has!' So in a public sermon he admonished that no work should be done when a Sunday was being celebrated.

1.11 His gloves supported by a sunbeam.

At the monastery of Vignonet,[15] he was giving a sermon outside to the people. Two boy-clerics had found his gloves in the church. They were tossing them back and forth, and the gloves seemed to hang on a sunbeam. They were astonished by this and called out;

12. This might be the castle of Busséol.

13. See the story about Elisha and the son of the Shunammite woman in 2 Kings 4:31–37.

14. According to AA SS OSB 9:217, this priory of La Chaise-Dieu, under the patronage of St. Martin, was located in the diocese of Limoges. It was founded on land given by Raoul "Little Sparrow" upon his entry at La Chaise-Dieu (see below 2.2; see also Gaussin, 114).

15. AA SS OSB 9:917 notes that Seguin, the fourth abbot of La Chaise-Dieu, was received at this priory and died there. See below 3.8. This priory was founded c. 1060 in the diocese of Clermont (Gaussin, 139; *Gallia Christiana*, t. 2, cols. 330–331, which gives *Avinionensi* as Avignonnet.)

many people gathered there. Seeing the mighty works of Christ, they glorified him who works such wonders through his saints.

1.12 The place of his burial divinely indicated beforehand.

On Friday before Palm Sunday, the energetic general of the Exalted King, who was worthy to accept largess for his honorable military service, was speaking with some brothers who were with him in the western parlor of La Chaise-Dieu. A divine voice came to him as he was discussing the needs of the monastery. It said, 'As soon as possible go to the gates of the monastery to see the place in which you will soon rest.' While the others who were present listened, he responded, 'Thanks be to God.' When they asked what he wanted to say, this was the reply they heard, 'Let us go, brothers, to see the place God has prepared for me.' So they followed him and found there something like the handle of a plough, as long as a man. It was where his body is now buried. When they saw it, he said, 'Behold my place, the place of burial God has assigned me.'

1.13 Though he was sick, he did not cease celebrating Mass.

He continued to pray vigils, psalms and hymns devoutly in his usual manner during the following Holy Week. And so he came to Holy Saturday, the vigil of the Easter feast. When he completed the offices of the sacred feast, the children of the nobility of that region were brought to him for baptism, as was customary. He had barely baptized one of them when he was seized with a fever. Another took his place to do the baptizing, and when he had finished the rest of the holy rites, Robert was carried to his bed. On the following, most holy day, his strength returned. When he had finished celebrating Holy Mass, his brothers supported his weak limbs and led him to his bed.

1.14 Commendation of charity.

As his weakness increased, he said to all his disciples gathered around him, 'You know, brothers, that the love of Christ led you here, how he taught through us that you should have charity, and how he commanded us to give charitably what is ours to all, whether known or strangers, rich or poor, whether they ask or not. For this reason I arranged to have the high altar of this monastery consecrated in the principal name of the Great God, which is charity, so that His charity might have first place in this community and its members, and so that the evil of possessiveness and greed could find no corner in it. Finally, I declare plainly that if you have not observed these things that we have declared to you, you will inevitably undergo tribulation and lack everything. On the other hand, if you and your successors have observed these diligently, without any hedging, God will prepare temporal goods and eternal joys in abundance.'

1.15 The season, hour and day when he crossed over from this light.

'My passage from earth will, I hope, Christ willing, be at dawn on the third day after the octave of the Resurrection of the Lord.'[16]

1.16 How he commended his pastoral care to Christ and His Mother.

Finally, after being anointed, he had himself carried into the oratory. There he placed his pastoral staff in the arms of the infant Christ imagined sitting on the lap of His Mother, saying as he did so, 'Jesus Christ, my Lord and my God,[17] from you I have received the staff of ruling over this monastery. To you and to our mother,[18] I hand it over. I will support with prayers those whom, insofar as it lies within my choice, I leave as rulers of this monastery.'

1.17 How he died.

When he had done this, fortified for his crossing by the divine sacraments, he kissed his brothers and said goodbye. At the time he had said, he passed over to the joys of the angels, while the boys in the choir sang psalms and said, 'Let every spirit praise the Lord.'[19]

16. The editors indicate that the text here is corrupt.
17. John 20:28.
18. John 19:26.
19. Ps 150:6.

1.18 The time and date when he sought the hermitage and heaven.

This blessed man went up into the mountains on the Nativity of Christ with two companions in the name of the holy and undivided Trinity. On the third day after the octave of the Resurrection, on the fifteenth day of the calends of May, he ascended the heights of heaven, and on the octave of that he was buried. Radulf's vision[20] declared that he was led along by the mother of the Lord, introduced into the heavenly palace, and exalted by the holy and ineffable Trinity, to Whom be honor and rule forever. Amen.

Chapters of Part Two

- 2.1 The multitude of people who gathered for his funeral.
- 2.2 Raoul's vision, who he was and what he did.
- 2.3 The appearance of the blessed man; the washing of his body.
- 2.4 The many miracles for which his tomb is renowned.
- 2.5 The visit of the archbishop of Embrun.
- 2.6 How his feast day was authorized.
- 2.7 The fish brought by an eagle.
- 2.8 Prohibition of miracles.
- 2.9 The vision of the archdeacon of Modena.
- 2.10 The homage of Raymond, count of St.-Gilles.
- 2.11 The affection that he had toward La Chaise-Dieu afterwards.
- 2.12 No one who hoped in the holy man was disappointed.
- 2.13 The contempt of Audebert, bishop of Agen.
- 2.14 A woman spinning on his feast day.
- 2.15 A soldier freed from chains.
- 2.16 The death of a haughty knight's horse.

2.1 The multitude of people who gathered for his funeral.

The death of Abbot Robert, the holy man beloved of God, called forth so many people from the surrounding dioceses and provinces that the multitude of people converging at La Chaise-Dieu would not fit into the village or on the length and breadth of the roads.

20. See Part 2.2 below.

Present for the funeral were people of every gender, age, rank, and a great multitude of the sick who wanted a relic of the holy man.

2.2 Raoul's vision; who he was and what he did.

In the middle of this, one of his earliest disciples, Raoul by name, whose cognomen was "Little Sparrow,"[21] weighed down with great anguish at the sudden death of his master, withdrew to a place apart and slept. He saw a wondrous vision of the Mother of God coming down over the holy body. This is described by Master Marbod, archdeacon of Angers and later bishop of Rennes, in the second book that he wrote about the miracles of blessed Robert.[22] The man came from the village of Saint Silvain, located in the territory of the Auvergne, near the town called Murat. Blessed Robert called him away from his shallow occupation as a mime to the service of Christ. As a result, more than the others he embraced his master with the arms of true love.

The Lord allowed him to add many possessions to the monastery of La Chaise-Dieu, specifically the church of Saint Silvain, just mentioned; the monastery of Port-Dieu; a monastery in the territory of Agenais called Caritas, along with two other churches; and in the Limonsin, the Chapelle-Fulcher, where living in honorable old age, he completed this life and was buried.[23]

2.3 The appearance of the blessed man; the washing of his body.

When the body of blessed Robert had been properly venerated until the eighth day after his passing,[24] it was consigned to the grave

21. Passerenus.

22. *The Life of Robert* 2.8.

23. Upon Raoul's entry into La Chaise-Dieu sometime before 1060, he donated all his goods and lands to the abbey, providing lands for several foundations: the church of Allanche (by 1067, a priory) in the diocese of Clermont; the land on which Port-Dieu would be founded (by 1060; see 1.10) and the church Chapelle-Fulcher (later, by 1067, the priory of Chapelle-St-Robert) in the diocese of Limoges; and the church Saint-Christophe-Cambes (by 1067, a priory) in the diocese of Agen. See Gaussin, 114.

24. The text here seems to be corrupt. I have chosen to read *venerande* as *venerandum*. This participial form adds a note of necessity or fittingness.

at the spot that had been divinely shown him beforehand. Afterwards, the saint appeared to some of his monastic disciples and told them that his head was being crushed by a rock that had been put over it. When the rock had been removed as he had requested, it was discovered that his nose was destroyed. Subsequently, because of the multitude of sick people seeking help, his clothes were kept for the benefit of present and future generations. The body was then washed with wine and carefully wrapped in a deer hide. After that, as was proper, it was carefully returned to its place.

2.4 The many miracles for which his tomb is renowned.

His tomb began to be renowned for divine miracles. So much so that if anyone (even if he were awash with the eloquence of Virgil or Cicero) tried to hand them on in writing for the benefit of future generations, he would be buried under the huge weight of material and sucked dry by the overflowing magnitude. So great was the magnitude of different maladies—an enormous number of the possessed, deaf, mute, crippled and those burdened by other calamities—that they would not be strong enough to resist one another's sicknesses. In fact, although the amount of illness and the suffering of the crowd seemed boundless, no one seemed to be deprived of the desired health, which was administered by the abundant grace of God and the care of blessed Robert.

2.5 The visit of the archbishop of Embrun.[25]

The happy report of such frequent miracles went out day by day, far and wide, not just to the neighboring provinces, but also to foreign and distant provinces. And so it happened that the Archbishop of Embrun, a city in the Maritime Alps, was disturbed by the reports about this. Because he had been acquainted with the blessed man when he was alive, he came to La Chaise-Dieu.

He entered the church seeking a place for prayer, and he remained alone before the tomb of the holy man. He devoutly prayed to God to show him the truth regarding this matter. In His kindness,

25. Embrun, in the French Alps, was the head of an archdiocese until the French Revolution. Most of its former territory is now in the diocese of Gap.

God did not want to postpone granting his desire. Two unmistakable miracles were soon worked in his presence. He was in awe, beyond belief. He was amazed that he was answered so quickly, and praising and glorifying God, he returned home happily, harboring no doubt.

2.6 How his feast day was authorized.

Gerald, whose cognomen, Laveine, derived from a village in the Auvergne located not far from the castle of Bulhon,[26] was a disciple and chaplain of blessed Robert. He wrote about his life and miracles. He went to Rome to the Apostolic See and made known to it the entire, holy story, carefully, step-by-step. When they had heard what he told them, the lord pope, with the whole gathering of cardinals, expressed thanks to God. Rising from the Apostolic See, he blessed for its holiness and devotion the Gaul in which blessed Robert had lived. He decreed with apostolic authority that henceforth the day of his death would be a solemn feast in the order of Holy Confessors. Gerald returned from the territory of St. Peter to La Chaise-Dieu. The community assembled, and it was decreed that in all the monasteries of La Chaise-Dieu in every land, the feast of the blessed master was to be celebrated in a manner worthy and praiseworthy before God and men. All accepted this most gladly, and each returned to the place entrusted to him.

2.7 The fish brought by an eagle.[27]

The prior of Allanche[28] had celebrated the feast in a festive way up to the Mass. Then a brother said to him, "What are we going to do today, since for us this is a solemn day? Little, if anything,

26. There was a priory subject to La Chaise-Dieu at Bulhon, founded by 1052 in the diocese of Clermont. See Gaussin, 399.

27. There is a similar story about an eagle delivering a fish in answer to prayer in Bede's prose *Life of St.Cuthbert*; the story is cited in David N. Bell's anthology, *Wholly Animals: A Book of Beastly Tales*, CS 128 (Kalamazoo: Cistercian, 1992) 51–52.

28. AA SS OSB 9:221 identifies Allanche as a priory in the diocese of Clermont. Its church was dedicated to St. John the Baptist. The priory was founded by 1067. See Gaussin, 399.

remains to eat.' The prior responded, using the words of the Lord, 'Brother, don't be anxious about what we will eat or what we will drink. Let us go into the church and sing the First Mass[29] in honor of God and blessed Robert, and all these things will be added to us in sufficiency through blessed Robert.'[30] This promise was quickly realized for those who believed it. As soon as the sequence of the Mass was begun, an immense fish, popularly called a pike,[31] was flung before the doors of the church by an eagle flying over the church. Those who went outside at the sound of this and saw the wondrous deeds of God brought the fish inside. As was proper they all happily celebrated the feast most devoutly with equal prayer and rejoicing, magnifying and praising God who always glorifies his saints.

2.8 The prohibition of miracles.

Meanwhile, the tomb of the venerable confessor of La Chaise-Dieu was so renowned for such frequent miracles that even someone endowed with an exceptional memory could scarcely or never relate them orally one by one or commend them in writing to the memory of future generations. So great was the abundance of offerings that it was received not by counting it as it was divided, but by measuring it with a bowl.

In the monastery the clamor and tumult of the sick, who arrived and then recovered their health and left, praising the power of blessed Robert and filling the ears of the inhabitants, was such and so great that only with difficulty could they hear each other and—what was unbearable—they could not render the divine services devoutly. So those senior by birth and more fervent in spirit came to the tomb of the blessed man and conversed with him as follows. They said, 'Lord, father, following your lead we chose the squalor of this deserted place and we entered it gladly so that we might gain pardon for our sins and the grace of the Redeemer.

29. In many medieval monasteries there were two or three Masses on a single day.

30. Mt 6:31–32.

31. The Latin name is *lucius*. On this fish see Hildegard von Bingen, *Heilkraft der Natur. Physica*, tr. Marie-Louise Portman (Augsburg: Pattloch, 1997) 354–355.

Because of the great number of miracles now, our divine services are growing more deficient; we can neither weep for our sins nor fittingly complete the divine services. We ask, therefore, that your merits would grant us that all these disturbances be laid to rest so that here we may serve Christ the Lord in peace and in the future find forgiveness for our sins.' For a time, it was feared that none of the poor would come to the tomb because the door would not be opened to them any more, and services would not be offered. Gradually the tumult quieted down and religious observance of holy quiet increased.

2.9 The vision of the archdeacon of Modena[32]

Divine providence determined to illumine with the grace of the merits of the blessed Robert not only the Cisalpine provinces of Gaul, but also foreign nations and regions. A prelate of Modena, while on his way to pray at St. James in Galicia, stopped as a guest at a church that was ruled by La Chaise-Dieu. He stayed there one night. When the priest of that church kept repeating over and over the name of Robert as he came and went, the bishop said, 'Lord priest, who is this holy Robert? Is he the one whose monastery is near the church of the Blessed Virgin at Le Puy?'[33] 'That is he, my lord bishop,' replied the priest. The bishop declared, 'It is not fitting to cover in silence what occurred recently in our city through this good man. On a feast day, some leading clerics and lay people of the town were sitting with us in our community. While they were dealing with some of their business, it happened that our archdeacon fell asleep for a while. When he woke up, he began to disclose carefully to us what he had seen and heard. He said, "I was just now led before the gates of a magnificent palace; its splendor exceeded the scope of the human senses. In the middle of it sat the lord of the palace, magnificent in countenance and dress. His name was Robert. Around the palace, on his right and left, sat a great concourse of distinguished men. While I observed them

32. The Casadean monastery of Saint-Peter of Frassinoro was located in Modena in northern Italy.

33. The church of Notre Dame at Le Puy-en-Velay was an ancient Marian pilgrimage site often visited by those on their way to Compostela.

carefully and willingly, behold, a man celebrated and well known in the city was led in by distinguished men and placed in view of the elder of the palace." He was then asked what he wanted. "Lord," he said, "a short time ago I wanted to be associated with the benefits of your monastery; now, if it please God, I desire to be joined to your community." "And this," he replied, "is pleasing to us." He then ordered him to sit with the rest. When I heard this, I immediately woke up.' When the archdeacon had recounted this, a great many bells began to ring throughout the city. While we were asking what was going on, the wife and sons and friends of the citizen who appeared in the vision that the archdeacon had recounted to us, entered our presence and with tears told us that he had died. When we inquired, they told us the following about the manner of his confession. They related that when he had begun to be very ill, he said, '"I wish to become a monk of Robert of La Chaise-Dieu. Once, when I was at Notre-Dame of Le Puy, I was drawn by the good repute of his monastery and decided to go to his monastery beyond the mountains. There with my companions I was charitably received. I offered myself as a monk, and so I want to become his monk." However, since we could not find a monk of that monastery, he had a Cluniac monk come and asked him to give him the religious habit in the name of blessed Robert. When that had been done, he was led out from this light.' If we look carefully at how this story agreed with the vision of the archdeacon, we can conclude from that how great is the merit of Robert in the sight of God, how certain is human salvation and how devoutly one should seek the company of religious men of holy repute.

2.10 Raymond, Count of St.-Gilles

The glory of the great confessor gradually diffused the sweet scent of his fame among the peoples. Raymond, who was first called count of St.-Gilles,[34] was deprived of all his paternal inheritance. With

34. Count Raymond IV of Toulouse (1041/2–1109) was a steadfast supporter of La Chaise-Dieu as is evidenced in his donations to the abbey, and in the fact that he made another pilgrimage to pay homage at the tomb of Saint Robert prior to his departure on crusade. For more on Count Raymond see, John Hugh and Laurita Lyttleton Hill, *Raymond IV de Saint-Gilles* (Toulouse: Édouard Privat, 1959).

one companion he came to La Chaise-Dieu, that is, to the abode of blessed Robert. He entered and kept watch before his holy tomb, pressing his case and need as though before a most certain helper and advocate. When Mass had been celebrated in the morning, he made homage to blessed Robert. He took his sword from above the altar and confirmed that he would have and hold the office of count of Toulouse from no one but blessed Robert, should God arrange to hand it over to him through Robert. He was not long in satisfying his desire, for after he left St. Robert's monastery and reached the boundary of his paternal lands, all the nobles, without objection, made homage to him. Giving him heartfelt adherence, in one rush they placed under him the city of Toulouse and the other provinces that were due him by paternal right. When he saw that, he gave great thanks to Christ the Lord, and as long as he lived he venerated the blessed confessor Robert with all his heart and with great devotion and veneration.

2.11 The affection that he had for La Chaise-Dieu afterwards.

It pleased Divine Providence to liberate His holy city, Jerusalem, which was oppressed by the wicked yoke of the pagans. He stirred up the hearts of some Christian princes to go in arms to the Lord's sepulcher to restore its former freedom. Among them was Raymond, count of St.-Gilles, about whom we are speaking. When he gave himself most zealously to this endeavor and took up the cross, he had a cup of blessed Robert. He took with him Arbert, the prior of Privezac,[35] a monastery of La Chaise-Dieu. The historians of the expedition give well-known accounts of how he distinguished himself on that expedition. When Monte-Peregrino[36] had been erected and the city of Tripoli captured, he made Arbert, the monk of La Chaise-Dieu just mentioned, the bishop of that city. When the count had been taken from this world, this bishop of Tripoli sent to La Chaise-Dieu the cup of blessed Robert, just as the count had ordered. The count, while he lived, cherished it among the relics of the saints that he brought back. The bishop

35. Privezac, in the diocese of Rodez, was founded by 1096.

36. San-Juan del Monte-Peregrino was a church built in Tripoli by the Crusaders.

sent many other ornaments and great riches to La Chaise-Dieu as well. Therefore, this outstanding man became ever more illustrious while he stood beneath the wings of the confessor of Christ, until Christ brought him into his kingdom.

2.12 No one who hoped in the holy man was disappointed.

In the same way, it is clearer than daylight to us that all those who implore his help because of some problem are never denied what they hope for. Many who came to him childless and asked for help merited to become fertile right away.

2.13 On the contempt of Audebert,[37] bishop of Agen.

The just providence of God arranged that as the subjects of the blessed man were exalted, so those who were arrogant toward him and proud were cast down and humbled.[38] A monk of La Chaise-Dieu, a man distinguished for his knowledge and piety attended a synod of Aldebert, bishop of Agen, because plunderers were treating the church of St. Livrade[39] and other churches of blessed Robert in his diocese unjustly. When the bishop spoke contemptuously of St. Robert, something invisible struck him and he fell backwards. The synod praised God and extolled the name of blessed Robert to the stars. Each returned home with joy and praise. Because the bishop was a prudent and reasonable man, he came to La Chaise-Dieu. In my presence he knelt before his tomb and declared him an excellent confessor.

2.14 A woman spinning on his feast day.

Although the person and cause are different from that of the previous account, a similar punishment of contempt toward the blessed confessor Robert was divinely manifest in the city of Clermont. Once, the priest of St. Genesius commanded the women to

37. He is called Aldebertus in the text of this chapter.

38. Lk 1:52.

39. In 1117 the canons of Livrade had decided to join La Chaise-Dieu. The priory of St. Liberata (Livrade) was one of the principal dependencies of La Chaise-Dieu.

celebrate the feast of St. Robert. One of the women of the parish spurned the command, took up her distaff and began to spin. When her daughter reproved her, she refused to correct her behavior. Immediately, her linen scarf caught on fire and gave off smoke. The girl saw this and ran to her right away. The two of them threw down the cloth and extinguished the flames. The woman again took up her distaff and spindle and began to spin again, because she thought that what had happened was an accident and not God's doing. The avenging punishment started up at once, setting fire to the whole covering of her head; it seemed to be burning up her hair and skin. The mother and daughter shouted out together and a crowd gathered from all around. The truth of the matter was laid bare, and the scarf that had been destroyed by the punishing fire was taken to the church, and all proclaimed the power of Christ in St. Robert.

2.15 A soldier freed from his chains.

Another time Armand, who is still viscount of Polignac,[40] cast into prison a soldier whose cognomen was "Fox." He refused to listen to his parents, relatives, and friends about setting him free. The abbot of La Chaise-Dieu interceded for him that in answer to their prayers he might be set free for love of God and blessed Robert, but they could not gain what they asked. However, on the First Sunday of the Lord's Advent, as dawn was breaking, the viscount went down to the prison and reinforced the place with even more irons and bars. Then he went up to La Chaise-Dieu. Blessed Robert, with a staff in his hand, stood by the soldier who often called upon him from his prison. At his command the chains fell away. The door opened, and bearing his fetters he passed through

40. The viscounts of Polignac, whose castle was near Le Puy, had a continuing power struggle with the bishop. This castle was also in a position to menace La Chaise-Dieu, although there is no evidence for this before the second half of the twelfth century (Christian Lauranson-Rosaz, *L'Auvergne et ses Marges: Velay, Gévaudan du VIIIe au XIe siėle: La Fin du Monde Antique?* [Le Puy-en-Velay: Les Cahiers de la Haute-Loire, 1987): 103, 129; see also, *Historiae Francorvm Scriptores Coaetanei*, eds. Franciscus Duchesne and Andreas Duchesne, vol. 4 [Paris: Cramoisy, 1636]: 682). According to AA SS OSB 9:225, this castle was about twelve miles from La Chaise-Dieu.

the middle of the guards.[41] The soldier went to La Chaise-Dieu and met the viscount who was coming back down when he noticed him. The viscount went straight to him, and had hardly asked 'What is going on?' when he heard, 'Blessed Robert freed me.' Then with profuse tears he prostrated before the tomb of the holy confessor. Everywhere praises and boundless thanks were rendered to Christ, the Supreme King, and to blessed Robert by those many of us who were present. After these things had happened, the soldier returned home rejoicing and happy.

2.16 The death of a proud knight's horse.

The feast day dawned and a huge crowd of people stood before the gates of the monastery of La Chaise-Dieu. Behold, a noble knight named Pons, whose cognomen was de Clavenaco, was coming up from the north, riding a very good horse along that level area. Many people told him that no one would have dared ride farther there. When he heard that he took it badly. He answered haughtily and refused to change his course. However, the heavenly Judge decided to correct him quickly. Immediately, at the procession two large bells that were located above the monastery in a bell tower began to sound. The clapper in one of them fell during the ringing and hit the forehead of the horse and hurled its brain and its whole body to the ground. When those present saw this they were afraid and began to declare that God is wonderful in his works.[42] The proud horseman who had ascended the steps descended as a humble pedestrian. For the power of Christ the Lord corrects those who disdain it; it casts down the mighty and raises the humble[43] to the stars. To him be glory and honor forever. Amen.

41. This story recalls the account in Acts 12:7–10 of an angel who freed Peter from prison.

42. Ps 67:36, Apoc 15:3.

43. Lk 1:52.

Chapters of Part Three

3.1 Blessed Robert and his successor, Durand, and two Roberts, one a count and the other a prior.
3.2 A demon discovered in the cloister.
3.3 A prophecy about the episcopacy of Durand.
3.4 The divine offices for the vigils of Easter and Pentecost.
3.5 The abbot, Dom Seguin, and a prophecy against a certain tyrant.
3.6 Likewise, a prophecy of his regarding the abbey of St. Illidius.
3.7 A thief expelled by excommunication.
3.8 His death, and his successor Pons.
3.9 A deceased brother, a deacon, seen clearly.
3.10 Abbot Aimeric.
3.11 Abbot Stephen.
3.12 Brother Bernard on whose joined hands the body of the Lord appeared.
3.13 A spider someone had swallowed came out of his arm.
3.14 A poor man's leg healed by God.
3.15 A monk led out of his body without pain.
3.16 John, the prior of the monastery of Lieutadès.
3.17 Godfrey, priest Meursac.
3.18 Abbot Jordan.[44]

3.1 Blessed Robert, his successor Durand, and two Roberts, one a count the other a prior.

The blessed friend of God and priest, Robert, founded the monastery of La Chaise-Dieu and endowed it with abbeys, churches, and other possessions. The grace of God was particularly active in him, and he traveled to its end the road that leads to the highest good. After he had been taken into heaven and his disciple Durand had been chosen for the pastoral administration, Robert, count of the Auvergne, and in his train, Robert, the claustral prior, took up the work with might and main, in so far as heaven granted it. Count Robert himself was an invincible shield against the visible enemies

44. According to the editors of the AA SS OSB 9:226, this chapter is found in no manuscript or edition and so perhaps was never written.

of La Chaise-Dieu, while Prior Robert, as a soldier of Christ, took up all the panoply of faith[45] against invisible enemies.

3.2 A demon discovered in the cloister.

Once, when as was customary the prior checked all the monastery workshops after Compline, lest anything should be out of order there, he found the Enemy of the human race wandering in the cloister in a monk's habit, huge in stature, dark of face with a mutilated nose. He drew him outside and asked him what he presumed to look for there. He replied, 'I was going through Cluny and Marmoutier and Marseilles and have turned toward this monastery to see if I can find anything here that belongs to me.' He replied in turn, 'Here, by Christ's will, you will never be able to find anything that belongs to you.' When he raised his hand and made the sign of the cross, that terrible vision fled through the school of novices with a great crash, which frightened the entire community of brothers when they heard it. The next day the prior explained it all step-by-step to those who inquired.

3.3 A prophecy about the episcopacy of Durand.

After ruling the monastery of La Chaise-Dieu for almost ten years, Durand was enthroned as bishop of the Auvergne in accord with a true prophecy of his master, Robert. Durand was from an undistinguished family of Clermont. Robert had trained him in his holy resolve. Once when he was with Robert while he was eating, the holy man offered him a piece of bread to eat. He opened his mouth and ate. Then immediately he heard the blessed man say: 'Because you did this, you have merited the episcopate.' The fulfillment of this prophecy proved that the early event was not insignificant.

3.4 The divine offices for the vigils of Easter and Pentecost.

Although Robert, the man of God, left the habit of the canons, still he did not want to change the office on the vigils of Holy

45. Eph 6:11-17.

Easter and Pentecost. When he had died and was established in heaven, his disciples said: 'Because we are monks, on such solemn feasts we should do twelve lessons, as is the practice of monks, and not three according to the usage of canons.' When all agreed to this, it happened that on the following day of Holy Easter—and not without God's willing it, so we believe—no one of the whole multitude woke up before the break of dawn. They could not say twelve lessons. So, divinely corrected, gratefully they began to do three lessons as their father had done—and so it has been done ever since.

3.5 The abbot, Dom Seguin, and a prophecy against a certain tyrant.

Durand was followed in the abbatial care of La Chaise-Dieu by Seguin, a renowned man of Lyons, who hailed from a castle called Escotay.[46] He was beloved of God and men. During his time, the monastery of La Chaise-Dieu grew in its religious reputation and in its very extensive possessions. And he himself was highly regarded in the world because of striking signs. When the prior of Carennac[47] met him passing through his land, he devoutly beseeched him to come to Carennac and celebrate the feast of Pentecost, which was to occur on the next day. Seeing his devotion, Abbot Seguin turned aside to the place and spent the holy day there. A multitude of nobles and ordinary people from the surrounding places poured into Carennac, drawn by the feast day and the fame of the abbot who was there. It happened that present there was a tyrant who had a reputation of inflicting unremitting evils on that monastery. The prior alerted the abbot so he could meet with the man and beseech him, because perhaps then the man would quit his wickedness. When the abbot had spent a long time doing what he had been asked, the knight was not moved to promise peace or good either out of love of the feast or from reverence for the venerable man. Instead, furious, he left even more threatening. To the prior, who was very frightened by this, Abbot Seguin said, 'Don't be afraid,

46. Escotay was near the town of Montbrison, roughly thirty miles northeast of La Chaise-Dieu.

47. According to AA SS OSB 9:227, Carennac was village on the Dordogne River, in the diocese of Cahors.

brother. This man has come to the end of his wicked course; he will not be able to harm you or your monastery any longer.' The just sentence of the Supreme Judge declared that this prophecy was completely true. For when the tyrant had haughtily left the abbot, near a river he launched a falcon at some birds. When he followed it, he fell into the river and promptly died. This instilled great fear in the persecutors of that place and provided the inhabitants with great peace.

3.6 Likewise, a prophecy of his regarding the abbey of St. Illidius.[48]

One time Seguin, a kindly man, arose from prayer at the monastery of Illidius, situated in the city of Clermont. He met a young monk of La Chaise-Dieu, called Peter of Pontgibaud.[49] Smiling, he said to him on the spot, 'Brother, you must implore God's help because next year you will receive from God the abbatial care of this monastery.' To be sure no creature can stand without God's help, but the help of Christ was especially necessary for this man. When he had accepted the abbacy, he was worn down by bodily weakness, and the bellicose crowd of the count of Clermont and of the canons oppressed his monastery.

3.7 A thief expelled by excommunication.

Similarly, the violence of robbers weighed heavily on those serving Christ in the monastery of La Chaise-Dieu. They had suffered this injury for a long time, and they could find no remedy for this plague. On the holy day of the Lord's Supper, the abbot, Dom Seguin, ordered his stole and pastoral staff brought to him. Standing up, he said: 'Because the son of iniquity doesn't stop disturbing the sons of God, by the authority of God the Father and the Son and the Holy Spirit, we restrain him from staying here any longer.' As soon as he had finished these words, in the sight of all, the refectorian left the chapter and never showed himself again. Because this made a deep impression, his accomplices outside revealed the thefts he

48. Bishop Illidius (Allyre) of Clermont, died 385.

49. Pontgibaud is located nearly 25 kilometers west-northwest of Clermont.

had committed in the cloister. Thus was fulfilled a true statement: 'There is nothing hidden that will not be revealed.'[50]

3.8 His death, and his successor Pons.

Abbot Seguin, beloved of God and men, exercised pastoral care of La Chaise-Dieu for almost fifteen years. He left the governance of the monastery to Pons and was buried in Vignonet. Regarding his death, we have written a few things in the life of the man of God, Stephen, the disciple of Blessed Robert.[51]

3.9 A deceased brother, a deacon, seen clearly.

Meanwhile, the prior of Vignonet, who wished to spend his time with God alone, sent a messenger to La Chaise-Dieu, asking that a brother be sent to him who was suitable to take over governance of the whole monastery. A young man of good character was sent to him and to him he was subject in everything. The prior told him, 'Brother, you are sent to us so that you can receive management of this house, and you may provide me with just the necessities.' The young man replied, 'Father, there is no way that it is going to happen that I give you orders or that I have priority over you during your lifetime.' Neither would accept precedence over the other. So they both agreed to do what a monk of Cluny who lived in the region recommended to them. They agreed with his suggestion that the elder would take care of all interior matters and the youth would see to all external affairs, and so it happened. The younger man asked the senior to permit him to go to La Chaise-Dieu to celebrate Holy Thursday there. He completed Holy Thursday at La Chaise-Dieu, as he had wished. The next day, the day of the Lord's Passion, he was seized with a fever and taken to the monastery infirmary. His illness advanced. He was anointed, and, fortified by the sacraments of Christ, he gave his spirit to God and was buried on Holy Saturday. On the next day, Holy Easter, a sacristan opened the door of the church to see if daylight had broken so that the

50. Mt 10:26 | | Luke 12:2.

51. The Latin reads: *De cujus transitu in vita viri Dei Stephani discipuli beati Rotberti nonnulla edidimus*. Cf. note 1 above.

hymn *'Aurora lucis'* could be begun in the customary way. Behold, the deceased youth, who had been buried the day before on Saturday, appeared, standing there before his eyes, clothed like a deacon with white vestments. He said to him, 'The Lord has risen.' At this the sacristan was shaking. When he had recovered his senses, he asked him who he was and how he had come there. He answered, 'The Queen of Heaven, with the holy apostles and angelic powers, is going to celebrate the divine offices here today. I have been ordered to come for this and to complete my diaconate.' When he heard this, the sacristan brought the prior, who heard the aforesaid things from the same one who had appeared alive. After that, he disappeared from them. This astonished all. Some of the brothers wanted to see if they could find in its tomb the body that appeared so clearly before their eyes. The abbot, Dom Pons, a man of great discretion and piety, kept that from happening, so there would be no note of presumption. Later, after seven years he was raised to the cathedral of Le Puy-en-Velay. He left the management of the abbey to Aimeric.

3.10 Abbot Aimeric

Aimeric then exercised the pastoral care for seven years before handing it over to Stephen, when he agreed to rule the church of the Auvergne.

3.11 Abbot Stephen

While Venerable Stephen was in charge of the administration of La Chaise-Dieu, its religious reputation and the monastery's possessions expanded far and wide.

3.12 Brother Bernard on whose joined hands the body of Christ appeared.

At this time there lived under the prior at Saint Privat[52] a brother of great simplicity and purity. His name was Bernard, but he was given the cognomen 'Baptist,' because when he was still a boy he

52. Saint-Privat d'Allier was founded by the beginning of the twelfth century in the diocese of Le Puy-en-Velay.

transmitted the grace of baptism to a child in an emergency. On the day of the Holy Pasch, he and all the people experienced great anxiety, because the priest had lost the body of Christ from the altar and could not explain what had happened to it. Bernard knelt before the altar and prayed to God in tears very contritely. Wondrously, he saw that the Lord's Body was at the end of the fingers of his joined hands. Out of joy he called out in a loud voice, and the priest who had lost it came running and acknowledged it. The great joy and exultation with which all there danced is better intimated by silence than it could be expressed in words.

3.13 A spider someone had swallowed came out of his arm.

Another surprising thing is told of this Brother Bernard. One day when he had celebrated Mass, a spider fell into the chalice of the Lord's blood. When he saw that, he didn't know what counsel to follow, where to turn, or what to do. So he drank it all, and by God's doing he felt no bad effects from it afterwards. When some days had passed, his blood was let. Those who watched saw that the spider came out of his arm with the blood. Because he loved Christ, because he believed Christ's words, even though he drank something deadly, it could not hurt him.[53]

3.14 God heals a poor man's leg.

A young man from the Auvergne, Peter by name, lost a foot and a leg when they were burned by a fiery illness.[54] He came to La Chaise-Dieu, supported on crutches with his leg bone in his hand. The devout man, Gerald, the almoner, kept him there for many days and the leg bones were kept in a designated nook. The poor man heard that celebrated miracles occurred in a place called Saintes-Maries-de-la-Mer, not far from Arles. He went there with the bones of his leg. A certain knight, Peter, named Vulgarius, of the castle of Vivarais, gave him hospitality. A few days passed and one night the knight heard some people conversing around the bed of the poor man. He said, 'Why aren't you sleeping?' He

53. Mark 16:18.

54. From the symptoms it seems likely he had suffered from ergotism.

thought they, his retainers, were disturbing the poor man. 'Lord,' they said to him, 'we aren't saying anything, nor do we hear any people talking.' He went to sleep again, and again he awoke. He heard what he had heard earlier. Calling the poor man, he said, 'Who are those speaking to you, Peter?' He said, 'Lord, the Blessed Mother of God and St. Hippolytus, the martyr, are putting together my leg and foot and restoring them.' The knight thought that this was vain and silly and said: 'Go to sleep, Peter, go to sleep.' But he said, 'Come and see that what I say is true.' So the knight got up and so did his wife and family, and they found—wonderful to say—a new leg with a proper, white foot reconstructed on it, just as he had said. However, they never did find again the bone of his leg that had been placed in the opening in the wall. All those who were there fell down and began to make much of this wonderful event, the like of which was almost or totally unknown in earlier centuries. They began to praise God.

3.15 A monk led out of his body without pain.

One Easter, in the monastery of La Chaise-Dieu, a brother novice saw all the brothers were rejoicing as they completed the divine praises. He began to ask earnestly for the place where the brothers departed their bodies. They asked him why he inquired about this. He said, 'I desire to be dissolved and to be with Christ.'[55] A bed was shown him, and he lay down on it. He devoutly asked that the brothers come and do for him what was customarily done for the dying. The brothers were astonished at this, but did it. In their presence, joyously and without pain, he slept in Christ.

3.16 John, the prior of the monastery of Lieutadès.

John, the prior of the monastery of Lieutadès[56] in the Auvergne, fell into a grave illness. When he seemed to be nearing the end, three brothers stood before him: Andrew, his nephew, Peter, the son of Rainard, and I, Bernard, who have written this. He had lost his appetite long before. He said twice, 'Bernard, Bernard.' A half

55. Phil 1:23.

56. Lieutadès was founded by the eleventh century in the diocese of Clermont.

hour later, his strength revived and he began to speak. He was asked why a little before he had twice called out 'Bernard.' He said, 'I saw a certain resplendent bishop—who seemed to me to be Blessed Nicholas, and I loved him with all my heart—and myself before the doors of a temple of such beauty, brightness and scent that scarcely anyone could describe it. He said to me, 'I have acquired this dwelling from God for you, or if you wish, you can live in the body. You have a choice between those two." "Lord," I said to him, "I have a friend, Bernard, and what he recommends to me I will choose." He said, "You have spoken well. Whatever he recommends to you, do it."' So Prior John said to me, 'Tell me, which of these am I to choose.' When I heard that, I confess that at first I was divided. Then I called on God, saying, 'Although by this I will suffer many serious inconveniences, I don't want your rest to be put off on my account. Enter into the place of God's tent.' This made him happy, and he said, 'Blessed be God, because this I chose, the other I feared.' A little later he happily went out of the body.

3.17 Godfrey, a priest of Meursac.[57]

A priest of the church of Meursac in the Saintonge, Godfrey by name, was overcome by a serious illness and sank down on his bed. When he heard that Bernard, the prior of St. Gemme, had come, he humbly asked through friends that he come to him. He had been infinitely troublesome to him and to the other brothers of La Chaise-Dieu, from the time they had accepted him into their church at Meursac. The prior came to him, and the priest said to him: 'I give thanks to my God and to you that you have chosen to visit me, for I have committed many wrongs against God and against you. But I entrust myself to God, to the Blessed Virgin Mary, to St. Robert, and to you in this life and in death.' Then he was carried to the monastery of St. Gemme, where he received the monastic habit. He was approaching death. When we saw that, we began to sing *Credo Deum*[58] and the litany around him. A little later, the sick man, who had seemed to be dead already, moved his hand.

57. This priory, dedicated to St. Martin, was founded by 1100.

58. According to AA SS OSB 9:231, there are textual variants here. The author may have written that they sang the '*Te deum*.'

Then he made a sign that those singing should be quiet. When they didn't do that, he caught his breath and said, 'Be quiet!' Then I approached him and said, 'What is this? What do you want?' He replied, 'Judgment has been passed, and I am saved.' And I said to him, 'And how is this?' He said, 'Blessed Robert received me from your hand and set me before God the Judge. And so when my whole case regarding how I had entrusted myself to you was carefully set out, the Judge of all decreed without any reservation that I was to share forever the lot of the elect.' A short time after he said this, he happily ended the present life.

The Life of Stephen of Obazine

Introduction to
The Life of Saint Stephen of Obazine

FOR THE MONASTERY OF OBAZINE and its founder there are two ancient and complementary sources: *The Life of Stephen of Obazine*, which is translated in this volume, and the extensive cartulary of the monastery of Obazine, which was redacted toward the end of the twelfth century. The cartulary reveals much about the history of the abbey under its first four abbots. The first of its two parts is a chronological collection of some seven hundred seventy-two charters. Generally, these are dated only if they originated after 1153. The second part of the cartulary is a topological collection of charters grouped according to place and monastic grange.[1]

There are three modern books that collect what is known of Stephen of Obazine. These include editions of the two works just discussed: *Vie de Saint Étienne d'Obazine*, edited by Michel Aubrun, Publications de l'Institut d'Études du Massif Central, 6 (Clermont-Ferrand: Institut d'Études du Massif Central, 1970), and *Le cartulaire de l'abbaye cistercienne d'Obazine (xiie–xiiie siècle)*, edited by Bernadette Barrière, Publications de l'Institut d'Études du Massif Central, 33 (Clermont-Ferrand: Université de Clermont-Ferrand II, 1989).[2] The third source is Bernadette Barrière's careful study of the early

1. Bernadette Barrière, *L'abbaye cistercienne d'Obazine en Bas-Limousin* (Tulle, 1977) 11–14.

2. Thirteen of the charters are translated and discussed in *Women and Monasticism in Medieval Europe: Sisters and Patrons of the Cistercian Reform*, edited and translated by Constance H. Berman, TEAMS (Kalamazoo: Medieval Institute Publications, 2002) 77–86.

history of Obazine, *L'abbaye cistercienne d'Obazine en Bas-Limousin: les origins–le patrimonie* (Tulle, 1977).[3]

This introduction will first discuss *The Life of Saint Stephen of Obazine* and its author, then Stephen and his monasteries. The latter section will treat successively of Stephen's life and foundations, his character, the religious and political backdrop for Stephen's life and foundations, and the growth, monastic observance and economic organization of Obazine / Coyroux and its foundations and dependencies.

The Author and His Book

The name of the author of *The Life of Saint Stephen of Obazine* is unknown. He reports that in his youth he was brought up at a monastery connected with La Chaise-Dieu, perhaps Port-Dieu (founded 1060) or one of its two dependencies, Saint-Robert or Védrennes. When he left there, he spent a short time in secular life. Then, on the advice of Stephen, he went to Cîteaux during the abbacy of Rainard (1133–1150). After two years there, he was sent to Obazine at Stephen's request and remained there for the rest of his life. Hence, he knew Stephen personally for many years (2.11).[4]

The *Life of Saint Stephen* is divided into three books and totals one hundred twenty-six chapters. The first book was written during the abbacy of Stephen's disciple Gerard, former abbot of Obazine's foundation of Garde-Dieu, who succeeded Stephen at Obazine in 1159. Fourteen years later, the author took up his work again and completed the second and third books. His purposes in writing, he says, were to make Stephen known and to edify the faithful. The energy he expends recounting Stephen's virtues and miracles suggests that he might also have been seeking to further Stephen's official recognition as a saint or to provide a source of readings for his feast day.

In the preface to the first book, the author of *The Life of Saint Stephen of Obazine* includes a number of commonplaces found in

3. These three works will be referenced in the notes as *Vie, Cartulaire* and *Abbaye*.

4. The historical information contained in *Abbaye* is summarized in *Vie*, 7–35 and *Cartulaire* 9–26. References to the translation of the *Life* are by book and chapter, e.g., 2.29. These divisions correspond to those in the Latin text in the *Vie*, which is the basis for this translation.

introductions to many medieval saints' lives: his style is inadequate; he is writing only because commanded to do so by his superiors or pressured by his brethren; and he writes at some length to satisfy the desires of the devout (2.11; 3. pref.). Less usual is his complaint that not many people are writing saints' lives anymore, because of a lack of either saints or authors. He says there are many recent saints who are recognized both by God and by the Church. Their lives have not been written since they preferred to keep their light hidden under a basket (Mk 4:21 par.) or because they are not renowned for miracles, which, the author says, are required for saints' lives in his time. Exceptions are Saint Bernard of Clairvaux about whom there exists a three-part life,[5] and Saint Malachy of Armagh whose life Bernard wrote.[6]

In the preface to the first book, the author anticipates future criticisms. The preface to the second indicates that the criticisms that his first book attracted were one reason he waited almost a decade and a half to write the second book. To forestall some of these criticisms, he assures his readers that he is writing, not to make himself known, but to publicize to others Stephen's life, death, and good deeds. Some critics also argue that recent saints' lives, like the author's first book of the *Life of Saint Stephen*, are badly written, false, or too long. He replies that the plain style reflects the way Stephen himself spoke.[7] In this the author finds one of several parallels between his work and Sulpicius Severus' *Life of Saint Martin*.[8] Everything he has written is supported by reliable

5. It is not clear what the author had in mind when he mentioned a three-part life of Saint Bernard.

6. *Vita Sancti Malachiae*, ed. Albericus Gwynn; *Sancti Bernardi Opera*, eds. J. Leclerq and H. M. Rochais (Rome: Editiones Cistercienses, 1963) 3:295–378; translated by Robert T. Meyer, *The Life and Death of Saint Malachy the Irishman*, CF 10 (Kalamazoo: Cistercian Publications, 1978).

7. At a few places in the text, the author reveals a fondness for Latin puns:

Book Two, Chapter 22, line 12	*presentiam . . . presentare*
Book Two, Chapter 22, line 28	*tulisti . . . retulisti*
Book Three, Preface, line 34	*dignas . . . dignis . . . dignum*
Book Three, Chapter 20, line 14	*precibus non pedibus*

8. Sulpicius Severus, *Vie de Saint Martin*, ed. and tr. Jacques Fontaine, SCh 133–135 (Paris: Cerf, 1967–1969) 1:248–345; *Life of St Martin*, tr. F. R. Hoare, *Lives of the Western Fathers* (New York: Sheed and Ward, 1954) 3–44.

testimony. He is writing now precisely because there are still people who knew Stephen while he was alive. A good chronicler does not just tell the facts, but highlights meaning. The author has imitated the evangelists, who did not all describe an event in exactly the same way. Finally, in the preface to the third book he admits that he has written at length of Stephen's death, but he has done so because it will be of interest to those who love the saint.

Book One[9] tells the story of Stephen's life up to the construction of the monastery at Obazine and the founding of the nearby women's monastery of Coyroux. Its *leitmotiv* is Stephen's 'wisdom', a wisdom that to many twenty-first century readers will seem very close to folly.[10] Another recurrent theme of Book 1 is the contrast between those early, heroic times and the slackness of monks at the time when the author was writing (1.16,19; 2.49). This theme, beloved of monastic moralists of all eras, was sounded already in the *Rule of Saint Benedict*, who observed that monks of old said one hundred fifty psalms a day, whereas he asked only one hundred fifty per week; similarly, monks of old abstained from wine, whereas Benedict asked only for moderation.[11] Later the author will contrast

9. The following emendations have been made to the Latin text by the translator; many are merely misprints:

Preface, line 1	*gesta* (for *geste*)
Chapter 5, line 17	*jacebant* (for *jacebat*)
Chapter 5, line 18	*mollitiem* (for *molitiem*)
Chapter 5, line 25	*necessitas* (for *nocessaitas*)
Chapter 7, line 39	*sedente* (for *sedento*)
Chapter 9, line 25	*indicant* (for *incidant*)
Chapter 16, line 26	*liquantes* (for *licantes*)
Chapter 23, line 6	*tempestate* (for *tempeste*)
Chapter 23, line 8	*turma* (for *turmam*)
Chapter 23, line 16	*quedam* (for *quodam*)
Chapter 26, line 10	*labentur* (for *laborentur*)
Chapter 27, line 18	*contra* (for *conta*)
Chapter 28, line 16	*trahi* (for *traheas*)
Chapter 30, line 2	*dextera* (for *dextere*)
Chapter 30, line 9	*nunc* (for *nonc*)
Chapter 30, line 23	*quodam* (for *quondam*)

10. 1.2,9,14,22; 2.45,47, where Stephen teaches wisdom to boys.

11. RB, 18.24–25, 40.6; Kardong, 198–203, 327–331.

Stephen's advisors with those of later times who seek victory for their ideas rather than the best solution (2.17).

Book 2[12] tells of Stephen's installation as abbot, the first foundations, the attachment of Obazine to Cîteaux (1147), and miracles that he worked during his lifetime. This was a period of swift growth for Obazine. In this second book, Stephen is no longer depicted as a fierce ascetic living in a secluded forest in very primitive conditions. Now he is the head of a growing monastic family which eats regularly and with cloths on the refectory table. He is portrayed as an important personage in the area, a very efficient manager who overlooked nothing and was able to give expert advice on everything from construction to agriculture. As abbot, he inspired great fear, but also great love. One look from him was enough to unnerve a man.

Book 3[13] begins with Stephen's death and funeral, then recounts his posthumous appearances and miracles. The theme of this book

12. The following emendations have been made to the Latin text by the translator; many are merely misprints:

Chapter 2, line12	*feminarum* (for *fominarum*)
Chapter 4, line 38	*ab* (for *ad*)
Chapter 10, line 8	*que* (for *quo*)
Chapter 11, line 13	the name *Renardus* here is given in Chapter 12 as *Rainardus*
Chapter 14, line 39	*qua* (for *quo*)
Chapter 15, line 74	*juvamen* (for *juvamem*)
Chapter 19, line 9	*otiose* (for *otiosa*)
Chapter 30, line 35	*ipse* (for *ipso*)
Chapter 30, line 37	*profundum* (for *profondum*)
Chapter 33, line 3	*laicis* (for *laicus*)
Chapter 36, line 12	*rustico* (for *rusticio*)
Chapter 38, line 9	*responsum* (for *respondum*)
Chapter 41, line 3	*ipso* (for *ipse*)
Chapter 41, line 12	*prepositus* (for *propositus*)
Chapter 55, line 8	*amplectens* (for *amplectans*) [as correctly in line 10]
Chapter 58, line 24	*facies* (for *facie*)

13. The following emendations have been made to the Latin text by the translator; many are merely misprints:

Preface, line 20	*angustia* (for *augustia*)
Chapter 2, line 49	*consummationem* (for *consommationem*)
Chapter 5, line 66	*sciamus* [or *sciatur*] (for *sciant*)
Chapter 5, line 95	*habebant* (for *habebat*)

is Stephen's continued presence within the community. The author draws a parallel between Christ's presence with his disciples after the Ascension and Stephen's presence to his community after his death. Stephen is still there in all the guises he assumed during life: father, mother, teacher, shepherd, protector, ruler, and pilot (3.2).

The author's style is clear and direct for the most part. He refers to the Bible, to the *Rule of Saint Benedict*, to Sulpicius Severus' *Life of Saint Martin*, and to lives of Saints Benedict (1.4), Bernard (1.1) and Columbanus (2.41). He is not widely read, but he does cite Pseudo-Chrysostom (1. preface) and Tertullian (2.17).

The author likes to connect the events he describes to liturgical days and seasons, especially Lent. Thus Stephen left his parish on the Thursday after Ash Wednesday, reached his hermitage near Obazine on Good Friday, and celebrated Mass near there on Easter Sunday (1.3,4). The community became monks following the *Rule of Saint Benedict* on Palm Sunday. The cornerstone of their new basilica was set down on the Friday before Palm Sunday (2.18). Stephen left for Bonnaigue on Ash Wednesday and died there on the Second Sunday of Lent.[14]

Stephen's hagiographer is careful to cite witnesses such as his abbot or *confrères*. Sometimes he claims to have been an eyewitness of improbable events. He tells us that Bernard, one of Stephen's first companions, provided him with information about the early days of the monastery. Sometimes what he reports can be confirmed in other documents. For example, his account of the sudden death of the abbot of Tulle at Limoges is confirmed in the contemporary chronicle by the prior of Vigeois.[15] What he tells us of Chartreuse is confirmed by the reports of other visitors.[16]

Chapter 9, line 5 *sarcophago* (for *sacrophago*)
Chapter 12, line 25 *increpitum* (for *increpatum*)
Chapter 20, line 24 *tentaret* (for *tantaret*)
Chapter 26, line 19 *detentum* (for *dotentum*)
Chapter 33, line 6 *custodire* (for *custodies*)
Chapter 34, line 28 *vocibus* (for *vocis*)

14. RB, 49.1, Kardong, 401–402.

15. Aubrun, *Vie*, 157, cites Geoffroy, prior of Vigeois, *Chronicon lemovicense*, ed. Labbe, in *Nova bibliotheca manuscriptorum*, (I657) II, 307.

16. See references in *Vie*, 81, 83.

Only two manuscripts of Stephen's *Life* survive, both from the library of Cîteaux. A third manuscript, now lost, was transcribed for a seventeenth-century printed version and seems to provide local details that were deliberately omitted in the Cîteaux manuscripts; hence, it serves as the basis for the critical edition.

Stephen of Obazine: The Man and His Monastery[17]

Stephen's Origins and Priestly Ordination

The *Life* is our primary source of information about Stephen, though the cartulary of Obazine and other sources, literary and archaeological, supplement what it tells us.[18] Stephen was born of respectable parents named Stephen and Gauberte near the end of the eleventh century in Xaintrie in the village of Vielzot at the border between the Auvergne and the Limousin. Like the mothers of other saints, his mother had a prophetic dream about her son's future. Stephen was sent to school to study sacred literature, perhaps at Pleaux, a priory of the Benedictine monastery of Charroux. When his father died, he took over the family estates for a while. He was kind to the poor, orphans, travellers and widows (1.1). Then he was ordained priest and served in the ministry, proving himself a talented preacher, who taught by word and example. However, like others of his time and locale,[19] Stephen felt drawn to a life of meditation, asceticism, and solitude.

Eremitical Life

Stephen proceeded toward his new way of life in prudent fashion by seeking expert guidance. Stephen of Mercoeur, abbot of La

17. This section is based on the text of the *Life* itself, but draws also on *Abbaye*, 43–108, and the introductions to the *Cartulaire* and the *Vie*.

18. On these other sources, see the introduction to Barrière, *Cartulaire*, 10.

19. *Abbaye*, 43–44, cites as examples Gerard de Sales, Geoffrey of Chalard, Stephen of Muret, and Gaucher d'Aureil. These men drew disciples and their eremitical life evolved quickly toward community life according to canonial or monastic precedents.

Chaise-Dieu (1111–1146), advised Stephen to take up the religious way of life (1.2).[20] So Stephen and a friend, the priest Peter, visited various hermitages and religious places, but none of the communities they visited was challenging enough. While they were discerning what to do next, they received guidance from a hermit for ten months (1.3).[21]

About 1120, the two priests decided to retire to the forest of Obazine, where they had to earn the acceptance of the inhabitants, who had had bad experiences with an unworthy hermit (1.5). As had happened with Saint Benedict, Stephen and his companion were fed by a neighbor and gradually attracted disciples. They lived in extreme deprivation (1.5-7).

A Community of Hermits

They decided to establish a community for those who joined them. Stephen obtained permission to do so from Eustorgus, the bishop of Limoges (1106–1137), who asked only that Stephen respect the customs of the fathers (*ita dumtaxat ut morem a patribus traditum per omnia sequerentur*).[22] Probably between 1125 and 1127, they built a monastery with a chapel, dormitory, refectory, and kitchen surrounding a central cloister. Stephen adopted the form of liturgical offices in use among canons, but kept an eremitical lifestyle that included personal prayer and reading, meditation and the manual labor that was an important component in their lives. They lived in austerity and silence (1.9,12,23). In these observances, the author of the *Life* notes, they were very different from canons regular who praise God, but have plenty of food and rest and do little manual labor (1.7; cf. 1.25, for another disparaging reference to canons).

New members arrived, both men and women. Stephen felt a conflict between his desire for silence and asceticism and his responsibilities for the growing community. His followers convinced

20. La Chaise-Dieu's priory of Port-Dieu was located in the southeast of the diocese of Limoges, eighty kilometers from Xaintrie. Bishop Aimeric of Clermont (1111–1150), had been abbot of La Chaise-Dieu (1102–1111).

21. According to *Abbaye*, 47, this hermit was Bertrand de Griffeville.

22. Barrière, *Abbaye*, 50, thinks that Eustorgus had in mind the rules that governed the life of canons. Stephen and his first disciples were clerics.

him to moderate his own austerities (1.10), but he would not give up his habit of cooking for the community. As still more people joined them, in about 1130 the community had to move to another nearby location. Stephen called it Obazine (1.11,14). The papal legate, Geoffrey of Lèves, bishop of Chartres, put Stephen in charge (1.14). Observance remained the same, except that now the meals were more ample (1.15). Unlike the fickle hermit who had lived there before them, Stephen and his disciples were committed to stability (1.15). At night, Stephen sometimes carted away the excrement from the monastery privy (1.20). Stephen often visited other monasteries to learn from them (1.23). Perhaps this was how the practice of a chapter of faults was introduced at Obazine (1.17).

In Search of an Ordo[23]

In 1135 Stephen travelled to look for a religious group to which he could attach his community or which could provide a model for organizing his followers. During a visit with Guigo,[24] the prior of the Grand Chartreuse near Grenoble, Stephen realized that his community could not affiliate with the Carthusian order. Prior Guigo mentioned as obstacles the large size of the community of Obazine and the possessions needed to support it. Stephen's emphasis on severe penance and manual labor, the common buildings they had already erected, and the lack of solitude and intellectual pursuits at Obazine also made them a poor match for the Carthusians. In addition, Obazine was far from the Grand Chartreuse, and it had women as members. The *Life* reports that Guigo suggested that Obazine join the order of Cîteaux (1.24–26). The number of men and women who wished to join the community at Obazine was still increasing, so Stephen decided it was time to expand the buildings there one more time (1.27). One noble, who had been a model

23. *Ordo* meant both a rule of life and a polity connecting several monasteries. Stephen was in search of both.

24. Guigo I was born in 1083. He entered the monastery at the Grand Chartreuse in 1106 at the age of 23. Three years later he was elected prior. He began writing the customs of Carthusians when he was about forty and completed them about 1128. He died in 1136, not long after Stephen's visit.

layman, joined with his whole household (1.29). The entry of a whole household into the community was not unique.[25]

Expansion

In the period 1136–1142, Stephen was very busy with construction projects. At Obazine the previous oratory was replaced by a church dedicated to the Virgin (1.27), and a second church, dedicated to Saint Peter, was built to serve the needs of guests (1.28). For two years the brothers worked on the construction of a monastery for nuns (1.30) at Coyroux. All was ready by Palm Sunday, 1142, when Bishop Gerard of Limoges (1142–1177) came and blessed the new churches. On this occasion, the bishop received Stephen's monastic vows and blessed him as abbot. Stephen then received the monastic vows of the other members of the community (2.12).

The community was now sure enough of itself to found new monasteries. Stephen founded two new monasteries, Bonnaigue and Valette, in the south-eastern part of the diocese of Limoges. He blessed the new sites and helped with the initial stages of their construction (2.8-9).

Incorporation into the Cistercian Ordo

In 1147, Stephen attended the General Chapter at Cîteaux. With the support of Rainard, abbot of Cîteaux (1133–1150), and of Pope Eugene III, who also attended, Obazine was admitted into the filiation of Cîteaux. There were, however, discrepancies between the monastic observances of Cîteaux and Obazine. The latter was more austere in diet, children were being raised at the monastery, and the abbot of Obazine was also abbot of Coyroux, the monastery for women that Stephen had founded. Coyroux was also admitted to the Cistercian order, provided it remained an integral part of a double monastery subject to the abbot of Obazine. Stephen had already taken steps to meet requirements for the material support and complete enclosure of the women at Coyroux. The congregation of Savigny, which also included a house of women, was admitted to the Cistercian federation at the same time. Monks and *conversi* (lay

25. *Abbaye*, 65, 124–25; *Vie* 1.29; and charters cited in note 31 below.

brothers) were to be sent from Cîteaux to help bring all liturgical and economic practices at Obazine-Coyroux in line with Cistercian usages (2.12). This involved revising the liturgical books so they would conform to the recent reforms undertaken under the aegis of Saint Bernard of Clairvaux (2.13). Another change was that the sick were now allowed meat. This was difficult for Stephen, who had been adamant against the eating of meat on the monastery premises (2.14).[26]

Stephen saw to the elevation to the rank of Cistercian abbeys of two of the monasteries dependent on Obazine: Garde-Dieu, for which he appointed as abbot Gerard, his long-time companion who later succeeded him as abbot of Obazine, and La Frenade in the Saintonge, for which he appointed as abbot Robert, who was abbot of Obazine when the *Life of Saint Stephen* was completed. At the time La Frenade was raised to abbatial status there was a fierce dispute with a lay magnate over land there. Stephen appealed to the pope and won the case (2.16). Grosbot, another dependency of Obazine, became an abbey in 1166.[27] The Cistercian abbey of Landais had been attempting to make a foundation, Sourdain, in the Limousin. To firm up the economic underpinnings of Obazine, Soudain was closed and its holdings transferred to Obazine.[28]

It was time to enlarge the monastery at Obazine once again. The cornerstone of a new church was laid in the presence of the bishop of Limoges on 6 April, 1156. Stephen devoted much of the last three years of his life to this project (2.18–19). The construction of this large, austere, well-designed church (2.19) probably took about twenty years. This was the first and last time the monastery did fund raising for a project. The bishop wanted to offer indulgences to donors, but Stephen refused (2.18). A number of miracles occurred to speed Stephen's building projects (1.28; 2.29–33). This extensive construction project, like others Stephen undertook, makes clear the economic ties between the monastery and its surroundings. On such projects the monastery employed local peasants and skilled workmen (1.12; 2.14). The projects required wood, stone, sand, and lime (1.30; 2.18).

26. RB 36.9; 39.11; Kardong, 300–304, 322–326.

27. *Abbaye*, 93–86.

28. *Cartulaire* #26 (pp. 76–77); *Abbaye*, 120–121.

Obazine's Relations with Its Neighbors

During this time, there was a long and severe famine in the area. Stephen mobilized the not inconsiderable economic resources of Obazine to help those who were suffering. He employed many needy people on the construction of the monastery's new basilica and provided them with food as recompense. He bought stores of food to sell or give to the needy. Whatever money he received for this food, he spent to buy still more food. Some he bought on credit. Those who fell under his care included not just his monks, nuns, and workers, but also guests, the *familia* of the monastery,[29] and the poor. On several occasions during the famine, food supplies were miraculously augmented, not only at Obazine, but also at the monastery's granges and at the monastic foundations at Grosbot and Bonnaigue (2.20–27).

The world in which Stephen lived was controlled by warlike and suspicious local lords (1.27). Once Stephen settled a war that had started over a falcon (2.39). In dealing with these lords and knights, Stephen used diplomacy, legal proceedings, anger and subterfuge (2.15–16). He was usually calm when they were upset (2.35–36), but he could be harsh and angry as well (2.37). During times of civil unrest and pillage by contesting local armies or brigands, many people flocked to the monastery for safety and succor (2.27–28,34; cf. 1.23). Stephen's miracles brought healing to the sick of high and low estate (2.34,42), children (2.43,45,46), and nuns (2.44). In working these cures, Stephen usually laid hands on the afflicted person.

Stephen's Death (1159)

At various places, the author of the *Life* describes Stephen's physical appearance. He was short of stature and balding, and had a plain, prematurely wrinkled face, though in other respects he never really looked old (1.6,22; 2.12,50).

The author deliberately devoted considerable space to Stephen's death and burial (3. pref.). On Ash Wednesday, Stephen left with

29. Ursmer Berlière, *La familia dans les monastères Bénédictins du moyen age*, Académie Royale de Belgique, Classe des letters et des sciences morales et politiques, Memoires 29:2, #1422 (Bruxelles: Maurice Lamertin, 1931).

some other abbots to preside at the election and installation of a new abbot at Bonnaigue. There Stephen took sick. Many of his monks, deeply saddened, came to visit (3.1–2). He instructed them and told them that if they would pray for him, he would obtain from God the salvation of all of them, especially those who died in the monastery (3.3,13). He was anointed, received communion, and died (3.4), and so passed from this wicked world to eternal happiness (3.34).

There was a great procession back to Obazine, over forty miles away. The procession carried his body quickly past the monastery at Tulle, because they feared that monks from there would steal his body (3.6). People wept; some were cured (3.5,8). His tomb at Obazine became a pilgrimage destination and the source of many miracles. Lay people and clergy who sought a miracle or had received one put candles at his tomb (3.10,20–21,29–31). In miraculous appearances, Stephen assured his community he would be with them always (3.11,14,15,34). He also appeared to the nuns at Coyroux, especially when one of them was dying (3.16–19). After his death, he continued to protect people from brigands (3.20–24) and oppressive landlords (3.32). His healing powers extended to animals as well (3.27–28).

Stephen was succeeded by Gerard I (1159–1164), who had been the first about of Garde-Dieu; Robert (1164–1188), who had been the first abbot of La Frenade; and Gerard II (1188–1204 or later).

The Enigma of Stephen of Obazine

In spite of the length and detail of the *Life*, Stephen remains an enigmatic character. How much of the enigma is attributable to Stephen himself and how much reflects the author's own personality rather than Stephen's is very difficult to judge. Stephen appears as a man of charismatic attractiveness, a man of God full of the Holy Spirit (2.12), possessed of a wisdom not of our world. He was a much loved parish priest, whose parishioners did not want him to leave. Having become a hermit, he attracted many followers, whose numbers continued to increase after the community became monks. He was a very imperious superior. Until the community adopted the *Rule of Saint Benedict*, his will was the rule (1.16). When the abbot of Tulle, Eble of Turenne, brother of Raymond II, count of Turenne, insulted him, Stephen remained calm; Abbot Eble died that same night (2.35).

Stephen doled out fierce punishments on some to strike fear in the rest (1.9,16,17; 2.10,50,54–57). Even after his death he appeared to terrify negligent monks (2.6). There were two mitigations in his practice of physical and psychological punishment: he reached out to console those he had saddened by his severity (2.57), and sometimes he inflicted on himself the same punishments he decreed for others (1.17). Perhaps one can say that Stephen lived in fierce times that required fierce measures, and people appreciated his forcefulness because anything less would have been ineffective.

On the other hand, the author of the *Life* points out that Stephen's followers preserved their own personalities (1.9), and says that Stephen was not cruel (1.15) and commanded more by love than by fear (2.51).

We are told explicitly that Stephen wished to mortify the body so that the spirit might live (1.7,14,15). During his hermit days he underwent extremely severe mortifications. Life was difficult for many people in those times, and severe restrictions in food, heat, and clothing were the lot of many of the poor. Stephen himself said that he wished to be a poor follower of the poor Christ (1.2). He thought that prayer and mortifications like restricted diet and sleep were the best or perhaps the only way to be poor with Christ. Perhaps one could compare Stephen's ascetical practices and aims to those of people today who engage in extreme sports. They risk life and limb for the 'rush' that comes from parachuting off bridges or jumping from helicopters to snowboard down precipitous mountains. In his younger days, Stephen was an extreme athlete of God who sought to purify and intensify his mental gaze in order to experience God.

The author of the *Life* presents Stephen as a very emotional man given to tears. The author sometimes surmises that when he was alone, Stephen must have been praying with tears, which suggests that this dimension of Stephen's personality may have been exaggerated by the author (1.18; 2.60). Equally striking is the extreme grief that Stephen's death aroused not just in the communities of Obazine but also in the whole area.

Although charged with administration, Stephen did not allow the monastery's supplies to be counted or measured in his presence, at least when it was a matter of tallying up the good the monastery had done for others (2.20). Nevertheless, he must have been an effective administrator. He oversaw the foundation of most of the economic underpinnings that sustained Obazine for centuries. He seems to have been a very hands-on and sometimes even micromanaging supervisor, not just of Obazine itself, but also of its dependencies (2.9,53). He was a person of immense energy who had to be doing something wherever he was (1.21; 2.9,19). He was especially meticulous in all that concerned the furnishing of the church (1.2; 2.60). He was careful to put on shoes before celebrating Mass (1.4,7), and in general insisted on good behavior in church (1.16; 2.60). So exacting was the discipline at Obazine that outsiders could distinguish its monks from a distance by the way they rode their horses (2.58).

The *Life* is replete with dreams and visions that bridge the gap between this world and the next. Visits to the tomb of a saint brought one in contact with healing power (2.10). The dead came back to warn and console the living (2.6). After his death, Stephen himself was always present to the community of Obazine. Stephen was acutely aware of the decisive alternative that faced human beings: heaven or hell. Stephen was not at all optimistic about this world. The cloister was a protection against its seductions (1.2; 2.4). Nor was Stephen optimistic about the number to be saved (1.9). The author celebrates the naiveté and simplicity of many of the monks and nuns who were raised in the cloister and had no experience of the wider world (2.5,47,48).

The author seems ambivalent about cheerfulness. He says Stephen punished any laughter or smiling in church and any loud laughter anywhere (1.16). Stephen himself avoided laughter, yet he seems to have smiled and had a sense of humor (2.2,9; 2.50).

Stephen did not have an extensive education (2, pref.). The author tells us that he mastered the sacred learning offered him by his teachers. When he left them he was sufficiently prepared to serve as a parish priest. Because Obazine had the practice of admitting whole families, it had to provide upbringing for children of all ages. When they reached adolescence they had the choice of entering

Obazine or Coyroux or making their way in the world. Since their families had entered the monastery and disposed of their material possessions, the worldly prospects for such children were limited. Not all of the boys who were educated at the monastery were honest (3.25). The *Life* does mention a scriptorium and the copying of books (1.15), but nothing indicates that Stephen encouraged learning and study. John, the first abbot of Bonnaigue, by contrast, is described as learned and cultivated (2.8).

Stephen and Obazine in their Setting

Geography

Obazine is located on the banks of the River Corrèze, which snakes down a valley running to the southwest. Gradually the valley widens and the hills become lower. Further south is the valley of the Dordogne. It is a land of mild climate, good soils, and relatively easy travel. This forested region has numerous springs. The first entry in the cartulary of Obazine (*c.* 1133–1137) declares that Archambaud IV, viscount of Comborn, donated to the Abbot Stephen part of the forest of Obazine (*quamdam partem Obazinensis silve*). An earlier entry in the cartulary of the Benedictine monastery of Tulle also refers to the forest called Obazine.

The *Life* (1.4) describes the place of their hermitage as forested, covered with briars, and difficult to reach. However, the hermitage was not in a virgin forest or an uninhabited region. Not far from the site of Stephen's hermitage were villages such as Vergonzac, Pauliat, and Roche (later called Palazinges). Roche had an ancient church. Stephen's hermitage was above Vergonzac; to the northwest the horizon was traced by the hills that line the right bank of the Corrèze. When the growth of the community required a larger site, Stephen looked for another spot with a level area big enough for a monastery. The one he chose was about two kilometers south of the hermitage. Like the hermitage, it had a view to the west and a dominant position. This new site did not have a stream nearby, but for the present there were ample springs (1.19-21). Later the monks built an aqueduct to provide more ample water supplies. Coyroux was located a kilometer southeast of the monastery at Obazine, at the mouth of a steep canyon (1.27).[30]

Politics

At the beginning of the twelfth century, the Limousin was part of the Duchy of Aquitaine. In 1137, with the death of the Duke William X of Aquitaine and the marriage of his daughter Eleanor to Louis VII, the latter gained direct rule over the area. He did not, however, interfere much with the traditional independence of the magnates in the Duchy. The never-congenial marriage of Eleanor and Louis was dissolved. In 1152 Eleanor married Henry, count of Anjou and duke of Normandy, who in 1154 became Henry II of England. Henry II was much more involved in the Limousin, and from 1158–1159 the area was mixed up in the ongoing struggle between the kings of France and England. Traces of the conflict show up in a charter of Obazine from 1159, 'when the two kings, of the French and the English, entered this land.'[31] In January 1169, at Montmirail, Louis VII received the homage of the sons of Henry II for their continental possessions. During the next twenty years the Limousin suffered greatly as Henry's sons unsuccessfully revolted against their father, and one of them, Richard, was installed as duke of Aquitaine. The viscounts Archambaud V of Comborn, Eble IV of Ventadour, and Raymond II of Turenne were allied with Adémar V, viscount of Limoges, in his struggle against Richard. Richard's brigands were entrenched at the castle of Malemort, six miles from Obazine. In April 1177, Richard's soldiers suffered a serious defeat at the hands of an army of Limousin knights, organized at the behest of the bishop of Limoges and the abbot of Saint-Martial.[32] In 1182 Henry II's eldest son, Henry the Younger, joined his brother Geoffrey in a revolt of the barons of Aquitaine against their brother

30. *Abbaye*, 17–24.

31. *Cartulaire*, #131 (p. 135).

32. *Vie* 2.27; *Cartulaire* #406 (pp. 276–77), a donation from Eble IV, viscount of Ventadour and his brother in reparation for damage that their army inflicted on the grange of Croisy and other granges of the monastery'; *Cartulaire* #568 (pp. 350–51) which grants donors right of refuge in the grange of Serre for themselves, their animals and goods during the time barbarians enter their territory.

Richard. Mercenaries entered the region in support of the rebellious brothers and their local allies, and in support of Richard and Henry II. In 1183, to support his army, Henry the Younger appropriated wealth from the abbeys of Saint-Martial, Grandmont, Uzerche, Dalon, and Obazine, as well as from the Marian pilgrimage shrine of Rocamadour.[33] After Henry the Younger died in 1183, Henry II took control of the situation and the fighting in the Limousin lessened somewhat.[34]

There was a wide divide between the nobility and the peasantry. The nobility could be both generous and imperious toward religious communities. War was endemic and a primary activity of the nobility. Brigandage was a constant problem. Stephen used his moral authority to try to limit the savagery of war and pillage. Peasants sought refuge near his monasteries. The peasants were mostly poor, and Stephen tried to protect them from war, pillage and famine. He could offer them help, both because of his moral authority and because of the economic resources of Obazine and its foundations.

Religion

The *Life of Saint Stephen* provides precious, if selective information about the religious world in which Stephen lived. Because of their widespread domains, Stephen and the monks of Obazine dealt not only with their own bishops of Limoges, Gerard du Cher (ca. 1137–1177) and Sébrand Chabot (1178–1198), but also with the bishops of Cahors, Saintes and Clermont. As we have seen, local bishops were usually supportive of Stephen. The bishop of Saintes, beholden to local magnates, was not.

There were many monastic communities in the Limousin, especially in the southwest, where Obazine was located: Benedictine (e.g, Tulle and the Casadean community of Port-Dieu), canonial (e.g., Lesterps, Aureil, Le Chalard), and eremitical (L'Artige and Grandmont). The Cistercians were just entering the area during Stephen's lifetime. The author does not present the communities

33. The events described in *Vie*, 2.28, probably occurred at this time.

34. *Abbaye*, 25–33.

of canons in a favorable light. The monks of Dalon, who adopted Cistercian customs before Obazine did, proved poor mentors when Obazine wished to learn those customs from them. The abbot of Cîteaux and the Cistercian pope Eugene III were very supportive of Stephen, and mentors sent from Cîteaux were much more sympathetic than those from Dalon had been. Stephen's final journey was made in the company of other abbots going to preside at the election of a new abbot according to Cistercian practice. In the *Life* the abbot and monks of Benedictine Tulle are portrayed as hostile and untrustworthy, though the cartulary indicates that they gave some generous economic support to Obazine during the abbacy of Gerard d'Escorailles (1152–1188).[35] La Chaise-Dieu and its dependencies are mentioned several times without any negative comments. The author makes reference neither to nearby Beaulieu nor to Grandmont, whose founder, Stephen of Muret, had died in 1124, when Stephen was pondering his vocation. There were not, however, many religious communities of women in the Limousin.[36]

In describing the entrance of a layman and his family into the monastery, the author of the *Life* gives an interesting description of an exemplary nobleman. He showed no bias toward the powerful or toward his friends in judicial decisions. He extended generous hospitality to all pilgrims, especially religious and poor clerics. The latter he invited to stay a while so he could learn from them. He had a rule in his household that the first person to hear someone asking for alms at the door should immediately see to the petitioner's needs. He was so zealous about religious services that he not only attended the parish Mass, but went two miles to the monastery to participate in the main Mass there on Sundays and feast days. It was while offering Stephen hospitality that he decided to enter Obazine instead of another monastery he had been considering. The monks then transformed his fortified house into the grange of Montredon and dismantled his weapons.[37]

35. *Cartulaire*, #129 (pp. 133–34), #478 (pp. 310–11), #562 (p. 347), #661 (pp. 403–4).

36. *Abbaye*, 38–40.

37. *Vie*, 1.29; *Cartulaire* #51 (pp. 88–89); *Abbaye*, 124.

Life at Obazine

In the midst of this tumultuous and insecure world, Stephen created at Obazine a place of rigid and reassuring order. He was a strict disciplinarian, who insisted that things be done in what he considered to be the proper way. There was a great deal of singing, though more at the men's monastery than at the women's (1.22; 2.3). The *Life* gives some indications of the daily order observed after the community had been well established as a monastery at Obazine (1.7,17):

- During the night and early morning: Vigils and Lauds of the day, and of the Virgin and all saints, as well as the Office of the Dead and the *psalmi familiares.*[38]
- Prime, followed by the seven penitential psalms and the litanies.[39]
- Mass
- Chapter meeting
- Work
- Meal (with reading) and Vespers
- Compline
- In winter, work together after Compline until half the psalter had been recited.

On Saturday there were more solemn services, but the monks worked on that day also. On Sunday, there was a procession to bless the cloister (1.22).

Life at Coyroux[40]

As we have seen, Stephen, like other charismatic founders of his era, had to provide for the women who joined him. He prepared for them their own monastery, Coyroux, situated a half-mile from

38. The *psalmi familiares* were a series of prayers said for a monastery's friends and benefactors (its *familia*). They were said in conjunction with a liturgical hour, but were not an integral part of the liturgy.

39. The seven penitential psalms (Pss 6, 32, 38, 51, 102, 130, 143) were prayed together from early Christian times. Added to them was a litany. They were said especially during Lent. They appear in many books of hours. See www.medievalist.net/hourstxt.

40. *Abbaye*, 91–108.

Obazine, in a narrow, secluded spot from which the only view was up. The place was at a spot where the rapids of the Coyroux River emerge from a narrow gorge. The valley is less than one hundred yards wide and the steep slopes block out the horizon. The women's monastery was constructed on an artificial terrace, four to five yards high, located on the north bank. The terrace forced the stream against the south side of the valley. Upon this terrace was constructed a cloister, about sixty feet square, with the church to the north, the nuns' residence to the east, the parlor and refectory to the south, and the kitchen and storehouse to the west. The nuns' monastery was about half the size of the men's monastery and it was built more roughly and with less technical skill.[41] It was completed in a two-year construction project (1.30). He built an enclosure, from which the nuns never emerged (2.2). The author says that Stephen's purpose in this was to protect the women from assault, temptation, and criticism (2.4). The two monasteries were close enough that the bells of each place could usually be heard at the other (2.1). The nuns' contacts with members of the men's monastery were, however, very limited.

The community consisted of women from different social strata (1.29; 2.4). There were one hundred fifty nuns when the community adopted the *Rule of Saint Benedict* in 1142. Their new church was about seven by thirty yards. A wall completely separated the much smaller, eastern part of the church, the chancel, from the long narrow nave to the west of it. The monks who served as chaplain entered the chancel through a door leading to the path which connected the two monasteries. In the wall there was a window covered with a grille through which communion could be distributed (2.3).[42]

The abbot was the superior of the women's community; under him, a prioress was in charge of the women. Some of the nuns came accompanied with donations that went to the common treasury of the two communities. Because of their strict enclosure, the nuns had to rely completely on the monks to meet their material

41. Bernadette Barrière, 'The Cistercian Convent of Coyroux in the Twelfth and Thirteenth Centuries', *Gesta* 31/2 (1992): 76–82.

42. Barrière, 'Cistercian Convent', 76–78.

and spiritual needs. It would thus have been practically impossible to separate the two communities. The monks provided liturgical ministries and spiritual guidance, preached sermons and heard confessions. One learned priest was assigned especially to serve the sisters' spiritual needs. A monk procurator brought them food and other necessities, which he set in a room that had locked doors both to the outside and to the interior of the monastery (2.3). The author of the *Life* observes that, in spite of their dependent position, the nuns' virtues enabled some of these women to surpass men in holiness.

Garde-Dieu in the diocese of Cahors also had an associated women's community, Fontmourlhes. When some nuns at Coyroux heard a rumor that their community was not to be allowed to admit new members, some of them fled to Garde-Dieu (3.3). Fontmourlhes had originally been the site of a mixed community. The male members moved seventy miles to Garde-Dieu, but established a small priory of men a mile from Fortmourlhes to serve the spiritual and material needs of the women.

The Growth and Economy of Obazine[43]

Stephen's influence resulted in the quick multiplication of granges and cells attached to Obazine. As was noted earlier, one factor in this diffusion of the order was the entry into Stephen's religious community of whole families.[44] When this occurred, each person in the family had a place: the father went to Obazine; the mother to Coyroux. Children up to the age of five were raised at Coyroux, and in due course the daughters could remain there and become nuns. At the age of five the sons were sent to be raised in priories (*stationes puerorum*: 2.45, 47) devoted to that purpose. One of these is described in the *Life* (2.30) as located on the border of the Dordogne. It had a church and a cloister and was directed by a prior. This was almost certainly the priory of Saint-Jean-de-Nougein, which later became the grange of Couffinier. When they reached

43. *Cartulaire*, pp. 16–26; *Abbaye*, 82–183.

44. *Cartulaire*, #30 (pp. 78–80), #61 (pp. 94–95), #103 (pp. 120–22); *Abbaye*, 124–25.

adolescence, these young men could return to the world or enter the novitiate. Constance Berman speculates that some of the families who entered Obazine/Coyroux were the households of married priests, and that some of the women who entered on their own may have been wives or daughters of married priests or women who provided social services in their parishes.[45]

Obazine continued to flourish into the thirteenth century. *The Life of Saint Stephen* (2.27) says that there were one hundred twenty men in the community at the end of the twelfth century. In 1242 Obazine undertook yet another foundation, the New Abbey of Sainte-Marie-de-Gourdon. Coyroux, which had one hundred fifty members by 1200, counted one hundred in 1270.

In the cartulary of Obazine, there are one hundred sixty entries from the time of Stephen's abbacy, and most of the patrimony seems to have been acquired by the time the monastery affiliated with the Cistercians. The entries in the cartulary witness to the support of the viscounts of Comborn and Turenne and to the role played by families of the local aristocracy who entered together into the community and deeded to it all their goods. Another source of material support came from the dowries of women who entered Coyroux. Abbots Gerard I (1159–1164) and Robert (1164–1188) were faced with the immense task of organizing and securing clear title to a vast patrimony. The cartulary contains the record of over seven hundred transactions effected during the thirty years spanned by their abbacies.

Most of the patrimony of the double monastery of Obazine-Coyroux consisted of agricultural land that was already in production when it was given to the monastery. In addition, the community received privileges, especially exemption from tithes to the local churches. Throughout the twelfth century the monastery, in keeping with Cistercian legislation, seems to have avoided acquiring tithes and parish churches. There were many monasteries in the area when Obazine-Coyroux was founded, so the community was not able to form a compact network of granges in the immediate vicinity. Instead, it formed scattered clusters of granges. There were four major groups of granges in the Limousin, the major-

45. Berman, *Women*, 78.

ity of them the result of the patronage of the viscounts of Comborn. Two groups of granges in Quercy were largely the result of the patronage of the viscounts of Turenne. These were centered around Rocamadour, the Marian pilgrimage site to the south of Obazine.

These clusters of territory served many purposes. Grain was the principal crop, but according to the nature of the place, vegetables, grapes, and fish were raised as well. Each grange tried to be somewhat self-sufficient by acquiring forest lands and mills. The granges around Rocamadour were coordinated from a central grange at Alys. In spite of these extensive domains, the abbey was not yet completely self-sufficient economically. In the next century the monks of Obazine would seek to acquire new possessions to provide specialized products, such as wine, cheese, and salt. Like other abbeys, Obazine had establishments in towns near its land holdings. These served as warehouses and business centers. By the end of the twelfth century, Obazine had such houses at Martel (2.27,31), Cognac (Cart. #254) and Rocamadour (Cart. #1241) and, at least later, at Brive and Angoulême.

Conclusion

Like Robert of La Chaise-Dieu, Stephen of Obazine was a priest who followed a call to solitude, and like Robert, Stephen ended up founding a monastery which followed the *Rule of Saint Benedict*. Both monasteries founded other monasteries, but whereas La Chaise-Dieu became the head of a large congregation of monasteries, Stephen led Obazine and its foundations into the Cisterican Order. Their respective *Vitae* tell us much about a tumultuous time in the history of the Auvergne, which was also a time in which many men and women seeking to follow Christ explored new forms of dispossession, solitude and community. Their *Vitae* present both men as charismatic leaders, who won the hearts of their disciples. However, Stephen also appears as stern and harsh with himself and others. He was a man who had a sense of humor, but forbade loud laughter and smiling in church. Stephen remains an elusive figure, but his hagiographer finds a divine wisdom at work in what in Stephen's actions may seem contradictory or even foolish.

The Life of Saint Stephen of Obazine

Book One

Preface

Here begins the preface to the Life of Lord Stephen the Abbot.

Although it is not now the custom to write about the deeds of saints, or rather it has ceased, it is not clear that this has happened for any other reason except either the lack of writers or the rarity of saints themselves. These now have disappeared to such a degree that either those who write, or those about whom they write, are found to be few or almost none at all. Hence that outcry of the prophet, saying: 'Save me, Lord, since the saint has disappeared and since truths have been taken away from the sons of men' (Ps 11:2).[1] Yet there are still, or there were, some unknown saints who not only shine brightly before God's eyes in their life and deeds, but who also are considered saints in the Church. But their lives could not be written for an example to others, either because, fearing to be made known, they themselves preferred to be placed 'under a measure rather than on a lamp stand,' (Mk 4:21) or since they were not so famous for miracles as is now especially demanded by those who want to write saints' lives. They seem like the darkened moon or the old moon, of which nothing is visible at its rising, but then, when full, glows in the heavens. For those who appear glorious on earth and who ponder heavenly things are likened more to the full

1. Biblical references are to the Vulgate, *Bibliorum Sacrorum iuxta Vulgatam Clementinam*, Nova editio, ed. Aloisius Gramatica (Vatican City: Typis Polyglottis Vaticanis, 1951). Translations of the biblical texts have been made from the Latin text by the translator.

moon, which shows forth all the brightness of its light to the world, and the black color of darkness to heaven.

Yet, there were in our age saintly men who presented the appearance of both phases of the moon. These men were glorious before God by merit of their hidden sanctity, and they shone forth wondrously before men by their signs and miracles. The lives of these fittingly deserved to be written: that is, of Saint Bernard, Abbot, and Saint Malachy, Bishop. The first was published in three books, the other by Saint Bernard himself with so great an elegance of thought and style that it might be considered inferior to the works of none of the earlier, illustrious authors.

However, I was not moved by myself alone to write (in whatever style) the life of the lord and father Stephen of Obazine, as might be thought, but I was asked, indeed compelled, by the commands of my superiors and fathers. Although it was perilous to yield to them in so great a matter, it would be more perilous not to obey. Moreover, I have done it, not so that I might become known through these writings, but that the life and lifestyle of the saintly man might not lie hidden; so that people now and those to come might know who and what sort of man he was, how he lived, how he abandoned the world, and finally, how much he benefited not only himself, but many others; how wondrous and noble were the works he completed in his own time, or left to be completed; and, at the end, how he went forth from this life with a glorious, marvelous death.

But if this effort of ours perhaps is looked down upon by many, or even spurned, it will be no wonder, especially on account of the novelty of the work and the unworthiness of the writer. The human spirit has this characteristic, that it considers a work according to the author, and it approves antiquity more; it does not think that writing should be accepted readily as long as those who write or those about whom they write live upon earth. Hence John Chrysostom says: 'Just as the flesh of living animals is not eaten, unless they have been killed first, so the writings of our ancestors have not been accepted as authoritative, except after their death.'[2] Hence it is that the Lord commanded that those invited to supper be told: 'My oxen and fowl have been killed; come to the wedding feast' (Mt 22:4). That is, those

2. Pseudo-Chrysostom, *Opus imperfectum in Mattheum*, Hom. 41; PG 56:862.

through whom Scripture was composed for you are dead or killed, so that in reading you might perceive the banquet of the divine word not as human, but as truly divine. We do not say these things so that, since we cannot be accepted now, at least we might be accepted after death, but because we know that certain ones have grumbled about these words of ours. They say that we ought not to have written these things since we are unworthy or inexperienced, or since the one about whom we speak is not yet canonized among the saints (although we read about many of the saints whose lives were written in great part before they died). To these and others who complain in a similar way, we answer nothing, except this only, that if God wills, this work will endure, and if it is not God's will, it will not endure. Moreover, we believe and without doubt we expect that, lasting, it will endure and be useful, God granting, for the praise of him about whom we speak and for the edification of many people.

Here the Preface Ends

Here Begins His Life

1. First, Stephen was born in the region of Aquitaine, territory of the Limousin,[3] to parents who were noble and from a long line of Christians. His father was also Stephen; his mother was named Gauberta. Indeed, his parents were neither exceedingly rich nor wholly poor. They had enough to live on, and, commendable for other good deeds too, they brought forth this son, beloved of God, not only to be useful to themselves, but also to the Church of God.

It is said that his mother was shown a vision in the night when she was pregnant, carrying him in her swollen womb. In this dream it was as if she had given birth to a lamb in place of a son, and when he was fully-grown, a great flock of sheep was handed over to him. When she reported this to a certain holy man of God, she heard from him that she would bring forth a son, to whom a vast number of souls would be entrusted by Christ to be instructed by

3. Tradition has it that Stephen was born in Vielzo.

his heavenly teaching. However, others say that the aforementioned woman saw not a lamb, but a white puppy, as one reads about Saint Bernard. Yet, each of these appears true in its meaning, since he was a lamb in the purity of his innocence and a puppy, indeed a dog who was not silent in guarding his flock (Is 56:10), that is, in his constant care of souls. But it is not for us to report at length how much barking he did for the Lord and for the flock entrusted to him, since we are hastening on to other things.

After he was born and had grown up, he was entrusted to the teachers in a church school to be instructed in the sacred scriptures.[4] Well instructed by them, he quickly mastered their knowledge, that is, the content of the scriptures that pertains to the worship of God and the edification of souls.

When he reached the age of majority, after his father died, he took on the care of his whole household. He actively guided his mother and brothers and sisters and his entire family and ruled them with discipline. Since a more noble cause impelled him, he was more zealous in caring for the poor than for his relatives. For, he was drawn to the latter by human nature and to the former by mercy and the hope of an eternal reward. He was the father of orphans, nurturer of the poor, 'receiver of strangers' (Est 16:10), and tender comforter of widows. His hands were stretched forth more for giving than for receiving, so that he might fulfill that saying of the Psalmist: 'He divided his goods and gave them to the poor; his justice remains forever' (Ps 111:9). He showed himself to be chaste, sober and kind, affable to everyone and generous, so that all around him marveled at his diligence and great prudence. Yet, he still was attached to hunting and certain worldly trifles, and he was attentive to his clothes, though he was considered more attentive to his way of life. Indeed, he presented this view first of all to avoid vainglory, to conceal the intention of his heart, and so that others might not think more of him than he of himself.

2. Moreover, after he was uplifted by the grace of God to the priestly order, he completely abandoned his worldly life, and that which he had first disdained in his mind, he then renounced in his actions

4. This seems to have been the school of the priory of Pleaux, which belonged to the Benedictine abbey of Charroux.

and way of life. Now laughter and those former trifles were transformed into sorrow and rejoicing in lamentation; the hunting of wild beasts changed into the catching of souls. Now the adornment of expensive clothes was given up and the preparation of savory foods was shunned, for in place of soft garments he wore a hairshirt inside, next to his flesh, and in place of a sweet meal he took his bread with tears and his drink with weeping (Ps 79:6). Finally, he treated his own body with such great harshness that he almost killed it with cold and fasting. Indeed, in the middle of winter, when everything was bound by ice and cold, he used to break the ice with his sword and, immersed there right up to his neck, he endured a long time, until the force of the coldness penetrated to his inner parts. In a certain way, he was saying with the Psalmist: 'Since I have become like a wineskin in the snow, I have not forgotten your judgments' (Ps 118:83).

He excelled in fasting, was constant in vigils, eager in prayers. It was not the arrangement of words that offered these prayers to the divine ears, but the devotion of tears. His speech was seasoned with salt and inflamed with charity, infusing his hearers with the fire of divine love and the seasoning of wisdom. So great a gift for teaching was bestowed on him by the Lord, that no one ever had enough of listening to the words from his mouth. But if someone was speaking in the church when he was absent, the person was spurned by the people as if he were a country bumpkin, on account of Stephen's wondrous teaching inflamed by the spirit. Neither was this without cause, for he commended by his works what he taught with his mouth, and his worthy way of life showed that his sermons were entirely right. He was ever watchful and unwearied in assisting at the divine offices, letting no cares or employments interrupt its proper round, unless he was detained by serious sickness or an unavoidable cause. In fact, in these matters that pertain especially to service at the altar, that is, to the sacred vessels or vestments or any ornaments in churches that he served, he devoted such great carefulness that because of this he appeared admirable in other things and everywhere irreproachable. Just as in military service or in specific trade some men are considered so well prepared and experienced that they are then deservedly thought to be masters, so in the care of the altar he was considered a master and guide of all virtue and cleanliness. He was diligent in the reading of divine scriptures, especially those writers who explained the gospels. Thus, he prepared eternal salvation for himself by reading and for others by preaching. And since he found there many doctrines about contempt for the world and the glory of the life to come, his mind was intensely inflamed toward despising things of the present and desiring the things of the future. In a certain way he was saying with the prophet: 'When will I come and appear before the face of God?' (Psalm 41:3) and 'My eyes have failed before your word; they say, "when will you comfort me?"' (Ps 118:82).

Inflamed by longings of this kind, he was determined to renounce the world every day so that, when earthly cares had been cast aside, poor and naked he might follow Christ the pauper directly, with unimpeded steps. But lest he might seem to do this rashly and without deliberation, he approached a certain religious, a very holy man named Stephen of Mercoeur.[5] This man had been a pupil of Saint Robert, inasmuch as he had been reared by him. His reputation for sanctity was renowned in that whole region. When Stephen had come to him and revealed the plan in his mind, not wavering concerning his vow, but seeking counsel, the venerable old man answered him thus: 'Dearest Son, you should not defer for long the desire that has been divinely infused in you, nor should you put it off from day to day, knowing that it has always been harmful to put off what has been made ready. But rather, as you have planned, follow in the footsteps of Christ on your blessed course, with the cares of the world cast aside, so that by your example many may be converted to God.' Trusting in this response as if it were a divine oracle, he returned with joy to his own house.

Moreover, in this plan he had a certain companion and colleague named Peter, a man of wondrous simplicity, who had also been recently ordained a priest. To him alone he entrusted the secrets of his heart in a proposition such as this: renouncing the world together, they would without delay take the habit of holy religion and persevere in it right to life's end. Then the holy men hastened to fulfill what they had vowed to God. Freed from the bonds of this

5. Stephen of Mercoeur was abbot of La Chaise-Dieu, 1111–1146. Direct contact between Robert of La Chaise-Dieu and Stephen is unlikely. Robert died in 1067; Stephen was offered to the abbey in 1078.

world, with willing, unhalting steps, they set out upon the way of salvation so that they might come together to Christ.

3. Therefore, after a few days had passed, a week before Lent (when ashes are customarily given), on a Thursday, they were ready to say a final farewell to a multitude of relatives who had been called together. They gave them a festive banquet and divided whatever remained of their property among the poor. Indeed, they spent the following sleepless night in vigils and prayers, imploring God's mercy so that, with His assistance, they might pursue their desires, which He had instilled in their hearts beforehand. Then, putting on the religious habit, even before it grew light, they began their journey, barefooted, as if into exile, with their native land left behind.

There was in those parts a certain hermit named Bertrand.[6] He was concerned with instructing souls and had a few disciples who clung to his teaching. When they had sought out this man, they spent only ten months with him, not because they suffered weariness, but in order that, more tested, they might not go backward, but might seek ways more courageous and closer to salvation. In fact, they had come to him under this condition: if within this space of time they should not find life with him suitable, they might go elsewhere, free and without complaint. After they departed from there, they went around to religious houses everywhere, so that when a more perfect one had been found, they might serve God so much more perfectly and more courageously, according to their desire. Indeed, such a religious order as this was not yet flourishing in these regions. But Almighty God was not willing that they be subject then to anyone's teaching, so that He might fulfil what He had predestined for that blessed man.

4. Thus, going forth together with his venerable companion, the man of God came at last, after he had wandered all over the region, to the woodland of Obazine. It was called this, I believe, on account of the shade[7] of the forests and density of the brambles by which it was surrounded on every side. Besides the density of the forests, this place was encircled here and there by rugged rocks

6. This could be the Bertrand who lived as a hermit at Griffeville around 1120.

7. The Latin word is *'opacitate.'*

and by a certain river, called Corrèze, flowing farther down, which seemed to bestow a certain charm on the place. Arriving at this place on Good Friday, with their feet bare because it was before Easter, the blessed men entered its inner recesses without fear. Not far off, there was a small plain lying low among the valleys, but thick with a vastness of thorn-bushes and brambles, with a small stream flowing down through the middle. After following many winding ways and circling downward, they entered this plain through the rugged hollows of the valleys and mountains. On that day and the following one they remained there without food or comfort of any other kind.

On the third day, which was that of the Lord's resurrection, they proceeded to a nearby church[8] and, after they had received shoes from one another, one of them sang a mass and gave communion to his companion. When this had been done, after the shoes were returned, they started to go back to their starting point with sadness, since no one invited them to a meal.

While they were slowly climbing the ridges of a mountain, and, distressed by their toil and fasting, were resting a little at a summit, a certain woman from the neighboring countryside, which is called Paulhac, approached them. She offered them a half-loaf of bread and a cup of milk. They accepted these with such great joy that the holy man testified afterward that he had received nothing more desirable in his life as far as food is concerned. And so, they returned to their starting point and were refreshed by that food. Since as yet no one knew either who they were or where they were, they spent many days there without human food, except the roots of herbs or whatever can be found in the wilderness. But since the merciful God wanted to lessen their hardships and to instruct others around them by their example, He willed that they should come to the notice of men in the following way.

While the head of a family who lived in the vicinity was going to church on a certain day, it came into his mind, under God's inspiration, to bring nourishment to the poor living there. And while he thought that he was going there, suddenly he lost the way and came, as if wandering, to the same place. However, he had not lost

8. Probably the church of Cornil.

his way by mistake; he was led by that guide who once conveyed a priest to blessed Benedict on the holy day of Easter.

And so, seeing unknown persons in religious habits settled there, the aforementioned man marveled at first, and then had pity. He offered them the goods that he was carrying. These sustained them that day and the next. Not long after, they were found by shepherds. When they were made known by them throughout the nearby places, many people began to come to visit them. These people carried with them nourishment for the body, and they brought back nourishment for life from their words, although the people feared, based on some who had preceded these men, that they would not long persevere there.

5. Indeed, a certain false-hermit had come there once. Pretending that he wanted to remain there, he built a little cottage in the manner of an oratory. And when the people offered him many things, he gladly accepted them. What he could not consume, he sold for money. Then to those coming to him, he indicated a day on which they should all gather together, as if for new celebrations of mass. Then on the night that preceded the aforementioned day, thinking I know not what and taking along with him all the goods he had received, he suddenly disappeared. At his unexpected departure, both those who had gathered and those who heard about it were equally mocked and incensed. They began to be harsher toward Stephen and his companion, thinking that they would act in a similar manner.

Hence, neglected by those people, they endured such great suffering from hunger that they even eagerly plucked the tender shoots of trees and every living plant, and they set these before themselves as sweet food. Their drink was a very little water. Drinking this from a broken piece of earthenware, they satisfied nature. Indeed, they used the same earthenware for many days. The hard ground was their bed; on this they cast their limbs, worn out by fasts, to be bruised more than to rest. And lest they lack little pillows too, they put hard stones under their heads, which both prevented sleep and banished weakness. Their clothes clung to their flesh so long that either excess of dirt or of lice compelled them to change. Removing them then, they shook them over a fire or put them in water. After the clothes had been washed and wrung out a little, then they were dressed in them again, so that their bodies, drenched in the freezing clothes, almost perished as much by the weight as by the cold. They used to do this especially in the winter, when there was no necessity for washing, but only the desire for mortification. But since these were not enough, Father Stephen fitted on himself a hair-shirt, which he secretly wore near his flesh for many years, until little by little, worn out by age, it split. In such a way did the good saint punish himself in the flesh for Christ, so that his spirit might be saved on the day of the Lord.

6. Moreover, next to a small tree there he constructed a hut of wood covered with a flimsy roof. In this, together with his venerable companion, he persisted day and night in continuous prayers and chanting of the Psalms. In this place, they would arise for divine praises after a short rest by which they refreshed a little their weary limbs, then, as soon as they felt oppressed by sleep, they took up bundles of rods, bared their sides, and lashed each other in turn and whipped themselves. Thus, their flesh, worn out by fasts and fatigued by the burden of vigils and hardships, was also furrowed by lengthy scourging so that, brought to subjection by this, it might produce not carnal fruits, but spiritual fruits. Whence also the Apostle said of himself: 'I chastise my body and bring it into subjection, lest when I have preached to others, I might become blameworthy myself' (1 Cor 9:27). A clear indication of how Stephen did this was given when his holy face, furrowed with wrinkles and worn with the pallor of fasts, produced the most scattered and thin hair. But the hairs of his head, maintaining their condition, were not even changed in old age, so that they did not produce baldness or whiteness. Thus, he might have been thought of as a young man, except that his wrinkles, as was written above, bore witness to his old age.

7. After this, by mutual agreement, his companion (mentioned above) proceeded to the city of Limoges. He was joined by a cleric named Bernard who had recently come to them. After abandoning all his possessions, this man was admitted to the monastic life in the same place. He dwelt as a monk in this place to the end of his life and died a happy death. From his account I learned many things about the deeds of the saint, since he was his follower in this world and clung to him inseparably in religious life until the saint's death.

When they reached the city, they met with the bishop, who at that time was Eustorgius,[9] and carefully revealed to him their purpose and the saint's plan. Blessing them, the bishop consecrated the cross that they had brought, and gave it back to them with water blessed by him. He granted them the right to celebrate mass and to build a monastery, so long as they would follow in all things the custom handed down by the fathers. After they heard and accepted these conditions, they returned with rejoicing to their father. When he agreed to these conditions that they brought, the saint moved his dwelling to the farther part of that stream.

Then, cutting down all that was harmful and useless, he constructed buildings according to the likeness of a monastery, that is, an oratory, dormitory, refectory, kitchen, and in the middle of these a cloister, with all of them scarcely occupying the space of one, large building.

Now some who converted to God attached themselves to his band of disciples and, subject to the yoke of discipline, they led a monastic life with him that was very arduous and rigid. Therefore, there were few who would imitate them, unless they became enemies of their own flesh and did not think about the present life.

Receiving well what belongs to God and repudiating what belongs to the world, they followed the canonical rule in their offices and led an eremitical lifestyle. Although canons chant to God according to the rule, they have rich, plentiful food from carefully prepared meals, long rest, and no manual labor, or very little.

Abhorring this very much, the saint decreed that the space of the entire day should be spent in work with their hands, except what either divine reading or divine praise claimed for itself. And so, refreshed in the evening by a little food, when night fell they rested a little, until the time when they would rise to celebrate their morning offices. They added to these the vigils of Blessed Mary and all the saints, and even the office of the dead, along with psalms in honor of their patrons.[10] These consumed no small portion of the night. But even that interval that remained after the vigils was not allotted to rest or sleep, but it was devoted to private prayers or manual

9. Eustorgius was bishop of Limoges, 1106–1137.

10. *'Psalmi familiares.'*

labor. For whatever was necessary for the house and could be done by candlelight, took place not in the day, but at night, since then they were occupied with the more important tasks. After prime, the prostrate monks recited seven psalms and the litanies.[11] Mass followed immediately, unless they were without sandals, which happened often. After mass had been sung, they went directly to their manual labors. Sometimes the man of God remained within the monastery.

Who could determine how many tears, or how many groans and sighs he used during this time to satisfy his fervent longing, since, being alone, he feared neither witness nor judge? And who might think that he spent time then in sleep or rest, a man who, impatient of even a little rest, used to anticipate the nighttime hours in praying and reciting psalms? But we decline to expose these things fully, lest we be found to have written things supposed more than known, since they were done in secret. Hence, with these omitted, let us come rather to those that are known.

8. When he remained in the house while the brothers were absent, he not only spent time zealously on those things that we mentioned, but also earnestly carried out the duties of the kitchen. He diligently procured what seemed necessary for their refreshment. He gathered food and prepared it himself. He carried wood himself and cut it up, and he bore water on his own shoulders. Then at last, after a fire had been kindled, he carefully cooked vegetables or greens and set them before the brothers. With respect to their refreshment, he bustled about anxiously like Martha. When their refreshment was completed, after the dishes had been collected and cleaned, if any of the food was left, he distributed it to the poor, if they were present. If by chance they were absent, he carefully set it aside to be mixed into the brothers' meals a second time. His followers kept this practice for a long time, so that as often as it happened that the poor were absent, whatever was left of the food or bread was set before the brothers again, not because of greed, but because of humility, and lest any of those things, since they had been blessed, might be wasted through negligence.

11. These were the 'penitential psalms.'

9. Failures in discipline and transgressions by his followers, especially young men and boys, he corrected or censured so severely that terror was produced in those who saw it. So great was the severity of discipline that even to have raised the eyes a little bit, or to have smiled slightly, or to have done something without an order, was punished by stern chastisement. Limits were established which it was forbidden to go beyond, unless either a command or appointed work required it.

There was complete silence among them day and night, not only in the cloister, but everywhere that some study or work was carried out. They observed this silence so strictly in the first years that they did not return a greeting when they were greeted, nor did they answer anything when asked a question, but, as if mute and deprived of the use of the tongue, they held no conversation with those who were traveling there nor asked them questions. Finally, when many who came to them for a visit had returned home and were asked by their own people about them, who or what kind of men they were, or what was their mode of life, or who was their master, they answered: 'The way of life of those men cannot be described easily, since they are protected by so great a silence that not only are they not heard in speech, but, to a certain extent, not even in the sound of the voice. Yet, though their mouths are silent, their works are not silent, which, with God as their author, bear clear witness to the religious life of these men. Moreover, there is one among them who presides over the rest; thus they shine, informed by his teaching and instructed by his example. His speech so inflames the souls of his hearers like a glowing fire and fills them with so great a love that, though they remain distinct persons, they become in a certain way other men, and the quality of their life and morals is changed. But both his appearance and his gait, even all things that he does, are truly a sermon, and they reveal nothing but the ordered manner of his life and morals and the discipline of his actions. Hence it is no wonder that such are the disciples who have such a master, who can teach them sufficiently, even without words.' Indeed, all could not say such things about such men, but only those whom wisdom and goodness inspired, since in fact wicked men cannot say good things or talk about good men, because they are unwilling or unable. With a report of this kind traveling swiftly around, very many men were converted to the service of Christ and, having put aside the pomp of the world, they did not fear to submit to an arduous way of life and a hard rule. They knew that 'narrow is the way which leads to life, and few there are who go through it,' and again, 'wide and spacious is the way which leads to perdition, and many there are who enter through it' (Mt 7.13). And so they reckoned that it is better to be saved with the few than to be condemned with the multitude of those perishing.

10. Moreover, when that site was filled by a multitude of those who came and remained there, Father Stephen began to ponder where he could establish them suitably. Yet, his soul was vexed and tormented exceedingly by his longing for solitude. He was impatient of the cares, which he did not wish to endure, which stemmed from directing so many people. Indeed, he had not sought out this aforementioned place to gather many throngs of men there, but in order that, dwelling in solitude, he might devote himself more privately and freely to God, and might torture his flesh without restraint, since he would fear no one's praise or prohibition.

Indeed, as time went on, he was compelled by the warnings and entreaties of others to cease the many torments of the flesh that he inflicted exclusively upon himself. When they could not obtain this otherwise, then they themselves did the things that he did, and so, to spare them, not himself, he relaxed a little his harsh practices.

Speaking often to his companion about this, he strove to persuade him that they should go to the Saracens; perchance by preaching they could convert some of them, or they themselves might be killed for Christ by these non-believers. His venerable companion discouraged this plan with as many counsels as he could, saying that it was better by word and example to convert from their wicked deeds those who already believed, than to labor fruitlessly among those who still did not believe and perhaps were not predestined for eternal life.

Indeed, Almighty God, whose foresight in His own plan is not mistaken, had prepared an unknown flock for the shepherd who was predestined and revealed in His own time, so that he might say with the prophet: 'A people whom I have not known has served me; at the hearing of the ear it has obeyed me' (Ps 17:45), and again, 'Behold, I and my children whom God has given to me' (Is 8:18; Heb 2:13). But also, Christ wanted to build His city not in the depths, but on the heights, as He said Himself: 'A city set on a mountain cannot be hidden' (Mt 5:14). He made him climb from the lowest parts to the higher ones, so that, ascending from virtue to virtue, he might see the God of gods on Sion.

11. At length, while surveying the extent of this woodland, he quickly came to the higher parts of the mountain, which jutted out to the east. He found a certain promontory so positioned that there was a passage through the mountain for those ascending and descending. After the brothers had been called together in this place, he built dwellings in the manner of the earlier ones, but more in number and a little larger in space. And when these were filled again by the multitude of those inhabiting them, the inner parts were placed outside and the outer parts remained in place, and thus the enlarged dwellings held a more copious number of brothers. It is known that they did this two or three times, until finally they were brought to this state that is seen now. Yet, provoked by these buildings, the devil tried by many machinations to destroy them.

12. One day the devil, in the likeness of black men, approached a certain carpenter who was covering the inside of the roof of an oratory he was building with wooden boards. I once saw this poor man myself. Then, in the evening hour, the same man, gathering up his iron tools, was intending to return home. A demon who was loftier than the rest and more savage, accosted him thus: 'Who are you' he said, 'and what are you doing in this place?' The man answered that he was performing the aforementioned work at the bidding of the monks who lived in this forest, since he was a carpenter and was hired for pay. To him the devil said: 'It is not as you say, but they are impious and perverse, hypocrites and crafty men who have come here so that, while capturing men's praise, they might heap up possessions and riches. Rather now, listen to our counsels and set on fire all which has been built here, lest, while striving further for the praise of men, they might deceive all the simple folk.' To these words, that man responded: 'Now I know that you are wicked and filled with all spite, sons of the devil. You are trying to destroy the straight paths of holy men by such great malice; on account of this I'll not assent to your devilish counsel, but I'll obey the orders of the holy men better than when I began,

and I'll remain more devoted in their service.' Saying these words, he climbed a ladder, for he wanted to go up to the roof to place his iron tools there. Then the evil spirits, enraged with extreme fury, hurled him down from the ladder and inflicted such great blows on him that he lay on the ground, entirely black and blue and swollen, with his head seriously bruised. Then, finally, when he had recovered his breath a little, he rose and, as night was now falling, he came with great difficulty to the hospice, shouting and saying: 'Ah me! Ah, me! I am wretched and miserable!' Roused by his words, the brothers came quickly with the man of God and, finding him afflicted by the demons with such a severe beating and rendered almost senseless, they placed him on a bed. There, sprinkled with holy water and signed with the cross of Our Lord, and also strengthened by the prayers of God's servants, after the man of God had placed his hand on him, he recovered complete health in all his limbs in a few days.

I thought that this should be commemorated here so that we might recognize how much praise belonged to Stephen, for when demons strove to revile him, they proclaimed him all the more.

13. For when he had first begun to dwell in this wilderness, the devil persecuted him with such great vehemence that he did not even allow him to rest at night. Hence, roused by his outcries, the brothers used to leap up from their beds and spend almost the entire sleepless night in prayers and vigils. And when he sensed again the attack of an evil spirit, with spiritual weapons in hand, eyes uplifted and hands stretched toward heaven, he bravely fought against those assaulting him, crying out with confidence and saying: 'Lord, judge those who harm me, vanquish those who assail me; take up arms and shield, and rise up to help me' (Ps 34:1).

The devil feared that, because of his example, the wastelands themselves might be crowded with choirs of monks (which later happened), and that he might remain alone after losing those whom he had already caught. Thus was fulfilled what had been foretold by Isaiah: 'The wasteland and the trackless places will rejoice, and the desert will exult and flourish like the lily; sprouting forth, it will grow, and it will exult in praise and joy. The glory of Lebanon is given to it, the beauty of Carmel and Sharon. They will see the glory of the Lord and the beauty of our God' (Is 35:1–2).

14. And so, after the monastery buildings had been reconstructed, the man of God, along with the brothers, moved without delay from the former place to that one, and he decided that this place should be called Obazine.

At that time a dispute arose between Lord Stephen and his venerable companion regarding which of them should assume the direction of the brothers. Yet, they did not contend with each other, as many do now, in claiming the honor for themselves, but in mutually declining the honor and subjecting themselves to one another for the sake of humility. For although all up to that time were subject to Father Stephen, yet he, remembering Him who came not to do His own will, but the will of Him by whom He was sent, was unwilling to be cheated of the sublimity of such great humility. He preferred to do the will of another rather than to impose his own on others. Therefore, while each one wanted the other to be preferred to him, and neither bore it calmly that he was put before the other, a dissension arose between them. It could not be settled until each was brought before the legate, the Bishop of Chartres, who was staying in those parts at that time.[12] But even there they were not able to arrive at a unanimous decision. While one proclaimed that the other was more learned in letters, the other declared that his companion was wiser in all things, nobler in his way of life and manners, and also more suited to directing others. Then the venerable legate, after the qualities of each man had been diligently examined, put an end to the debate. He entrusted the office of prior to Lord Stephen and enjoined upon him the care of the souls subject to him.

15. After he had become prior, Stephen lived according to the same manner of life and habits as before, and he taught others to live that way. The same observance of vigils and prayers, the same course of daytime and nighttime psalms, the same silence in all activities was preserved everywhere. The same custom of fasts and the same moderation in food remained, except that then they were richer in the abundance of these things than before. Indeed, observing their true and tested religious life and their firm stability, the people in

12. Geoffroy de Lèvres.

the vicinity brought so much that they were not able to consume it all. It now nearly reached the point when they would say that 'the people offer more than is necessary' (Ex 36:5). And yet the servants of God, not unmindful of their former poverty, by no means threw away the old as the new things arrived, but they first used the moldy, older provisions, and this in suitable measure. They did this not out of avarice, but for humility. Indeed, in this they curbed the appetite of gluttony, so that the palate, embittered in these ways, might be kept from the immoderate desire for food. All the provisions that were given were weighed on a scale. They were divided among them with such great uniformity that no one boasted, or indeed muttered, that he had more or less than others. No one, except on the Lord's Day, dared to break his fast, in summer just as in winter, unless he was prevented from keeping it by his youth or by serious sickness. Moreover, the one who established this rule, not content to fast just on these days, even fasted on Sundays, until finally, following the advice of the seniors, he resumed meals on those days and on the fifty days after Easter. Indeed, concerning Sundays, he easily gave assent; concerning the fifty days, he could not be prevailed upon until he was made a monk. So great an ardor for abstinence inflamed him, and he treated himself and others with such austerity, that the severity of his way of life scarcely could be endured by anyone, unless the help of Christ the Lord sustained him. But in no way was he cruel in this. What he took away from the flesh, he conferred on the soul, and he compensated for bodily loss with spiritual gain.

Manual labor was constant for him as well as the brothers, and more burdensome than what is customary. For this purpose, not even the span of an entire day was enough for them. Thus, they very often deferred their meal until evening, so that none of their daily tasks would be diminished because of it. In winter, when the nights were longer, after compline was finished, all of them, gathered in one place, directed their attention to the assigned task until they had completed half of the psalter. When their prayer was finished, they put an end to the aforementioned work and went to sleep. They constantly saw to it that reading was not absent from their meal nor psalms from their manual labor. During the daytime, they employed themselves zealously in the work of the fields: tilling the earth with hoes, completely cutting down thickets of unfruitful trees and thorns and brambles to enlarge the space for lodgings or gardens. They also built dwellings for themselves, breaking with hammers the stones that were cut from the mountain and carrying them to the building site on their own shoulders. It was a wonder to see these huge stones (since they could not be borne by many men) being carried by four brothers, and to see them marching along so easily that they thought they were bearing no burden at all. Although all devoted themselves to these tasks and labors of this kind as much as they could, the ones who were superior in swiftness and bodily strength especially worked at them. On the other hand, those who were weaker in body and did not have this skill were occupied rather with copying books or lesser tasks. And although they were indeed continually wearied by such great labors, neither was their fasting diminished nor their food increased, but the flesh was employed in labors so that it might not be pampered by better food or more food. Just as Pharaoh knew how to afflict the children of Israel and did not know how to aid them, so did the master of these men act in the same manner, but not with the same intention. He wanted his brothers to be content with little food, and he ordered much work so that they might afflict the flesh and strengthen the soul. Pharaoh, on the other hand, nourished the flesh among the females and destroyed the spirit among the males.

16. This man was zealous in discipline and very stern in correcting the faults of those who were lacking. Indeed, as we have said above, if anyone raised his eyes a little in church, or smiled a little, or dozed, or carelessly allowed the book he was holding to fall, or made any sound through negligence, or sang too quickly or ineptly, or made some irregular movements, he immediately felt a switch on his head or a slap on his face such that the sound of the blow reverberated in the ears of all. This discipline he applied especially to boys in their younger years, so that they might be corrected, and the others might be deterred by fear.

While a certain novice from the nobility was holding a book in church and, addressing a comrade positioned next to him, was showing him something in the book with his finger, the saint saw this. He did not want to punish the person, but seized the book from his hand, smashed it against a bench and then returned to his own place. This instilled so great a fear in the others that scarcely anyone dared to open a book in choir even out of necessity. This discipline was especially vigorous then, when it was flourishing as if in its blessed beginning, since they were fewer in number and more perfect in their way of life.

Since no rule of any order was established, ordinances of the master served in place of a rule. These taught nothing other than humility, obedience, poverty and discipline, and beyond these, constant charity.

This, then, was the true and wholesome doctrine of the blessed man, which privately and publicly he pressed upon those who clung to him. This was the rule promulgated, and there was no concern for the teachings of the Pharisees. But while we are 'straining out a gnat and swallowing a camel,' and while we are busy 'tithing mint, rue and every herb' (Mt 23:24, 23) we despise justice and faith, since we neglect the greater goods while we advance the lesser ones. But also, wearied by the long duration of time and weighed down by the multitude of those dwelling together, we have forsaken our ancient vigor and conduct ourselves laxly and negligently. And while we wish to stoop down to the weak, we hasten to follow their negligence rather than to draw them toward perfection. This necessity did not exist at that time, since they were more perfect then, and a rare person, or no one, was there to confound them.

17. Every day after prime or mass, the brothers gathered in chapter. With the prior presiding, after a reading was concluded, or whatever things are customarily said there, then they discussed ordinances, discipline and order, and whatever was wrong was suitably corrected. Then if anyone knew that he was guilty of something, he made satisfaction of his own accord, or, accused by another, he accepted his punishment and, standing now as if before the divine judgment, he received a penance for his fault according to this manner: depending on whether he had sinned more or less, he underwent greater or lesser punishment. Moreover, one who increased his guilt by defending himself was chastised more vehemently, even if by chance he had sinned less. Indeed, one who devoutly made satisfaction, not unwillingly, but willingly, was reproved less, although he had transgressed more seriously. If anyone had to be scourged, after he was stripped, then the fiftieth Psalm was begun so that at the individual verses he might receive individual strokes.

But if the fault were greater, longer psalms were assigned, so that he might be furrowed by more scourgings.

In fact, on the day of the Lord's Supper, which is filled with mercy, pardon was sought by all through a general supplication, so that whatever they had committed through the course of the entire year might be effaced by this holy, solemn remission. Then the venerable old man, completely drenched in tears and recalling before his eyes his own sins, relying on God's mercy, granted remission to himself and others and loosed the bonds of sin with the word of God. O what great streams of tears were poured forth then, and what groans and what sighs of the soul were sent forth, since no one there had such a heart of iron that he was not moved to weeping by his conscience! Who then would believe that the Holy Spirit was absent there, in whom remission of sins is realized?

Indeed, when he had scourged anyone more severely than usual because the person's faults demanded it, then he made himself ready to endure similar scourges, and he ordered himself to be whipped by one or all. He used to do this lest one who judges others might himself remain free of their affliction, and if perchance he had failed in his judgment by excessive correction, he might make amends through punishment of his own body. Besides this, hardly any day was permitted to pass, especially in Lent, in which he did not receive discipline from someone secretly and in private. Thus privately and publicly cut by whips he bore on his own body the stigmata of Christ's sufferings, so that he could say with the Apostle: 'I chastise my body and reduce it to servitude, lest when I preach to others I might myself be rejected.'

18. After compline, when the brothers had gathered as usual for sleeping, the man of God very often remained in the chapel and diligently devoted himself for the whole night to vigils and prayers accompanied by tears. The grace of tears was granted to him by Heaven in such a way that as soon as he would prostrate himself for prayers, immediately his holy eyes sent forth streams of tears. I recall that once I had entered one of his churches (he was unaware of it), not really for prayer, but for carrying out a certain task in private. In fact, he was in the courtyard talking with laymen about certain matters. Then suddenly, leaving them there, he entered the church. Not knowing that anyone was there then, he prostrated

himself for prayer in a certain manner, with such great simplicity and modesty that no one could hear him, even if someone were present. Right away, when he had thrust his head on the ground, so great a flood of tears started to flow from his eyes, not in drops, but, so to speak, in rivers (as I myself truly saw), that it flowed over the top of his nose to the ground, although no cough, no clearing his throat, no sighing at all was heard. I stood fast in my place, like a thief, fearing and trembling, yet not seen by him until, after he had wept sufficiently, he went back with the same simplicity as he had come, with no one at all knowing it, as if he had attended to the necessities of nature. We have mentioned this so that it might be known with what devotion he always applied himself to prayer, and at the same time we might consider how much grace he possessed, so that when free even a moment (he was a man bound by so many cares), he was not kept away from his spiritual zeal.

19. Indeed, one cannot easily describe how he assailed the divine ears with many tears and sighs while spending the night alone in church, and with a certain importunity he overcame them, so that the Father of the world was compelled to rise up and give him whatever needful thing he had requested (see Lk 11:8). Truly, Father Stephen was never undeserving of God's blessings, either temporal or eternal, as it was written: Nothing is lacking to those who fear God, nor to those who love Him in truth (see 1 Kg 12:24) And again: 'Those seeking the Lord will not be deprived of every blessing' (Ps 33:11). He sought 'first the kingdom of God and His justice' (Mt 6:33). Certainly, he did not doubt that he would obtain from his good Father eternal and true blessings, and, for the rest, all good things. Now, however, while we are anxious about earthly matters and perishable things more than is fitting, and we do not think about heavenly things, it happens that, to a certain degree, we are rich neither in these nor in those. Since we have been commanded to seek heavenly blessings first—that is, above all—we ought to entrust our concern for the other things that remain to divine providence. Hence Saint Peter admonishes that 'we thrust our every concern upon God, since care for us belongs to Him' (1 Pet 5:7).

When Stephen prayed for a long time, he was beset very much by the cold. Rising up directly, he did not cease to genuflect until his whole body was drenched by his sweat. Then, when he had put off his cape, he repeated the same process again, until, finally, worn out by exertion and fatigued by the burden of his vigils, he would cease, or even fall asleep. As a result, when the brothers came to vigils, they often found him fallen asleep in a praying position.

20. Beyond this, at night, if by chance the situation demanded and he could do it secretly, he even cleaned the latrines of the house diligently and properly, which no one else ventured to attempt. Having taken a basket, he heaped in it all the horrible-looking filth and, placing this on his own shoulders, he took it far away.

And when anyone discovered him carrying such filth and asked with much amazement why so great a man had subjected himself to such a great ignominy, he instantly responded: 'Brother, it is no wonder that earth is carried by earth or shit by shit, since we are going to return to this filth and much more filth.' Yet, truly, in this he was imitating Him who, not shrinking back from the filth of our sins, did not refuse to bear them on His own sacred shoulders.

21. During the daytime hours he toiled, often alone, often with the brothers, in such a way that two could hardly attempt what he did alone. He attained this strength not by more or better food, but by an inner force of spirit that was so great that it also strengthened his outer limbs not a little. Although they were weakened more than other people's by vigils and fasts, they were full of greater vigor than theirs, and they endured greater hardship, so that he could say with the Apostle: 'I have toiled more than all, yet, not I, but God's grace in me' (1 Cor 15:10).

Moreover, he frequently did kitchen duty. He carefully served the brothers as they refreshed themselves and, after they were refreshed, he prepared a meal for himself from nothing else than their leavings. In this, he wanted to give an example not only of abstinence, but also of humility and vileness, just as it is taught in the sixth step of humility that a monk should be content with every vileness and the lowest place.[13] Indeed, as far as human appearances are concerned, what can be more vile or more lowly than to eat the leavings from the meals of subordinates and to clean all the latrines? It is no wonder that the Apostle says of himself and those

13. RB 7.49; see Kardong 131, 153.

like him: 'We have become as the offscourings of this world, even until now the refuse of all' (1 Cor 4:13).

22. On Sundays, he and the brothers devoted themselves to readings and celebrations of masses, leading a procession through the cloister and purifying the individual buildings with individual blessings.

Also, on Saturday, they celebrated with nine readings and two masses in honor of Blessed Mary, Our Lady, embellishing these with certain joyous hymns in honor of the gracious Mother of God and reverence for her. Yet, on that day they did not rest from work, lest they might seem to act like the Jews. But also on other feast days, they devoted themselves to divine praises with such grand melodies that they seemed to imitate the manner of the large monasteries.

This monastery was great, not in quantity, but in merit; expansive, not in space, but in sanctity; copious in virtues, not in estates. The rector of this place was ordinary in body, but large in spirit; small of stature, but great of soul; despicable in appearance, but outstanding in moral integrity; vile in habit, but distinguished in the precedence of his works; lowly in lineage, but lofty in the nobility of his virtues. Although he was considered worthy, in fact desirable, to be imitated by all for the merit of his blessed poverty and his teachings of divine wisdom, yet, as if rich in treasures and poor in graces, he visited diverse houses of religious men with gifts, so that he might bring aid to them and obtain for himself the patronage of their prayers.

23. He often went to the monastery of Dalon,[14] which was about nine miles away, and from these things which were offered to him, he gave what gifts he could to those brothers. Once, while he was on his way there, it happened that he was sitting near the river Vezère watching for a boat. He had in his retinue a boy with a donkey laden with breads. Behold, while he was singing psalms to God at the proper time in the stillness of the night (for at that time they were accustomed to travel at night; this was changed later), at a distance was seen a band of robbers with captured booty hurrying

14. Dalon was founded in 1114 by Gérard de Sales. The abbot at this time was Roger (1120–1159), a monk of Pontigny, sent to Dalon to teach the monks Cistercian customs.

toward him with a loud clattering. Then, surrounding him, they impudently inquired of him who he was, where he came from or what he was doing there. The holy man, prevented by the seriousness of the nightly silence and occupied with divine vigils, gave them no answer. Hence they were more irritated and provoked to more ferocious anger. With swords drawn, they began to threaten him with death unless he should speak quickly. But when necessity forced him either to speak or to die, he chose death and, in fact, put forth his neck. Suddenly, a certain divine power struck such great fear in the robbers that all took flight as if enemies were chasing them, although no one was found to be pursuing them. Not only could they not injure him, but they could not even touch the breads that he was transporting; not a human hand, but a divine force protected them. In this was fulfilled what the Psalmist says: 'The Lord will send an angel in the way of those who fear Him, and he will deliver them' (Ps 33:8). And again Scripture says: 'The just man, like a bold lion, will be without fear' (Prv 28.1).

When Stephen told this plainly in the morning to the abbot to whom he came, the latter was greatly astonished. However, he advised that he did not think silence should be kept in such a circumstance, especially if he were asked, so that he might not irritate foolish men even more. Therefore, we have reported this, so that his followers to come might know with how great a zeal they ought to keep the appointed silence in safety, since their master chose rather to die than to break it.

It was his custom to survey monasteries all around and to propose to his own brothers that they observe whatever examples of probity or discipline he saw there. In this he very wisely imitated the work of a bee, choosing different flowers and from them making the sweetest honey.

24. Moreover, hearing about the reputation of the Carthusian monks, whom public opinion then made renowned before other religious, he undertook a pilgrimage to visit them that was indeed pleasing, but also difficult for him. On this journey he endured many pains of hunger and cold, because the places through which he would go, although they are always cold by nature, were then especially filled with the snows of winter. In fact, proceeding on this journey on foot and sometimes with bare feet, he carried nothing

with him in regard to provisions. His companions on the journey were two brothers, who were clerics. With them he continually chanted psalms; they had one of their servants with them who ministered to them in their needs.

Also, at that time he was wearing the hair-shirt (mentioned above), which brought him no small aggravation. One day, while he was walking alone behind the others, it suddenly was torn in the middle, as if someone had cut it all around, and the lower part fell straight to the ground. Saddened by this, he secretly called a certain one of his companions who was his confidant. With his help he tied the hair-shirt as best he could with some cords, and fitted it on himself again. When they had proceeded a little, again it broke apart and fell. And so, in the same way as before, but more firmly, he mended it again and put it back on. But when it burst apart for the third time, the saintly man understood (the brother also admonished him) that it was not God's will that he should wear it any longer. Therefore, in a nearby village it was torn apart and used for necessary purposes. Thus, although unwilling, he was nevertheless relieved of this burden by the will of God. For, before he had this hair-shirt, he is said to have worn iron chains on his flesh. When these had been broken for the third time in a short while, he put this hair-shirt on himself. However, besides its weight, this was so rough that it not only burdened his flesh, but lacerated it exceedingly.

25. When the requirements of the journey had led them now to Lyon, they approached a certain house of regular canons and asked for lodging. Not only did they not receive them, but they also drove them away with insults. While they were walking through the streets of the city, a certain one of the respected clerics of the Church at Lyon received them with hospitality and treated them kindly.

When they arose at night and were chanting the morning offices, suddenly a tumult arose in the city. Then the master of the house went to a window and asked the passers-by what was happening. A certain man told him that a fire was completely destroying the aforementioned house, and no one could come to its aid. Hearing this, the servant (mentioned above) of the man of God began to exult and to hurl certain curses against those canons, mindful of the insult that had been inflicted on them the day before. Hence, he was severely chastised afterward, because he presumed to exult over their sad misfortune, or rather to taunt them over it. Yet, it happened to them deservedly, so that those who had rejected Christ in his servants were themselves driven from their own dwellings by fire.

26. Arriving at Chartreuse, they were received courteously by those brothers. In fact, it was the feast of the dedication of their church;[15] this had brought them all together. Indeed, on other days, the individual brothers remain apart in their own private cells. However, on feast days or Sundays, all gather together in church and the refectory or in other customary meeting places. When the celebration is finished, they return to their own cells. Wintry mountains surround their dwelling; their cells are separated from each other by five cubits. It happened just during those days that vast piles of snow became loose and fell to the places below in heaps. When the brothers' cells were filled, the avalanche swept many of them away, with their dead occupants.[16] When those living nearby heard about this ten days later, they gathered from all sides to dig them out. Among the others who had been crushed, they found one still breathing. They rejoiced over him unexpectedly because in so great a disaster he had survived the others. They brought him immediately to a hearth where, after his breathing was recovered a little, as soon as he could speak, he made the prior come to him. He made his confession, accepted his penance, and, happy after he had received the viaticum, breathed forth his spirit. Who would doubt that the others were received into eternal rest, and he was saved for penance, and then died?

And so, the man of God spoke in a friendly way with the prior of the place, for he was prudent and grounded in religious life. Stephen sought his counsel about what manner of religious life the prior might determine that he should choose. Indeed, he said, it was in this way that he and his brothers might receive the customs of some order. He had come there so that according to their

15. The Carthusians celebrated the dedication on September 2.

16. On January 30, 1132, an avalanche destroyed the hermitage at the Grand Chartreuse and killed seven monks. Prior Guigo I, the fifth prior of the Grand Chartreuse, died July 27, 1136.

counsel he should accept their order and their will. Responding to this, the prior said that the Cistercians, who had been founded recently, held the royal way; their statutes could suffice bountifully for every perfection. 'As for us,' he said, 'there is an established limit in persons and in possessions. Truly, you, who have gathered many for God's service and have determined to accept still more, ought to seek a more coenobitic profession which is open both to many and to few, since it is determined not by number, but by religious life, and it is measured by virtues, not by possessions.' Hearing these words, Stephen accepted the prior's counsel with joy as if it had been divinely given, and he returned to his own place.

27. After he returned from Chartreuse, the man of God decided to enlarge the monastery buildings, which were small, since the brothers had become more numerous. Starting first with the sanctuary, he began to construct a church in honor of the holy mother of God, Mary, like the church at Chartreuse.

While the brothers were erecting it, one of the lords of that land, fearing that this building would be a refuge for his enemies and ruin for himself, came with a great force to stop them. Terrified by his threats, the brothers carried on this work for almost two days with less vigor than they had begun and without using the right cement, for the man of God was away. When he returned, he saw that the walls were joined not with cement, but with mud; that they were not only deformed, but also weak. After he had chided the brothers, he then restored the material and the method of building to their original state. When he heard this, that powerful lord returned again to oppose them. Thus the holy man addressed him: 'O wicked man, full of every malice, why do you persecute God's servants? Why do you attempt to destroy a holy work? Is it because the devil could not find another through whom he might hinder us? Indeed, this is not being erected for the devil, but for God; not against fleshly enemies, but against spiritual wickedness. Therefore, depart from the servants of God and do not dare again to act maliciously toward them. Truly, they do you no harm, but, if you are willing, they will plead much before God on your behalf. But if you persist, you will see what God can do against you, and the prayers of his servants, which had been for your salvation, will be for your destruction.'

At first moved, then overcome by these rebukes, and in the end obedient and suppliant, that powerful lord pleaded for pardon; when this was obtained, he set aside his initial malice and then provided assistance.

When that structure was rising higher, and the brothers were using moving equipment to transport a very large stone destined to serve as a support, the engines, creaking under the weight, began to fall and, giving way, were thrown down to the ground. Seeing this from far off, the saintly man ran up quickly and, making the sign of the cross first, he put himself under that burden. Suddenly, he applied such great strength that the engines were fortified more quickly than could be said, and the brothers, made stronger, moved along as if without a burden. Thus, the man of virtues brought lightness in place of weight, and they were unburdened where they ought to have been more burdened.

28. At the side of this church, he also constructed another in honor of Saint Peter the Apostle, on account of the guests and whoever else came to them, so that he might officiate at the celebration of masses and defend the brothers' church from the persistent requests of strangers.

He also built a cloister and regular dwellings around; among these he made a fishpond with an elegant fountain. For this he brought a stone of immense weight, which thirty teams of oxen could scarcely move, along with a very large altar-table. He did this for a mile and more through some unfrequented, rough places, with toil no less astonishing than great. However, he had no small number of oxen and peasants for reinforcement.

But, in order that God might show that human strength without His help is worth nothing, they were dragging the aforementioned stones over the level ground, where it seemed easy, with difficulty and the greatest toil. However, when they had begun to climb the steep places in the mountains, as their journey required, they continued with such great ease that, unless you saw the mountains, you would think that the stones were being drawn downward rather than upward. For then the holy man ran up and, having first made the sign of the cross, as we said above, with an invocation of Christ's name, he immediately positioned himself on the side and provided the greatest strength, with the assistance of God. Thus, at last, the aforementioned stones were brought and suitably shaped or hollowed out, then fitted suitably in their proper places. Even to this day they offer much loveliness and usefulness to the place.

29. At that time, nobles and lowborn persons, men as well as women, began to leave the world. They flocked to the monastery from all sides and submitted their humble necks to the yoke of Christ (Si 51:34). We should not pass over in silence that among them there was a certain man, noble according to the ranks of this world, who converted along with his entire household to the service of God. While he yet served the world, he was esteemed for such great integrity in morals that many in the religious habit considered him worthy of imitation. Noted for justice and for favoring no person in a judgment, since he was very often a witness in public cases, he was sometimes chosen to be a judge. Hence, his own people often reproached him, because he did not defer to friends in such a matter, but rendered a wholly just judgment. He generously offered hospitality to all strangers, especially to religious and to poor clerics, whom he even detained in his house out of zeal for learning, and he provided all their necessities. And lest those passing by or crying at the gate should go away empty or cry out for long, it was decreed that whoever in his household should first hear a pauper crying out, he should immediately give him alms, which were always ready, without awaiting anyone's order.

He was so zealous and devout in divine offices that it was not enough for him to have heard public masses in the churches of clerics, unless from there he continued on directly to the monastery, which was two miles away. After he had heard high mass, always fasting on Sundays and feast days, he would return to his own home.

While he was attentive to these good works and ones such as these, it happened that the venerable Father Stephen took a journey into those parts. When that man received him most graciously with hospitality, he was delighted so much by Stephen's behavior and speech that, putting aside his intention to go to another monastery, he immediately entrusted himself, with all his household, to him.

Therefore, when brothers were sent to him on an appointed day, he sent ahead to the monastery in wagons his little children, along with his wife and household members of each sex, and all his furniture, his animals and beasts of burden, his herds or whatever pertained to daily sustenance. The brothers who had come took down the fortifications and high walls in his presence. From a worldly dwelling, they constructed religious ones, and habitations suited to the servants of God; these remain even to the present day.

Whatever there was of weapons or arms (with which the place was considered very well provided) was either cut up piece by piece or burned in the fire, except those which could be put to better uses. And so, the aforementioned man, along with many others, not counting those already named, entered the monastery and was immediately clothed in the religious habit. He progressed so much in doctrine and morals that, although he was already tending toward old age, he came through the various orders to the order of priesthood. He served happily in this rank for many years, and thus, having reached a most blessed death, he passed away to the Lord. I thought that his life should be touched on briefly here because of the novel, and in our days, unheard of example of conversion, and so that coming generations might learn that one who desires to be completely converted might, as much as is in him, leave behind no attachment that might lead his soul back to worldly cares. But now, let us return to our purpose.

30. The number of women converting from the world to the monastic life increased not a little. No one could worthily describe the wondrous change in them wrought by the hand of the Most High. Indeed, many of them were very illustrious, and there were wives of many noblemen. Although they had long lived otherwise, they willingly converted to this poverty and humility. Those who formerly were adorned in garments woven of silk and gold, now dressed in thin cloth or a cheap rag, preferred the appearance or attire of the poorest women. Those who once were accustomed to color their faces and look at themselves continually in mirrors and linger constantly in bed, now eagerly attended to kitchen duties, so that one who was blacker and, so to say, sootier than a cooking pot, considered herself more beautiful. Instead of musk and other perfumes, they breathed in smoky smells with delight, and instead of sumptuous, exquisite feasts, they received in moderation cheap foods and many leftovers. And while the brothers were busy with more vigorous labors, those women believed that lowly and unbecoming works belonged to them, such as to prepare vegetables and legumes,

to clean kitchen utensils, to wash clothes, to sweep out the dwellings, and to carry out other cleaning diligently. They performed all these tasks in their own houses, for they never entered the habitations of the brothers, nor did anyone approach these women except when the prior was present or with his permission, and this only for the sake of instruction or for assigning tasks.

They lived not far from the brothers, separated in their dwellings but joined together in religious life. Furthermore, realizing that these women could not long dwell virtuously among men, the man of complete religious life began to consider where he might suitably establish them. Since he was very troubled about this, one day he went out two or three furlongs from the monastery. In a remote part of that forest, he found a rocky place hemmed in by steep cliffs and surrounded on all sides by very high mountains. Those living there could see nothing except the sky and the mountains around them. Moreover, the place was encircled by a stream, small indeed, but with a loud roar; from this the place took its name. Therefore, the saintly man believed that this very place was more suited to his holy purpose, because he saw that it was more removed from people. Besides the advantage of solitude, the place was also rich in resources of wood and stone, so that nothing for building would need to be brought there from another place besides cement. And so the brothers were summoned, and immediately they began to clear the land, remove rocks and reclaim space according to what their spiritual master and wise architect showed them under the direction of the Holy Spirit. They made aqueducts for their many necessary uses; these conducted free-flowing water sufficiently through all the monastery buildings. But why do we prolong this? They worked with such great zeal and toiled with such great diligence that within two years, or not much longer, the construction of the entire monastery, with all its pertinent parts, was finished.

But now with each monastery completed, there must be a little rest in the course of this narrative, so that what follows next might begin with another preface. Likewise, it seems right that we should be mindful of our readers, so that, when the zeal for writing and reading has been restored by silence, the interruption of this work might be, in some way, an alleviation of our toil.

End of Book One

Book Two

Here Begins the Preface to the Second Book

We have already described in part the life of our lord, Stephen of Obazine, a saint and most blessed man, and truly our patron. We had been asked, in fact compelled, to do so by the prayers of certain religious brothers and especially by the orders of Lord Gerald,[17] his successor. When he died, as if deprived of a great patronage, we neglected our work on such a fruitful subject for almost fourteen years, for we feared the tongues of detractors, who always lie in wait for new works, so that they might depreciate them either as false or badly-written or strewn with an excess of words and deeds. Even this small part that we had done before, they used to carp at with envious talk then, and they do not cease to tear it apart yet. But if they do this because of the perverseness of my life, I do not blame them nor reproach them, but for that reason I accuse myself more. For it is right that one who is preparing to describe the life of a just man should cease to be unjust himself, or if he cannot do this, let him blush with shame.

If, however, they reproach this work on account of my lack of skill, let them hear what a certain wise man said to one who was hesitating in such matters: 'Truly,' he said, 'either speak commonly, or awkwardly, or, if you prefer, in French, but speak like Martin.'[18] And likewise, I do not hesitate to name this work of ours a 'Martin,' even though my speech is unskilled, since, as long as he lived, he exhibited nothing of secular wisdom in his conversations, but speaking 'in the

17. Previously abbot of La Garde Dieu (see 2.15, below).

18. Sulpicius Severus, *Dialogues* 20; PL 20:201 = *Dialogues,* Postumianus, 27, tr. F.R. Hoare, *The Western Fathers* (New York: Sheed and Ward, 1954) 100.

spirit of the living God' (2 Cor 3:3) he utterly eluded all the arrogance of worldly wisdom. I have named it a 'Martin' in virtue, not in name, in spirit, not in body, in the same way that John was an Elias in spirit, although not in person. Truly, as far as I have been able to learn, no one seems to have thus imitated Martin in his way of life, morals, conversation and the strength of his faith, and what is chief among these, in the wondrous end of his life in a happy death.

But if Martin raised the dead in body, it is certain that Stephen recalled to everlasting life many persons of each sex who were sunk in the depths of perdition, whose deeds were so wicked and whose life was so ruined that, as is said about people who are desperately ill, no sign of salvation was visible in them. Indeed, what shall I say about the common whores (although certain ones acknowledged publicly that they were from among the noble married women), since they caught so many men that scarcely any ruler could lead men against his foe? Let anyone reckon, if he can, how many of those women were sinning, when the number of men sinning with them cannot be determined. Therefore, I do not doubt that the one who made of such women chaste and most pure brides for Christ through the healing of penance and the gift of prevenient grace was of greater virtue than if he had raised them from bodily death.

Now the third calumny, concerning falsehood, remains. If anyone charges this, let him know that I have set forth nothing here except what I saw with my own eyes or heard from credible, truthful men who reported it. But if in their words anything is changed or lessened or increased, it is due to the licence of the writer, not falsity of the narrative, since it is the mark of an excellent translator not to carry over word for word, but sense for sense. For even those who wrote the Gospels did not use the same or just as many words, since one completed his purpose with these words, another with other words; this one with few and that one with more. But this beautiful variety of reporting could not lead to any falsity in the most holy Gospels, whose venerable text is the foundation of all truth, since what is dissimilar in words is found to be most harmonious in sense and in the truth of the action.

Nevertheless, this is the reason why we have now returned to this work that has been neglected for so long. Venerable Robert, formerly the abbot, and Master Gerald, who succeeded him, since they always strove to glorify our beneficent father, ordered this among other things, that what we had begun once concerning his life, we should continue in writing to the end, especially since Alexander, formerly the Cistercians' father of blessed memory,[19] had earnestly commanded this to be done. Joined to this are the prayers of the brothers entreating it in every way by declaring that unless we do this now, while those who saw Stephen present in body are still living, after their death there will be no one who can confirm this narrative. But now let us proceed with the course of the narrative.

Here the Preface Ends

Here Begins the Second Book

1. In the preceding book are contained those things about the blessed man which he is known to have done before he received the name or rank of abbot, up to the time when two monasteries were established for the growing number of brothers and sisters apart from each other only to such a degree that when a bell was struck in one monastery, its sound was heard in the other monastery, although slightly and not always.

Meanwhile, the brothers at Obazine were still bound by no written rules, but they used the arrangements of their venerable master in place of a rule. These were so strict and arduous that the severity of any rule at all could add nothing to them in the rigor of their discipline. 'Since the days of a man are truly brief' (Job 14:5), and human instructions would thrive only so long as the teacher lived or was present, it seemed good to adopt the profession of another order authorized by the Church, so that when their masters died, the undying authority of a written rule might remain for them. Although there was uncertainty for a long time about these, while certain ones embraced more the rule of monks and others the rule of canons, finally, with the inspiration of God and the counsel of wise men intervening, especially Lord Aimeric, the bishop of

19. Alexander, abbot of Cîteaux, 1168–1175.

Clermont,[20] who was very friendly toward them, all gave their assent to the rule of monks. At that time, there was no regular monastery in that region except Dalon, which was mentioned above. Therefore, a mission was dispatched there, and masters were accepted from there to teach about their order. Then they awaited the day on which they might receive the habit of monks and establish the nuns in the monastery that had been made ready.

2. And so, in the year 1142 from the Incarnation of Our Lord, on the Sunday before Easter (which we call Palm Sunday), in the presence of Lord Gerald, the Bishop of Limoges,[21] and many religious men, our venerable father Stephen was made a monk by a certain abbot who had come with the bishop. He was immediately promoted to abbot and consecrated by the bishop. All the brothers whom he had that were clerics, Stephen consecrated as monks, and the rest he designated to remain in their original condition. After these things were done, they formed a procession of palms, including loud singing of Psalms, from the men's monastery to the women's monastery, with the bishop and clerics going first, then the new abbot with his new monks and lay brothers, followed by the religious band of nuns. They were accompanied by many multitudes of people who had come on that day to so glorious a spectacle. What a day of exultation and veneration that was, on which, beyond the general solemnity of the Church, two tabernacles so perfect and so beloved of God were established!

Finally, after these things were thus done and all returned to their own places, our common father, Stephen, remained there with certain elders, and he ate with the handmaidens of God in the refectory on that day. He taught them in speech how they should live at all times from then on, and by example he showed them, and he made this known by the views he expressed in his own words. Then, he departed before sunset. He secured them in their perpetual enclosure, and then decreed in the strongest edict that none of them should leave the cloister of the monastery for all the

20. Aimeric, bishop of Clermont, 1111–1150, after preceding Stephen of Mercoeur as abbot of La Chaise-Dieu.

21. Géraud de Cher, 1142–1177.

days of her life, on any occasion or for any necessity of any kind. But since it seems extraordinary to many people, how so many women could be enclosed at the same time in one place (for indeed, after not much time they had reached up to one hundred and fifty in number), something about their state of life and the setting of the place must be recounted briefly.

3. Their church is sufficiently extended in length. A wall placed from top to bottom so divides its eastern part from the rest of the structure that it produces two whole, complete buildings on the inside, although from outside it appears to be only one. In the upper church, which is smaller and extends to the east, there is a door on the north side through which the brothers and those who are assigned for this purpose always enter for the nightly vigils and for celebrating masses.

Moreover, in this wall that divides each church from the other, there is a square window proceeding down; it is completely interlaced with iron and covered by a curtain on the inside or the women's part. In fact, in the lower portion there is only so much of an opening left that the hand of the priest with the Holy Eucharist can be put forth through it. Indeed, when they are to receive communion, either all together or specifically the sick ones, after communion is finished at the altar, the Lord's body is brought there with reverence by the priest, and thus, with the curtain removed, all approach the hand of the priest and receive communion with respect and fear.

In fact, if any nun is so sick that she cannot walk by herself, she is brought there by others, either by many between their hands or carried on a litter just like a corpse. She is placed at the window so that many have been seen to have expired right there in the hands of those carrying them after they have received the viaticum.

However, we have determined that it is unnecessary to describe in what way or how they are served each day by the monks, under the direction of the abbot, in divine offices, in holding chapter meetings, in hearing confessions and enjoining penances, in carrying out and burying the dead, or in providing other spiritual benefits in such a way that for those standing outside and those remaining inside, there is no access to each other, since this is clear to all and we are hastening on to other things. Nevertheless, they have for all these needs a learned, God-fearing priest who, after the abbot of the place, has the care of their souls especially entrusted to him.

Indeed, those who remain inside under the direction of the prioress conduct themselves according to their own manner as monks, in the daily hours, in silence, in discipline, in work, or in other assemblies which occur in church, in chapter, in cloister, in refectory, except that they never go outside and they chant softly. In fact they are not chanting, but they celebrate the hours of the day as if by reading with the greatest devotion.

Moreover, we should indicate briefly how they attend to bodily necessities in such a way that they do not go outside nor do others come inside. At the end of the cloister there are two doors, one opposite the other, and in between them there is a short, little corridor. The prioress keeps the key for the inner door, and an older, approved brother, who is appointed as steward of the place, keeps the key for the outer door. Now that priest-brother whom we mentioned above has in particular the care of souls. Specifically, it is his duty, with the aid of the monks, to chant the divine offices daily for the nuns, to celebrate masses, to hear confessions and give penance, and also on certain days to hold a chapter meeting after a sermon has preceded it. On the other hand, this brother whom we have called a steward or porter, since he is a lay-brother, is entrusted with the care of outside matters. He brings all necessary goods from the monastery, and seeks nothing from lay-people, except what they give or transmit to him of their own accord.

When he has gathered between the two doors various kinds of supplies, that is bread, wine, vegetables, wood, greens and other such things as are useful to the healthy as well as the sick, he immediately secures the outer door with the key that has been furnished and strikes the door with his staff. By this sound he summons the interior doorkeeper so that she might open her door and carry inside the things that have been put there. The two of them never dare to open their respective doors unless they know that the other door is locked.[22]

22. See Bernadette Barrière, "The Cistercian Convent of Coyroux in the Twelfth and Thirteenth Centuries," *Gesta* 31/2 (1992) 79–81. Archeological excavation indicates that this gatehouse was an underground passage, about ten yards long,

4. Who could expend such great and such cautious foresight on the female sex, unless Christ were granting it? Who could supply both spiritual and corporal benefits at the same time to so great a multitude of women remaining always in one place, without an intrusion on the cloister, without the loathing and muttering of the brothers, without danger to their souls and almost without a loss of goods, unless the Holy Spirit were showing the way? Who could so cloister four or five women, as here almost one hundred and fifty are secluded? Who could so close the chattering mouths of women (when one is scarcely restrained by walls and bolts), as here so many and such diverse women are not only shut up in the cloister, but also bound by perpetual silence? Who would not allow them to go out at least into the garden, to gather vegetables, to carry water or wood, especially in a place so far removed from people, so that no one visits them at all, except for the sake of devotion?

But it is no wonder that 'the good shepherd, not a hireling' (Jn 10.11–12) the true guardian did not allow them to go outside for temporal goods lest they incur spiritual losses. He preferred to supply all their needs himself rather than to suffer a loss of souls in any way. He knew well enough what might happen to wandering women, and especially to holy virgins, as is known to have happened to Dinah, the daughter of Jacob, when she went forth to see the women.

Would that this could not be proven by a thousand examples: how many women dedicated to God and nourished in monasteries from their very cradles, when they go outside to obtain any sorts of goods from their parents or strangers, lose their virginity either through their own wantonness or the carelessness of their superiors, and while they purchase corporal gains, at the same time they suffer irreparable losses of both body and soul!

Foreseeing from afar this harmful risk, the holy man provided for the women entrusted to him. He supported them in such a way that not only did they not go out, but also they remained inaccessible, in order that he might take away from those inside every occasion of sinning, and from others outside every occasion of detracting.

---

leading from the path to Obazine to the basement of the storeroom on the western side of the nuns' cloister.

No one, however unjust and hostile to our house, has ever been able to defame their holiness, even if he wanted to.

Really, how is room left for sinning, when even sight itself is restrained? For when you approach them to speak, indeed you can hear them; however, you cannot see them, so you know that it is granted to them to benefit by speech, not to harm by sight. But they guard no less against seeing people than being seen by them. And when, sitting in the cloister, they might by chance spy some people walking on the mountain peak, the only place they can see, immediately they lower their faces toward the earth or turn then in another direction, and remain so until those walkers have passed by.

5. Moreover, what should I report about their pleasing innocence, when certain of them are so innocent that they think that the cities and castles which they have learned about by reading or hearing are situated around their own mountains? No wonder the whole world has perished from their sight and recognition, as happened to Lot's daughters! Truly, many have been raised there from their infancy or from their very cradles. They are completely unknowing of what goes on in the world, for whatever they are not accustomed to see in their own cloister, they do not even suspect to exist.

As a result, it happens that, since they are utterly ignorant of the sins of the world, as much as they are far removed from them, so much the more profoundly do they lament that they are sinners. And so they bewail the least sins, just as foolish men do not know how to bewail the most grievous sins.

However, this must be understood concerning those who have spent almost their entire life there. Yet, there are among them many who have learned about almost the whole world. They have passed through all the whirlpools of sin, and no wickedness was unknown to them. But, 'when sin was abundant, grace was superabundant' (Rom 5:20). And to the extent that more was forgiven them, so much the more have they loved (see Lk 7:47).

6. Moreover, who could report the glorious death of these women without envious lamentation? As they are dying, they commend themselves to the prayers of those standing around them, and they ask for the alms of prayers and psalms. Then immediately, as if

taken up in ecstasy, praying with their eyes and hands raised up to Heaven, they send forth their spirit in that ardor of prayer.

Indeed, certain ones return after death to the living and, when questioned, eagerly reveal what has happened to themselves or to others, and what is still needful to those who asked. While visiting, they also greet their beloved sisters, and they make known what they particularly wish to be done for them by their sisters. They even tell about the glory and great happiness of certain fellow-sisters. As an inducement to the others, they are not silent about the merits by which they particularly earned these rewards. They also warn some to whom they appear about certain excesses. Through these, they correct certain others, bringing forth into their midst the secrets of their hearts in such a way that by this declaration many are convicted of sin. Through the confession of their mouth, these expel long-standing sins buried in their hearts, which they formerly committed in the world and consigned to oblivion, and through the ministry of the dead they escape the death of sin. They also speak about certain negligent sisters who lived here. Because of the disorder in their life, they could not bear the presence of Stephen, their holy father, standing there as he was accustomed to do while living, because he appeared frightful to the negligent. Moreover, those who went forth from this life in good progress, he embraced and loved, and 'he was pleased with them as fathers are with their sons' (Prv 3:12).

Finally, I would not have said all these things, God knows, unless I had learned them most certainly from the mouths of those sisters who saw them in a vision, or who heard them from those who saw them. But since we have tarried for a long time with women, (not women, for indeed they are women in sex, but they surpass men in their manly virtues), let us next come to other subjects.

7. Meanwhile, the brothers of Obazine were changed from hermits into monks. They were instructed daily in new rules and new customs. Although they were veterans in the service of Heaven, yet in monastic endeavors they still seemed untaught, and those who had already become perfect in religious life were unskilled as monks. However, they were instructed according to the judgment of teachers from Dalon, who taught them the life and profession of monks. They educated them in precepts of the rule, and, since they

were harsh and indiscreet in their ways, they assailed the simplicity of the brothers with sudden novelties and stern reprimands, and they led their hearts to bitterness. Indeed, they had not learned to draw them away from their customs in a pleasant manner and to lead them to unaccustomed ways gradually, but as if the brothers had always been nurtured in these, they demanded of them every observance of the monastic discipline without distinction. They used to confuse them, change them, and reprimand them without warning, in church just as in other places. However, these brothers had not been used to this, since they had been trained under a most pious and learned teacher. Hence, fleeing to him as if to an accustomed haven, they often grumbled in his presence about the harshness of their teachers. Then the holy man, like a pious father and wise physician, comforted the confused brothers and reproved them, saying that they should not bear disagreeably the learning of discipline, which is the mistress and governess of sanctity. Referring to the teachers' harshness as the censure of discipline and the vigor of religious life, which a slack lukewarmness had, as it were, extinguished, thus did his passion more eagerly burn. 'Even if,' he said, 'you have thus far sustained many difficulties and hard toil of body for God, it is not a great thing if you endure any other vexations from reprimands in the newly-received order, especially since healthful habits begin in bitterness, but end in sweetness. In fact, no skill is either acquired without difficulty or retained without effort. And so, you have been nourished by healthful endeavors. Whatever harsh thing has happened because of these, endure it with a brave heart so that you might be able at some time to bring forth sweet fruits from a bitter seed.' Saying these words, he strengthened those who were wavering and at the same time instructed them. He strongly admonished the teachers themselves to persist in their undertakings and to fear no one.

8. Then he began to build two monasteries, one established in Limousin,[23] another in the district of Auvergne.[24] After these were properly constructed, he immediately sent bands of monks there, with the best fathers appointed for them. One of these excelled,

23. Bonneaigue.

24. La Pestre.

beyond his personal refinement, in the knowledge of letters, eloquence, urbanity and fluency. He was esteemed in every religious matter, so that if you saw him, you would believe that he was a bishop in his teachings, a father in his compassion; you would think him a monk in his way of life, as he truly was.[25]

The other, although he was a high nobleman in the world and a knight distinguished for the worth of his military service, had converted to religion.[26] Indeed, he became a monk instead of a soldier, and from being a monk, he was promoted to abbot on account of the worthiness of his way of life. His monastery, since it was burdened by the harshness of the site and the lack of resources, was transferred by Lord Stephen after a few years, at the suggestion and direction of Lord Gerald, Bishop of Limoges, to the territory of his diocese.[27] As long as he lived, Stephen was solicitous for all the monasteries he established, and he showed concern for them as if they were his own.

9. As often as he was about to build any place, when the cross had been taken up and water blessed, he went there with a few brothers. After the land was measured out, according to what the kind or size of the future building demanded, he placed a cross there, where the altar should be set up. When he had seized an axe or any sort of tool, he constructed a hut, as is the custom of shepherds, and for many days he dwelt there toiling and building in great poverty and want until, after the buildings were enlarged, he appointed some vigorous brother there. When the place had been sufficiently prepared by the supplying of houses and the aid of possessions, he immediately honored it with the title of abbey, or if it was too near, he assigned it to the function of a grange, so that it might serve the uses of the brothers, and the opportunity for religious use would not be lacking to it.

10. Moreover, that venerable Peter, the companion who had been his first and only company as he left the world, was still living. Indeed, he had been appointed prior of the monastery of Obazine

25. The first abbot of Bonneaigue was named John.

26. Begon d'Escorailles.

27. At Valette.

at that time when the place was elevated to an abbey. Although he was religious and holy, he is said to have been so simple that he was persuaded by certain men of perverse mind that the Lord Abbot wished to appoint him abbot in a certain place from among those which were being built; hence he ought to prepare what was needed from those things which were entrusted to him. Believing this, and acting out of fear, not greed, he hid some gold coins from the money entrusted to him, to benefit somewhat the place to which he thought he would be sent. When this was made known to the abbot, he was so provoked that he removed him from his office and ordered him to live in a certain remote cell. Dwelling there for some years in much affliction, he finally departed happily from toil to rest, from wandering to his homeland, when the Lord called him from earthly affairs to Heaven.

The saint did all this to him, not out of an inclination to ill-will, since he knew that he was simple and innocent, but urged by zeal for the true way of religious life, so that an example might be given to those to come by which they might avoid deeds of this kind, knowing that if the saint did not spare a man so great and so dear to himself, they would be all the more certain that they would not be spared. Yet, at his tomb many cures take place, so that it might be recognized that whatever sanctity he lost through his negligence, he received all the more fully through his penitence.

11. At the same time in the city of Rome, when the Pope died, a venerable man, and one adorned with all virtues, Eugene, was elected to the apostolic see. He had been a monk at Clairvaux and had been sent by Saint Bernard into the Roman territories, whence afterward he was chosen and made Pope in the City.[28]

In the second year of his pontificate, he came to Gaul and held a council at Reims. Then Father Stephen of blessed memory, as he had once desired, came with certain brothers to Cîteaux and found there the aforementioned Pope. Indeed, for a long time he had been wishing to secure a union with that holy order and to submit to its direction all that belonged to him. At that time an abbot named

28. Eugene III, who was abbot of the monastery of Saints Vincent and Anastasius ad Aquas Salvias, when he was elected pope, February 25, 1145.

Rainard was the Cistercians' superior,[29] a man not easily compared to anyone else, as far as I could learn, and this was clear to many others also. In fact, he surpassed all the abbots over whom he presided (there were three hundred and more) in the refinement of his person, nobility of his race, beauty of his humility, and fervor of his religious life. Furthermore, he was so inflamed by the force of divine love and holy religion that he exceeded the heat of fire; he stood out with such great exterior charm that he surpassed the sweetness of honey.

From this man I myself, although unworthy, received the habit of this holy religion. For although I had been entrusted as a boy to a certain monastery of La Chaise-Dieu,[30] after some years I was removed from there by a faction of certain people, and I fell back into the world. After I was detained there by many misfortunes, I was received by the most benign Father Stephen for the love of God and for the sake of my parents, whom he utterly cherished, as was recounted far above.

Then he ordered me to go to Cîteaux where, after I had received the monk's habit, I was recalled to Obazine after two years by the aforementioned Lord Stephen. By him I was consecrated a monk according to the rule, and from then right to this very day I have lived with him or his successors. Whatever I saw or heard from others that was worthy of mention concerning him, I have not neglected to insert here, so that the zealous reader might choose what he wants and might leave it to others to read what he does not want.

Indeed, I have preferred to seem more prolix on account of devoted readers than too concise on account of disdainful ones, or, so to say, undeserving ones, especially since it is easier to choose a few things from many than to retain many things from a few. In fact, besides this loss to the reader, an excessive epitomiser is sometimes marked by the haughtiness of pride when he wishes to avoid rusticity more than is just and affects urbanity too much, seeking in all things not the benefit of others, but his own.

29. Rainard was abbot of Cîteaux, 1133–1150.

30. Port Dieu, founded in 1060, or one of its two dependencies in the region, Saint-Robert or Védrennes.

12. And so, as we began to say, when that blessed man had come to Cîteaux, he humbly approached the Pope mentioned before and brought to the apostolic ears what he had in mind. He humbly requested that his ardent wish be carried into effect through the Pope's authority.

Then the Pope commanded Lord Rainard to come to him, and the father of all commended the holy man to him as a son to a father. He ordered Rainard to make him an abbot in his convent and to unite him to their holy order. Receiving Stephen with joy from the Pope's hand, he led him into the chapter and, with a cheerful voice, he said in the presence of all the abbots: 'Behold, my Lords and Brothers; you observe this abbot small in body, short in stature, contemptible in appearance, ugly in looks, but whatever you see in him, you should know that he is filled with the Holy Spirit and with faith.' It is no wonder that one filled with the Holy Spirit could recognize Him, Whom he bore in himself, in the man of God, and could show Him to others. For such was the man of God, that blessed one, that whoever simply looked at him might declare without hesitation, from his habit alone or his appearance, that he was truly a servant of God.

Without delay, after the commands of the Lord Pope were made known and Stephen's petitions were announced (he also humbly made his request in person), he was amicably received into the fraternity of the order by the abbots, and assigned specifically to a Cistercian house. In this they certainly deferred no less to his religious way of life than to the Pope's command, although there were some customs in his house by which such reception could have been hindered, where these seemed opposed not to their religious way of life, but to their own customs. This surely brought greater ill-will or vexation—that the holy man had accepted men and women to be governed by him as master—which their order utterly forbade. However, for love of him, all his customs were granted admittance, when Lord Rainard, who loved him as his own soul, promised that all customs opposed to their order would be abolished gradually, and lest a still-new house might not be able to endure a sudden change, in this case, those holy women might always remain in the order.

13. Under such auspices and with his order accepted, our joyous agent returned to his own monastery, taking with him outstand-

ing teachers whom the Cistercian father had granted to him as a special gift for instructing his order. Of these, two were monks and priests, holy men; however, two were lay-brothers, no less religious and properly trained, each in his own craft. The fifth one, who remained here until his death, after the others returned to their own monastery when the time of their teaching was concluded, was skilled and very experienced in raising animals, besides other useful talents. Through his labor and industry, our house increased much in worldly goods.

Indeed, these teachers were not like the former ones, rude and harsh, but they were agreeable, pleasant and meek; for teaching our order, they were suitable and discreet. In fact, when they ordered many things to be changed through their teaching, even ones to which the monks had grown accustomed, this surely seemed most troublesome: books which they had recently completed with much toil according to the rule of monks, they were compelled to put aside and to refer to the Cistercians' model. Therefore, they began some books from their very beginnings, others they erased and rewrote again, others they abandoned entirely, and others they kept, with few parts unchanged.

But since these books had first been brought from Cîteaux by the monks of Dalon, it seems astonishing that they could be so unlike one another and so different. Yet, it should be known that the books that the Cistercians first used in their divine offices were very corrupt and defective, and they remained so even to the time of Saint Bernard. Then they were corrected and emended and arranged as they are now by that same holy abbot and his precentors through a common decree of the abbots.[31] Hence, it is clear that they were sought out before this emendation by the monks of Dalon, who, although they were not then of this order, yet desired to live according to its rule and secured for themselves the written customs of the order.[32]

14. Among other changes, even the use of meat was allowed to the infirm according to the rule. Until then, this had remained unknown

31. Chrysogonus Waddell, 'Chant cistercien et liturgie,' in *Bernard de Clairvaux: histoire, mentalités, spiritualité*, SCh 380: 287–306.

32. Dalon was affiliated to the Cistercians in 1163.

to our brothers. The holy man bore this change with great chagrin, so much so that, in his agitation when he saw some animal being slaughtered on account of the infirm, he used to say that they had brought a butcher-shop into the house of God. When the chapter of the rule for the infirm[33] was set before him, he remained silent, since that could not please him, nor could the authority of the rule displease him.

One who heard these events and saw them in person told me that when our church was being built, before the monks were there, the hired artisans could not endure the daily abstinence from meat. They bought a pig for themselves and ate its cooked flesh in the woods. Carrying back the leftovers to the guesthouse, they hid them so that they could eat them secretly on the next morning.

When this had been reported to the abbot, he was exceedingly upset. Taking certain brothers with him, he began to go around to the workshops. Coming to the guest house, he found the meat, just as he had been told, hidden in two small pots. Taking these and looking toward his companions, he asked what ought to be done about them. When some said that they should be given to the poor, and others said that they should be returned to the artisans so that they might not be distressed and leave, he answered: 'Brothers, by no means let it happen so, but let us make these meats go ahead on the way which they will have to come to a little later.' Saying these words, he ordered the meats to be thrown into the latrine, and he returned by the way which he had come.

When the artisans who were now employed in their work learned this, they were moved to very great rage. They threw down their tools, abandoned their work, and ranting and raving, began to grumble against the man of God and to utter angry words.

He came to pacify them. Although he had begun to appease their wrath with gentle words, they accosted him with insults and reproaches. They warned, moreover, that neither they nor others would toil in his employ hereafter, since he was a man who had done so great a wrong to them. Then, making light of their threats, he began to rebuke them for their weakness and their clandestine meals, saying that if they abandoned God's work on account of

33. RB 36.9; Kardong, 300.

the allurement of gluttony, the necessary builders would not be lacking to his house, who would without provisions of meat build it better than they themselves; that if they could not be found, it was better that God's house not be built than that the dwellings of His servants should be polluted by unclean foods. After these words, he turned and began to go away. However, the artisans were soon stung with remorse. They followed him and fell prostrate at his feet; they begged forgiveness for their foolish talk. After this was obtained, they immediately returned to their work. They were wholesomely reformed and beneficially chastised.

15. After these events, he decided to create two monasteries in places that had been built up before, one in the diocese of Cahors, another in the district of Saintonge.[34] When these had been properly furnished, he sent capable enough ministers, that is, pastors, with a complement of brothers, who might govern the places entrusted to them to which were given the title of abbey.

The first of these was named Gerard, a man of virtues and an exemplar of the entire religious way of life. Renowned for his life and words, he happily ruled the house of Obazine after him (Stephen), with whom he had built many places, and now with him he happily rests as his inseparable companion.

The next was a man truly to be honored for his life and deeds, Robert, by name. He is living even now and ruling our monastery as Gerard's successor. We shall talk about each shortly in his own place. This man received the abbey that was situated in the diocese of Saintes, which even for a long time before he had been in charge of without the title of abbot.

Now there was in his possession a fertile field that had formerly been handed over legally to Lord Stephen and had been held for a long time by the brothers. However, a certain powerful man in that region arose, who said that that field belonged to his property, and that it had once been owned by his ancestors. Hence, enticed by blind greed, he now brought that same field under his own dominion. When this was reported to the man of God, to whom it had been specifically transferred, he immediately proceeded to the

34. La Garde-Dieu (Cahors) and La Frenade (Saintonge).

place and approached the aforementioned man. He began to ask that he desist from this unjust trespass and that he not take away, to his own destruction, that which had been given by faithful people to the servants of God. In no way assenting to his words, that man refused to restore his possession. He said that he would never give it up unless the holy man could demonstrate that it was his through legal donation when the case had been brought to public trial. Wherefore, with friends advising them on both sides, a day was set to decide the case, and so both departed to their own places.

That powerful man was not careless; he hired for pay many learned lawyers and advocates. Moreover, he summoned certain bishops to the defense of his side. On the other hand, the man of God, as if having no knowledge of affairs and entrusting his cause to God alone, fortified himself with the prayers of the servants and the poor of God. As if he had many defenders, he went unconcerned to court.

When the appointed day had arrived and there were gathered together bishops, lords, magnates and people 'against the Lord and against His Christ' (Acts 4:26), so to speak, behold, the man of God came on the opposite side as if another David were about to fight against Goliath, not with a sword, not with a spear, but with faith and with only two companions, and these were not sufficiently skilled in law. When he came into view, astonishment and wonder gripped them all. Indeed, some were laughing and others were saying, 'Is this the man against whom so many leaders and powerful men and the whole populace are gathered?' To which one is reported to have said fitly enough and elegantly and no less truthfully: 'This man whom you see, poor and modest and almost alone, will overcome all these people today. For our plaintiff will scarcely feast today with his supporters and accomplices for one hundred *solidi*, not counting gifts and grants promised. But this simple, poor man will take care of his advocates for about three pennies, and without the expense of any gift giving. And what is greater than this, he alone will carry off the victory from this judgment.' Nor was he at all deceived when his words were spoken, although he was prophesying something uncertain.

Meanwhile, arguments were presented by the opposing side. By these the sluggards determined that, as though from the authority of the laws, an unjust trespass was like a just possession. This man claimed unjustly what that one possessed lawfully. He did not have a just complaint, but an unjust claim. On the other hand, the holy man humbly begged the bishop of Saintes[35] to provide some suitable executor from his staff to plead his case, so that he might not seem to have applauded himself too much concerning God's help or to have spurned human counsel. Considering this just, although he had been obligated to his adversary, the bishop sent to him his own archdeacon, a diligent man and one abundantly versed in such matters. Perceiving the shrewdness of his adversaries and how they were disposed to entrap the simple man, the archdeacon counseled him that for now he should plead his case not about the foundation of the land which he was seeking, but about its possession. Indeed, in this matter those men were trying to lead Stephen into a ditch they had prepared, so that when he innocently conceded that point to them, he would lose immediately the whole case at the same time by some arguments which I know not. When he proclaimed this openly, saying, 'We do not plead the case about the foundation of the land, but about its possession,' then all the advocates were incensed with rage. They began to act violently and, supporting themselves with false accusations, they cried out that the man of God had not spoken correctly, and they assailed him vehemently. However, the aforementioned archdeacon opposed them and nobly defended the cause that he had undertaken to support.

In truth, the bishops stood firm on that side. Although they did not doubt that the blessed man had the just cause, they brought him no help, since they had been swayed by that tyrant, that trespasser. When he considered this and perceived that he was being overwhelmed in that multitude, Stephen arose in their midst and said before all: 'My Lords and Brothers, I have come here to recover land for the sake of the poor, having faith in God's mercy, and in the protection of the justice of the bishops present. For I was hoping that they would not allow the "rod of sinners to rule over the lot of the just" (Ps 124.3) nor expose the property of Christ's sheep to the onslaught of wolves. But, "since they are not shepherds, but hirelings who see the wolf coming and flee" (Jn 10.12), and, while the sheep suffer violence, they conceal themselves in silence

35. Bernard, bishop of Saintes, 1141–1166.

and offer them no protection, constrained by necessity, I appeal to the Roman court, so that there I might receive what is just or pay what is just.'

At this speech, an uproar was raised by almost all crying out; certain ones were indignant and said, 'Who is this man? In this mighty court, against so many powerful men and nobles, he has appealed higher, and he has called the bishops hirelings and not shepherds.' Certain others were saying, 'Even if he has appealed, this man will zealously carry it out, and he will accomplish more with a single messenger distinguished by four patches on his feet than our lord with his eminent messengers weighed down with much money.'

While they were disputing in this manner, the bishop of Saintes addressed all (after silence was achieved) in this way: 'Brothers, you know that I undertook to have this quarrel ended under my authority, and that I have worked for peace and harmony on each side as much as I could. But since that man is afraid to be overwhelmed, he has appealed to a higher judgment. Now it is not for me to judge further in these matters, but neither is it for you to reproach his appeal rashly. Hence, we want both sides to be advised: namely, let him who has appealed and that man against whom he has appealed present themselves, either in person or through suitable executors, in the sight of the Pope by a set date.'

After these words were spoken, the court was dissolved, and all went back to their own places. The man of God returned to his own house with his small entourage. However, it came about, just as the cheerful seer had predicted, that Stephen paid almost nothing and obtained the victory, although his adversary had spent very much on his own supporters. For when Stephen had come according to custom to the chapter at Cîteaux, which was then taking place, and he had found there certain abbots and bishops prepared to go to Rome, he specifically assigned to them one of his own vigorous monks, a man learned in such matters. Supported by their stipends in going and returning, the monk was also much strengthened in the Roman court by their aid and counsel.

Returning successfully, he brought back such authority that, under the authority of the Bishop of Bourges, in whose court the case was heard again at the Pope's direction, the aforementioned trespasser was compelled to bring into the brothers' cellars all the produce which he had taken from that field by the hands of his servants and to relinquish the land to them in peace, free and unrestricted. Indeed, if the brothers had lost that land then, it is certain that there would never have been an abbey there, as it remains even to the present day.

Moreover, we have reported this not as a miracle, but as an example of Stephen's honesty and faith. Indeed, almost alone against so many nobles and powerful men, he obtained his possession and that of God from the hand of a tyrant; he did not place his hope in men, but entrusted his cause to God alone.

16. Also, at another time, a certain knight, constrained by poverty and swollen by greed, seized sheep and certain other livestock from a certain grange of ours. He took the opportunity because the land that the brothers then inhabited had once belonged to his ancestors. Moreover, he consumed certain animals from this plunder with his men; he agreed to consign the rest to the brothers, who claimed them, until a set day, when the abbot himself would come and answer him fully about this land.

By no means negligent, the abbot came on the established day with many others. Then the other man, in order to strike greater fear in them, refused to come to court unless he knew clearly what he might obtain from that same court. Indeed, he was hoping that he would receive much money if he would drop this false accusation against them in peace. Yet, compelled by his friends, reluctantly he finally agreed to come, but he did not bring fear, as he hoped. Rather, he became afraid himself.

The man of God saw him coming from a distance. As he was always affable and pleasant when the situation demanded it, he told his companions that they should hold him back when he rose up against him, as if they were calling him back from an attack. When he was near and positioned within earshot, the holy man assailed and accosted the knight, although he was still held back by his companions: 'Is this the man who seized our sheep as the wolves do and devoured them? Is this the man who has usurped the Lord's possession for himself? O unjust tyrant! What have you to do with the servants of God? Why do you misappropriate their property under an unfair law? Surely, if these men did not prevent me, I would excommunicate you and hand you over to the devil so that you might be an example to all who dwell in this land.'

That man was terrified by these reproaches. He became rigid and could not bear to look upon the face of the man of God. He did not dare to approach farther. He reproached himself first because he had come there; then he blamed the friends who had led him to such circumstances. Finally, moved by a divine impulse, and by all who were present interceding for him, he prostrated himself at the feet of the man of God and, crying out that he had sinned, that he had acted wickedly, he begged forgiveness. After this was obtained, he gave up the entire complaint of his unjust accusation. The man who had come as an enemy and a criminal went away as a friend, made sound again.

At different times, when Stephen came to court and saw that all favored his side, and indeed that his adversary was abandoned everywhere and by everyone, he was moved with compassion. Secretly, he used to direct some of his own advocates to defend the adversary's side and to contend against him on the adversary's behalf. He used to rejoice that he was conquered by them just as if he had conquered.

If any poor peasant, devoid of all skill except common ones, entreated him to be taken in, he would immediately direct him to the cellarer, saying, 'Go and plead with him to ask me on your behalf. But if he drives you away with disdain, tell him that you know very serviceably this or that skill, and then see what he answers you.' When the poor man would do this and be driven away at first, he would be heard most willingly afterward on account of his supposed knowledge of a skill. Immediately the cellarer, approaching the abbot, would ask that he not refuse to take in so indispensable a man. Taught the art of mercy, the cellarer would ask for what he had first prevented and then soon had repented.

17. Meanwhile, since the brothers at Obazine grew in number from day to day, the small houses of their original dwelling place could not hold them. A decision was reached to the effect that the dwellings would not be enlarged first, but that they would be moved elsewhere again. Now there was no doubt whether they would build, but plans were still being considered about the place. At the foot of the mountain there were pleasant-enough places, where the minds of certain ones were determined that they should build. Others with a sounder plan wanted them to build not far from the

first place, so that the old dwellings might serve the new buildings, and the old tombs of the brothers might be joined to the new ones. Moreover, they added to these reasons also the healthfulness of the air, the usefulness of the woods, the garden, the possession of vineyards and trees of diverse kinds which were fruitful enough and which had been cultivated for a long time. These could not be abandoned without loss nor overseen without difficulty by those who were situated at a distance.

Furthermore, in those chosen places, many peasants lived with their families. If these were forsaken, that would create a great danger to their souls; if, however, they were driven away, it would be nothing less than a grievous sin. The holy man considered these and many other things in his noble mind. Although he did not want to leave either the grove or the place where he had first come, yet he wished more to act according to the plan of others than according to his own judgment. Indeed, that maxim was thus fixed in his mind that says: 'Do all things with counsel, and you will not be sorry after the deed' (Si. 32:24). He was never willing to do anything, albeit a small thing, without another's counsel. Even if a matter was timely and would admit of no delay, and he did not have anyone present except one of the simple brothers or perchance one of the servants, he would not hesitate to seek counsel even from him. And when that man, trembling, would say: 'Father, are you asking me?' he would immediately set before him the chapter of the rule which says, 'The Lord often reveals what is better to the junior.'[36]

Let those give heed to this and be confounded, who do not fear to do great and lofty deeds without counsel, from which they do not go forward, but rather they fall; and those who, if they are prevented by another's good counsel, even if it pleased them before, now they do not deign to follow it, since they did not initiate it themselves. Hence the Roman senate refused to accept Christ for no other reason, except that this was not first initiated by the senate itself.[37] It is a shame to report here that there are certain men who

36. RB 3.3; Kardong, 69.

37. Cf. Tertullian, *Apologetica* 5.2, *Corpus Christianorum Series Latina* 1 (Turnhout: Brepols, 1954) 95; Eusebius of Caesarea, *Ecclesiastical History* 2,2, Nicene and Post-Nicene Fathers, ed. Philip Schaff and Henry Wace (Grand Rapids: Eerdmans, 1997) 105–106.

seem great to themselves, who give counsel not for utility, but for contrariness; who, when they hear that others have praised one way, do the opposite, and with all zeal contend mightily not that what is better might happen, but that what happens may show that they are victors and others are defeated. They bring forth in counsel their own opinion last, but want it to be first in execution, speaking to the point last so that they might tear down the prior counsels. For this purpose they are silent at first, so that they might conquer later. But, omitting these things that lead to bitterness, let us return to our purpose.

18. Therefore, after many deliberations, they decided to build on the upper grounds of our monastery, so that the outermost houses of the first settlement might be joined to the outermost buildings of the new monastery. Then, when a heap of stones and lime and sand had been brought together, on the Friday before the Passion, they began to break ground for the foundation of the basilica, after the cemetery had been consecrated first in the area by the bishop, Lord Gerald. It was the year 1156 of Christ's incarnation. Then, on the following Friday, which is before Palm Sunday, all processed devoutly from the monastery to the building site with the cross and holy water. Then, after litanies and pertinent psalms for the occasion had been recited, the first stone was placed in the foundation by the bishop, the abbot and the chosen overseer of the work with an invocation of the Triune Majesty. Justly was that stone set with such great veneration; it eminently symbolized that One of whom the Apostle says: 'No one can place another foundation besides that which was placed, which is Christ Jesus' (1 Cor 3:11).

An inestimable crowd of people of different classes and ages, with a vast company of nobles, came to the start of this great building. Some of the more powerful of these were offering help and protection. The rich offered money. The poor supplied by their prayers what they could not supply in material things; with their hands stretched forth to Heaven, they prayed that Almighty God would bring to completion so holy a work that He had begun in their sight.

With us, however, this day was the beginning and the end of seeking and obtaining help in so great a task. It is the custom for almost all who build to solicit the people through the churches.

Although the bishop often advised this, rather I should say ordered this, with letters given that were filled with an abundance of indulgences, yet the holy man never wanted to acquiesce in this, saying: 'We do not want to introduce such a custom, so that we give scandal to the people and procure shame for ourselves by going around the churches promising blessings and bestowing indulgences, which no one can grant, except God alone.'

Yet, I have heard it reported by those who were present, that when he was building a new house in a certain diocese, he was persuaded, in fact compelled by certain ones, to request letters of solicitation from the bishop, so that the people might bestow benefits on that house as long as it was being built.

The bishop gladly approved his request (although Stephen was reluctant and did not do this on his own), and he immediately ordered these letters to be written. When it came to the part about indulgences, he entrusted to the abbot how much indulgence he wanted to be credited to those who would enroll themselves in this fraternity. That holy man sent back a reply to him. He said: 'Lord, our own sins still weigh us down, and we are not able to lighten the sins of others.' Hearing this, the bishop blushed with joy and did not doubt that Stephen was truly a man of God, as indeed he was, a servant of God, and a man filled with the fear of God.

19. Now after the building of the monastery had begun, who could worthily describe the austerity with which Stephen bruised that small body, which had been weakened before by many afflictions? He was at work the whole day, not bearing a rod, as is the custom for many men who sit in a higher place and call for others to toil with words, not deeds; with a finger, not work; with a rod, not a hand. He stood working, indifferent to the sun and rain, in such a way that he might observe all those laboring or not laboring, and show them more by works than words what each ought to do. When he saw some men standing idly or perhaps sitting and talking at leisure, he did not reproach them immediately, but passing before them, he first offered an opportunity to cower and blush. But if they did not reform themselves, he used to upbraid them with harsh words so that all who heard were afraid. If he saw men worn out by work, he called them to rest and refreshed their glum spirits with soothing speech. Those who were stubborn and unwill-

ing to work he upbraided harshly. Those who were ashamed and willing to work, but not able, he comforted and soothed, and so dealt with them as if they had done the greater part of the work. He even invited certain ones who were still carnal to carnal appeasements, saying that those who had toiled so strenuously should be well rewarded in the refectory. Some were striving for praise and were accustomed to work more on this account. Although he reproached them strongly for this, yet he much preferred them to those who gave themselves over wholly to laziness and negligence, unconcerned about the fear of God or human shame.

That most discreet man used to do outwardly these and similar things to relieve the toil, and he so made himself like all others that he showed himself infirm to the infirm, strong to the strong, happy to the happy and sad to the sad. But also he seemed in a certain way carnal to the carnal, and to those seeking glory, as if he were pursuing the same thing with all zeal, fulfilling that which the Apostle said of himself: 'I have become all things to all men so that I might save all' (1 Cor 9:22).

However, when he was at home, he put aside all these things just as if they were worldly garments, and in word and deed he exhibited the kind of religious life that he bore inwardly. He showed that he was a man to be feared; he was pleasant outside so that he attracted inwardly by his gentleness those whom he might correct in his charity. Indeed, he was perfectly mindful of souls. Moreover, he was mindful of what is outside, that is, he provided also for bodies, or, I should say, for their labors; so that these might happen more freely, he used to relax a little of the rigor of discipline. That basilica, perfect in every part, is a witness to his virtue and to the brothers' toil. In many provinces, there is no basilica easily found like this one in its beauty, it elegance, its charm, and what is greater than these, the durability of its work and its most immovable soundness. Those people who have travelled through many provinces beyond the sea and on this side of it offer testimony to this.

20. At that same time, there was so great a famine and so great a scarcity of produce that grains were sold at a higher price, by more than double what they now cost. Hardly anyone was found who had food, and those who had food concealed it as if they had nothing at all. For they were awaiting a better time for selling, just as the

prophet says, so that 'they might increase the shekel and decrease the measure' (Am 8:5), and they might empty the pouches of the poor and fill their own sacks from the sustenance of the needy.

Then the holy man, little regarding the onset of the famine, brought in from everywhere so many peasant workmen to bear the burdens that if you saw them, you would think that the whole parish had arrived. He hired them for bread alone. He gathered so many that he might feed them and accelerate the work of building.

So many poor people flocked together from all sides at the gate of the monastery that they could not be counted. They did not lament that they had come in vain. No one ever went away unfed. Indeed, from the ninth hour of the day, all the brothers (whoever could be present) were occupied in distributing food and were barely finished at a late hour. Besides the remains of meals, this food was continually supplied from the cellar and the oven, so that nearly every day all that was cooked in the entire furnace was given out, although it was ready for baking bread two or three times a day.

This custom toward the poor was always preserved at all times, but especially in time of famine: namely, if bread were lacking, meats were given out. In fact, pottage with bread was always given. The brothers assigned to this task scurried about everywhere: the cellars of all houses and the hidden storage places were searched, and old supplies of food were brought forth from pits and holes hidden in the ground. Nothing was imposed upon those about to buy, except that however and at whatever price they bought, they would not increase the public market price nor return empty-handed. But if they did not have the price, they should not hesitate to accept it on credit from somewhere, having confidence in that one who always rescued them from unjust usury and never permitted them to be in wretched want. Furthermore, if a sum of money remained, the holy man did not put it in the treasury, but summoned his buyers and stewards and handed it over to them without weighing or counting it. The breads brought from the oven and distributed throughout the required places were never counted.

No one dared to compute the daily expenses or disbursements, especially in the presence of the man of God, but the weight, number and measure of all these things was reserved to God, their Giver. Granted this freedom, the servants became more cautious and more solicitous, and in the affairs entrusted to them they feared no less to commit fraud than to incur it. Now, however, when we trust no one and count everything, it happens that we are not even trusted ourselves, so that we make unfaithful servants out of faithful ones. We offend God, the Giver of good things, rather than please Him, whose blessings we count as if they are from us.

21. Although the man of God was burdened by the care of his monks, both the brothers and the sisters, his guests and household, and laborers of different kinds, for whom daily subsistence was prepared with great effort, yet his greatest concern was for the poor. He knew without a doubt that nothing would be lacking to the others as long as he had something to give to these. Hence, not only in the abbey, but also in all the granges, he ordered a generous distribution, especially in time of famine, so that these places might obtain a blessing in these poor.

Once, a brother, the steward of those granges that are beyond Dordogne,[38] came to him saying that he did not have anything either to set before the brothers or to disburse to the poor. Yet, the holy man did not respond to him about the brothers, but concerning the poor he commanded him, saying: 'Go, and if you do not have bread, kill the animals and give them to the poor, except the plough-oxen. In the end, if you do not have anything, use the oxen without hesitation.'

That brother went away ready to do as he had been ordered. But since he had a little wheat, which could suffice barely for three days, he immediately decided that the wheat should be consumed, so that afterward he might buy provisions for the brothers and give meat to the poor, just as had been directed. And behold, while the deficiency of that wheat was expected daily, (even more, it was feared), it increased so much (with God granting it and the faith of the holy man cooperating with God's grace), that all the way to the harvest time, which was far off, the brothers and the poor had enough bread, according to what that time of year permitted.

22. At that time, as the famine was growing worse, the man of God heard that in the village called Martel, two men (one was a priest,

38. Two granges existed there in Stephen's time: Allis-Saint-Sauveur and La Dame.

the other a layman) had in common forty measures of mixed grain, single portions of which weighed down four or five animals. He went there in haste. Even though he had nothing to meet the price or the terms at which it was valued, he reserved the forenamed grain for himself and sent it to the monastery. Although the grains were badly heaped together, yet through the faith of the good buyer, they were increased. They refreshed and sufficiently nourished the whole monastery in its greatest need for a long time.

But when the time for paying had come, he had nothing with which to pay. For a long time he was uncertain what to do. Finally, he went to the village so that he might at least show his presence to those men, even though he could not offer them anything. When he arrived there, he greatly feared to face those demanding payment, in particular the one who was greedy and avaricious, stern, crude and churlish. He went to the church and, as it is told, then celebrated mass.

After this was finished, he went outside. When almost all the inhabitants of that village rushed up to him, among the rest came that creditor whom he especially feared. Then, seeing the man of God humbly standing there and, as it seemed to him, troubled over the payment of the debt, he said to him in front of everyone: 'What is this, Lord Abbot? Have you brought the money that you are aware that you owe to me and to the priest? For you should know that from this hour we shall accept nothing from you without interest.' The man of God said to him: 'Truly, I tell you that I have nothing that I can pay you at this time. Thus, I ask that you still have patience with us until the Lord deigns to bestow His bounty on us. Then we can appease you.' Then that creditor, as if irritated, although he was made milder by God, responded to him in front of everyone, saying: 'So far as I hear, Lord, you have come here to mock us! You took our grain, and you have not repaid us. I cannot be appeased except under this condition: that all the monks who consumed my produce be handed over to me as hostages, so that in the meantime I might feed them until I receive what is owed to me.' All the people broke into laughter at this speech. When the priest, his partner in the sale, was summoned, he said to him: 'Mark (for so he was called), does this agreement which I have made with the abbot please you?' 'What sort of agreement?' he asked. His brother said to him: 'Such that he surrender his brothers to us as hostages, so that we might feed them for so long as it takes until we receive what is owed to us.' But the priest replied: 'You keep this agreement; you proposed it. For I shall never keep it.' Then that man, no longer an exactor, but now made a defender, said to the man of God: 'Go now where you will, free from care, Lord Abbot. On behalf of myself and the priest, I assure you that you shall pay nothing of that debt except what you wish or what you can.' Then all who were present gave glory to God when they saw in that excessively greedy man so great a change 'through the right hand of the Most High' (Ps 76:11).

After a little time had passed, that man died. He bequeathed to the monastery half the price that was owed to him, that is, five hundred *solidi*; he provided for the remaining five hundred to be paid to his son. Since this son was more agreeable than his father and more lavish in giving, he forgave those five hundred *solidi* that were to be paid to him, and he often gave many other things from his own possessions. Indeed, when he attended the funeral of the blessed man, he donated so much from his own possessions that for the entire span of his own life a light would never be lacking at the blessed man's tomb.

The priest had a cleric assigned to him whom he entrusted to the monastery. He remitted the thousand *solidi* that were owed to him from the aforementioned sale, and beyond that he added many measures of mixed grain for his sustenance. Thus was fulfilled in the man of God what the Apostle said: 'To those who love God, all things work together toward the good' (Rom 8:28).

23. At a certain other time when the holy man was sitting in the infirmary, the cellarer came to him, and with a sad face and silent tongue he sat next to him. The man of God said to him: 'Why is it that you sit here so sad and say nothing, Brother?' To him that brother answered: 'I am sad, Lord, because the brothers will eat nothing today. Indeed, the hour for our meal is upon us, and we do not have bread to set before the brothers to refresh them.' Then Stephen, with his eyes and hands raised toward Heaven, as was his custom, sighed deeply. Finally, he turned to the doubting brother. Chiding him, he admonished him and said: 'Therefore, Brother, has it been revealed to you alone that the brothers will not eat today? Is the hand of the Lord not strong? Or since you do not have bread,

will the Lord on that account have nothing to bestow? Go, then, without hesitating, and make haste to prepare the tables as usual. I hope and trust in God, that He will not allow those who serve Him to remain without food.' The cellarer believed and obeyed. He quickly prepared the refectory and provided the tables with tablecloths. Behold, while the brothers were chanting in church at the hour which is before meal-time, suddenly there appeared animals laden with breads which certain faithful men, inspired by God, as it is believed, had sent to them as a supplement to their provisions. Although the brothers did not expect that they were going to eat then, when they came out of the church, they found the tables full of unusual bread. Hence they were refreshed enough and more than enough. They gave thanks to God the Giver, and thereafter they could not doubt His abundance, even in their poverty.

24. We have heard from those who were there, that such a thing happened once in the monastery of Grosbot, which was handed over long ago to our jurisdiction. Indeed, on a certain day, the cellarer came to the abbot of that place, who had been one of Lord Stephen's pupils. He said that in the entire monastery there were no breads of any kind to be had, except three. Hence, he asked him whether the bell ought to be rung for the meal, since there were no breads, and what should be done about the three that had been found. Then the abbot, after he had first gone to a higher counsel, ordered that three pounds be placed among the allowances of the dead, as was the custom, and also that, after the hour, the bell be rung for washing. He also ordered porridge to be set on the tables in place of bread.

While they were in church, chanting the hour, which was near its end, the lord of the land, the founder of that place, arrived unexpectedly. In his usual way, he entered the cloister, and he went through other buildings also, as he was accustomed to do, for no one dared prevent him. He entered the refectory. When he saw that only porridge had been served up, without bread, he quickly went out and sent his own horses and those of his companions to the nearest village. He caused all the bread for sale to be snatched up, after the price was paid, and to be brought to the monastery.

After the hour was finished, the brothers entered the refectory; they were making themselves ready to eat. Suddenly, amidst their eating, the unexpected bread arrived in full baskets. This fed them sufficiently on that day and the following day.

25. Likewise, in the monastery of Bonneaigue (where some time ago the holy man departed from this world), a countless throng of poor people, more than usual, had crowded together on the day of the Lord's Supper. After as many breads as could be found were given out, the brothers, constrained by necessity, since there were still poor people remaining, distributed all the bread which had been set out for their own refreshment. Since they now had nothing to eat, the abbot brought forth money and ordered that breads be bought for the use of the brothers. Behold! The box in the monastery in which breads were customarily stored was found to be full right to the top; from this they were refreshed on that day and the following day. Thus, it was not enough for the man of God to demonstrate the signs of his faith in his own monastery. In other monasteries that belonged to him he also showed these same signs through his disciples after his death.

26. Also, in our monastery during the time of famine, especially from Easter right to harvest-season, so great a throng of poor people used to gather daily that it generally exceeded three thousand in number. On account of this, buyers hurried about everywhere with their animals, as we said above, and they brought to the monastery as much grain as they could find, after the price was paid or promised. Then bread was provided for the brothers as well as for guests and for the poor, so that they could live from that sufficiently, even if they had nothing else. At the end of that period, when the debts they had then contracted began to be computed, they determined that more than three thousand *solidi* had been added up, they rejoiced that not even one *solidus* was in excess: indeed, the man to whom they were paid forgave the debt.

When a mighty famine was devastating this land exceedingly at the time of the annual celebration of the saint's feast, which they were celebrating, as was their custom, so great a throng of poor people gathered that they were estimated to number fifteen thousand by the laymen who had come, although they were estimated by others to be fewer. Indeed, all said without doubt that there were more than ten thousand. However, to each person was given, as always happens, a one-and-a-half pound twisted-loaf of bread and the customary measure of beans, with wine. As was always done and is even today, an equal measure is given to an older person as to a younger one, so that women receive as many portions as they have children, even in their cradles. However, the knights and many other distinguished guests who had come to this spectacle from many places, and who were accustomed to distribute the portions with the brothers, seeing the throng of poor people and considering the small number of breads which had been prepared, began to cry out, saying that the bread could not suffice for one tenth of the people. Hence they advised that the bread be broken into small pieces so that everyone might then receive a little. But in this they were not heard. Rather, trusting in the name of God and the power of the saint and having implored his help, they began to distribute the portions with great hope, confidence and joy: first the bread, then the beans, and afterward the wine. When the customary measure had been distributed before sunset to all, from first to last, from the oldest to the youngest, the poor people surged forward. So great a cry arose from those praising God for His bounty and blessing the holy father that the earth itself seemed to be shaken by their clamor. Indeed, they wept then more for joy and for so great a miracle than they had wept previously for fear, especially those who urged them to divide the bread into small pieces. They were declaring openly that if the distribution were continued even to the morning, the breads would not be lacking as long as the poor were not lacking. Moreover, it has been proven that this happened many times on this saint's day and many other days. The more the breads to be distributed to the poor were thought to be few, the more they abounded.

27. But also at the time of the barbarian persecution, when these same barbarians were ravaging this entire region far and wide, the peasants who were fleeing the barbarians sought out our monastery with their wives and children and herds. They filled all the places inside and outside to such an extent that we could scarcely go out or in. Thus, constrained by necessity and moved by pity, not only did we not keep them away, but also we even encouraged them, and without sparing we set before them whatever provisions could be found. At last, on a certain Saturday, when we had given away so many breads that almost nothing remained for the next day, it

was decided that we should cook on the Lord's Day, contrary to our custom. However, when morning came, so great a supply of breads was found in the storage boxes that they would suffice in the customary measure either for us, that is, for the entire convent, or for the refugees and the poor, if they received the whole amount. But when they were now set out to be divided between us and them, it seemed good to the Higher Counsel that they should receive a whole bread, since it was just so much; however, we would be content with two porridges which were then ready. Thus, all the breads were brought whole to the gate, so that not even one of them was left.

After tierce, they again entered the bakery. They found so great a supply of breads that the whole convent, which then numbered one hundred twenty and more, had each a pound and a half of bread as usual. Indeed, on account of the holy communion, there were very many gathered together, seeing that it was the eighth day of Pentecost.

Several times we have even seen this happen with our own eyes, that scarcely anything was left after charity had been practiced, but when morning came, all had enough from this, and more was left over. But also, the bakers very often recounted to me that in the time of the above-mentioned famine, the grains estimated for barely one week carried us through two months, and they sufficiently fed us, so that they were not augmented from outside nor were those consuming them lessened in number.

Also, in a cellar at Martel, in which grains from the granges situated beyond there were stored, at the time of building as well as of famine, the grains were carried with animals from there to the monastery. After many days or weeks, when it was believed that nothing was left of these grains (in fact, all were astonished that they had lasted so long), the brother who used to transport them was questioned. He said that he could find no diminution of these grains from the time when he began to transport them. Then the same brother was ordered to measure the same grains again. When this had been done, and the Giver had been offended, the gifts ceased and the grains were quickly consumed.

We have told these things not because they were done through or for us who are now, but by the merit and power of that one who works wondrously not only among us, but in many other places.

28. Recently, I heard this reported by the brothers. In certain granges near the aforementioned devastation, when the brothers were generously handing out to the poor, the prisoners and the refugees fleeing to them bread which they had prepared for themselves, the baked bread, which usually sufficed for four or five days, still sufficed that long even when it was divided into so many parts beyond what was customary. But that merciful Recompenser rewarded this generosity, not only in the future, but also in the present, since neither was the supply that was widely expended nor were those expending the supply diminished. And these same barbarians, who were plundering churches, stripping altars, concealing broken chalices in their pouches, touching holy objects with their unworthy, defiled hands, like pigs, were also binding and dragging off priests themselves, despoiled of their property and vestments, and keeping them for ransom under the most bitter hardships. These same barbarians, I say, who were doing such things, when they passed by our houses and saw the yards full of people and cattle or herds fleeing from their face, not only did not carry off what was ours, but they did not dare to touch anything belonging to those people. They were frightened, not by our holiness, but rather by the divine power, and by the merit and virtue of that saint. But since these things happened to us or our regions after his death, let us return to those that were done when he was present and active.

29. At that time, the porter, a faithful and religious man, was surrounding the abbey with a wall. In that place the mass of a huge rock rose up, which, joined to the earth on every side, presented the appearance of some mountain. Since the wall was going to pass through there in such a way that it could not be turned aside from that place, that same porter and his companions had tried and failed to break up the stone in many days of useless toil. Not only could it not be broken up, but also it had often broken many hammers into pieces. However, it happened that the man of God was passing by this place on his way to an appointment. The porter, filled with faith, directly seized the bridle of his horse and commanded, rather than requested, that he dismount.

Then the saint, smiling a little, was moved to dismount from his horse. He marveled at the boldness of the porter's faith and asked, as if he were captured, what he wanted him to do. When he had picked up a hammer, the porter put it in his hands and ordered him to climb to the top of that rock and strike the stone with the hammer. When he had done this and had struck the stone with three blows, then the porter took back the hammer and said to him: 'That is enough. Go now happily on your way.' Saying farewell and blessing him, Stephen finished the journey that he had begun.

After his departure, that venerable porter summoned his workmen; they began not only to cut this same stone, but also to demolish it entirely. They broke it into pieces with such great ease, right to the very roots, so to say, that in the evening nothing of it remained to be broken up. The stone, which had been harder than the hardest iron before, now was easy to break up, as if it were barley-bread. From its fragments they made a mighty heap and from that built a great part of the wall. There is no doubt that this was done through the power of the saint and the faith of the porter.

30. There is a certain grange situated beside the river Dordogne. It had been built formerly for an abbey, but afterwards was set up for teaching children. When this was being built on the right side of the church, a rock (as we have said about the other place) rose up like a mountain and occupied a great part of that place. And since it was necessary for the cloister to be made in the same way, the brothers were striving as much as they could by pounding that rock with hammers to bring it down to the ground and make it level with the land. They seemed to do this in vain, so great was the size and hardness of this rock.

And so, after the church was already constructed, the prior of the place went to the abbot, asking what they might do about that rock, or whether they ought to build the cloister on the other side, that is the left side. Since this was unsuitable, he ordered that a very deep ditch be made on the side of the rock, and that the rock be buried in it when all pushed against it.

The prior accepted the order, although it seemed impossible to him. However, since he did not dare to speak in opposition, he returned to his place. According to the abbot's command, he made a very deep ditch next to the stone. Then, after all were gathered together, not only from that place but also from the neighboring farms, as they were pushing that rock with their shoulders and with levers, using all their strength, it seemed to them as if they were trying to move a mighty mountain. Many were laughing and saying that they were crazy to have attempted things that were not so much difficult as impossible.

So, abandoning the work, all returned to their own places. However, they left the ditch as evidence; because of this, the saint could not accuse them of disobedience when he arrived. Several days later, when he came and saw the ditch remaining thus, after a prayer was said, he summoned the prior, along with the brothers. Provoked, he asked them why they had thus abandoned that stone and not buried it in the earth, as he had commanded them. But they reported to him all that had been done, and how with so many men gathered from everywhere and pushing, it could not be moved. Then, reproaching them, he said: 'Call the men to me, as many as we have, and the brothers who live here, and you will see that the stone could not be moved not because of impossibility, as you say, but because of your disbelief, and your faith in men, not in God.'

When this had been done, the man of God made the sign of the cross and uttered his usual acclamation, that is: 'In the name of the Lord.' While he was pushing along with the rest, that rock was moved with so great a speed that it was thrust down into the pit in a moment and without difficulty. After this happened, the cloister, just like the other buildings, was constructed according to the wishes of the man of God.

31. At Martel, which was mentioned above,[39] a house was kept outside the walls. It was designated for the uses of the brothers of Obazine and advantageously managed for purchasing or selling necessary goods. The lord Stephen went to this house once to set something in order there. Then the brother who was in charge of the house began to complain openly to him that he was spending much on bread and wood and even water. Hence, he was less able to procure the common necessities of the monastery.

Then, since these complaints were brought to him in a reasonable way, Stephen did not pass over them with a deaf ear, as certain men do, but thought in silence how he might suitably aid in the

39. 2.22,27.

needs of all. Indeed, he gave satisfaction immediately concerning bread and wood by assigning to the brother one of the nearby granges so that he might take these things from there advantageously. But since he was still concerned about water, he went out before the gates on the side of the house; he found a suitable place from which water could be conveniently supplied. A spring could be heard in that area, but not seen. Thus, after a prayer had been offered, he commanded those standing around to dig there. When he had begun this first, and they had penetrated deeper in their digging, they found running water. Then, with great gladness, they made a well there which remains even to the present day.

32. Again, at a certain time, our memorable father went to one of his granges that is situated near the village of Saint-Michel.[40] While he was talking with the brothers there, he looked into the distance and saw far off that some men were carrying water with great effort. He immediately turned to the brothers and asked of them why they were bringing water from far away, since they had a spring at hand. But they said to him: 'Lord, the water of this spring is indeed suitable for all purposes, but in fact it cannot be used to cook pottage or any other thing at all, nor could it ever, as far as we have heard.' Then Stephen marveled much at this, and, as if displeased at that water, he went up to the spring. After he had said a prayer there with his hands placed under the water, he blessed it. Then, when the brothers were summoned, he ordered water from it to be drawn right away and poured into cooking-pots. He advised them that henceforth the water would never be unusable for cooking. When this had been done, from then on that water so kept the command of the saint that in that land even to the present day none is held to be more suitable for cooking as well as for drinking.

33. In the region of Cahors, not far from the river Tarn, a cell was built with a view toward making an abbey. A few monks were staying there, along with some lay brothers. Since the place was arid and waterless, the brothers dug a well for their necessary uses in a suitable spot. But when they had reached deep down in their dig-

40. Banière.

ging and had already completed forty feet and beyond, the deeper they went, the more were they throwing out parched, dry earth. Hence, overcome by weariness, they completely abandoned their toil and sent the workers to other labors.

Meanwhile, Stephen, our common father, decided to visit that place. When he completed a journey of three days, he arrived on the fourth day, a Sunday, at the fourth hour.

When they heard of his coming, the brothers eagerly went to meet him and led him with joy to the cell. After a prayer was offered in the oratory that had been built, Stephen went out and stood in front of the doors. When he had briefly addressed the brothers, he ordered them to prepare for him what was needed to celebrate mass. Meanwhile, as he looked about while washing his hands, he saw not far off the piles of earth that they had thrown out from that well and placed in a circle around its edge. Thus, he asked what they wanted these for. Then, showing him the well that they had dug, they reported how they had sweat in that fruitless toil for such a long span of time.

But, reproving them for deserting so necessary a work so quickly and without success, he ordered the workers to be called immediately and sent into the well. He commanded that they dig until they found water. What need of more words? He went to mass, and before he had finished it, they brought truly fresh water from the well to him for washing his hands and his chalice. Then, after the recitation of the hour, he entered the refectory and ordered some of that water to be given to all for a blessing. That well, full of sweet, unfailing waters, remains even to this very day.

34. Once, when Stephen was going to the city of Limoges, he came to a certain town on his journey where a certain noblewoman was burning up with a great fever. She had a daughter who was possessed by a similar sickness in Limoges. She wished to visit this daughter, although she did not dare to go there, either on account of the illness or on account of the invading barbarians. Hearing that the man of God was proceeding there in haste, she immediately left her bed and, weary in body and panting for breath, she joined herself to his entourage. And since the brothers could not tolerate the company of a woman, she rode with her companions at a distance behind them, yet in such a way that she might see them.

After they had travelled a certain distance on the journey, she could not bear the burden of her sickness. She dismounted from her horse and rested for a while in the bosom of a knight. Then the holy man, when he looked back and did not see her, began to regret that he had removed her from his company; he feared that some misfortune had befallen her on the way. However, the noblewoman ordered one of the boys to run after him, asking either that he wait for her or that he send her some item of his as a blessing.

Seeing the boy running, the brothers stopped for a while, thinking that the woman was either dead or near death. But when they understood the situation more clearly, at the command of the man of God, they turned into a suitable place, and there, having loosed the horses, they waited for the woman.

When she appeared in a short time, she immediately dropped to the ground, and so great a weakness seized her that she was thought to be about to die right away. When the holy man looked at her and asked about her state, she could not even respond. This alone she begged with her lips barely open, that he assist her as she was about to die, or if he decided to leave, that he cast upon her some item of his. Then, with his hands placed upon her head, he handed over to her the wool cincture that he wore, and gave himself over, along with the brothers, to prayer for her. After this was finished, they chanted in the usual way the hour that was then turning. They scarcely completed it when that woman was so restored to health that she mounted her horse on her own. Giving thanks for her recovery, she happily finished her journey. She, who followed with difficulty before, now went far ahead, carrying with her the cincture of the man of God as a token of her regained health.

35. Also, at another time, as the story is told, when there was a synod in the same city and Stephen was there, the abbot of Tulle, who then was Eble by name,[41] very unjustly stirred up strife against him. He began to threaten him vehemently before all who were present. When the holy man answered him with gentle words and refuted his unjust reproaches prudently and advantageously, then Eble became puffed up with the pride of his worldly power and

41. Eble of Turenne, brother of Raymond II.

incensed with the fury of his wrath. He threatened that he was going to do to him things so great and of such kinds, that the report of this deed resounded in all the parts of Limousin. But the man of God was not at all frightened by his threats; armed then with greater confidence, he is said to have responded to him: 'O mighty Lord, do not threaten such powerful things for the future, since you do not know what the coming day might bring' (Prv 27.1). While they were contending in such a manner, their friends intervened, so that they were calmed and parted from each other.

On the following night, a cry arose in the city, along with wailing and bells ringing everywhere. In this way it was made known that the forenamed abbot had died suddenly, and although he seemed to have caused his own death by a drink of poison, yet all who had been present at the aforementioned quarrel marveled that the speech of the man of God (although he grieved much), had been fulfilled so quickly, and he had been swiftly delivered from the harm that had been proposed.

36. In his conversations with worldly men, Stephen was so effective and urbane that if anyone unjustly accused him or assailed him vehemently, he immediately beat him back with such speech that the man blushed in confusion, and others, astonished, kept his words as if they were a proverb. Accordingly, Viscount Archambaud[42] (to whose dominion belongs the place in which we abide), when he was arguing with him harshly for certain reasons and hurled against him rude and almost abusive words, Stephen confounded him in this way: he said that he should not be so treated by him, who was more powerful than all his tenants and who did not have in his whole territory so honest a peasant. Thus, the holy man seemed by this to be exalted, as it were, after he truly humbled himself, by comparing himself to a peasant and to villeins, a man to whom scarcely any of the magnates and nobles dared to be compared because of his incomparable virtues. Hence, the forenamed Viscount, although he loved him incomparably for his holiness, and feared him, yet was much confounded by this incident, and loved him even more.

42. Archambaud V of Comborn.

37. Likewise, when Stephen was present at a certain court for the sake of his affairs, a certain judge stood opposed to him. This man, who was a potent speaker and puffed up with bragging about his riches, yet deprived of his sight, had been appointed judge in the case. When he had brought forth an unjust judgment against the man of God, Stephen did not hesitate. He replied to him with a common proverb, saying: 'Friend, thus he strikes who does not see.' The judge was silenced and derided by this saying. He was so confounded that he did not presume to say anything for the rest of the time in that court. His blindness was a reproach to him, along with the falsity of his unjust judgment. Yet, afterward, either moved by that saying, or rather goaded by the fear of God, he became a monk in our monastery, in which he persevered in a praiseworthy way, with the admiration of many, to the end of his life.

Indeed, divine mercy is accustomed to lead to itself, through reproofs or rebukes, certain ones who act wickedly, so that those who are unwilling of their own accord are at least provoked by reproaches, and returned to the path of justice.

38. For instance, I recall seeing a certain young knight who had once become a monk in our monastery, and then later, through the promptings of the devil, he had fallen back into his old ways of the world.

On a certain day, when he was going to ride in a large gathering of knights, he ordered, with arrogance born of pride, that his horse be displayed before him, along with his arms. In front of all who were there, his page immediately bowed deeply and responded to him with '*Benedicite*,' thus reminding him indirectly of what he had once been, and that now he ought in no way to do such things.

At this response, he was confounded and troubled beyond belief. Rather, in fact, he was beneficially warned. He immediately removed himself from the sight of men and, rising at night, he returned humbled and chastened to the old place from which he had departed in pride.

39. Furthermore, that holy man was watchful with great care and solicitude for peace, not only at home, but also in the entire province, as will be evident more clearly than the light of day through the following example.

Once there arose a dispute between Raymond, the Viscount of Turenne,[43] and a certain other illustrious man named William. This was the cause of the trouble: this same William had caught a falcon that had been released; it belonged to the Viscount, and the proud man refused to return it to him. Indeed, nothing hinders the devil, whether he incites great mischief through trifling affairs or through important ones.

Therefore, the aforementioned Viscount bore it grievously that the falcon was stolen, not only for the loss, but also for the insult to him. He declared war and threatened that he would ravage all the property under the jurisdiction of the robber, unless the falcon were restored to him quickly. Not only would small rural holdings be laid waste in this destruction, but almost an entire province, and not only for those who were in conflict, but also for those who were coming together from elsewhere to bring aid.

However, William then held on to the falcon all the more, because he was desirous of war, so that he could use this opportunity to invade the Viscount's fertile lands and to destroy everything suddenly. In fact, fearing that the falcon could be stolen from him in some way, and thus he might lose the occasion for the war he wanted, he took pains to entrust it to a certain powerful man who resided far off. This man burned for war no less, and he ardently gaped at plunder.

But indeed the holy man saw that wicked deeds were increased, for all the land was filled with armed soldiers committing acts of plunder, and they were being multiplied from day to day. He did not avoid going to face so many calamities. In fact, first he went to the Viscount and chided him, asking why he was harassing and destroying so great a Christian populace on account of a single small bird. Then he asked that pardon be granted for the theft, or if not, that punishment for the injury be exacted from the robber alone, not from innocent people. But when the venerable man accomplished nothing in this effort, he tried by the only other way that was open to him. He promised that he would restore the bird, as long as the assembled armies would be discharged and sent back to their own lands.

43. Raymond II succeeded his father, Boson II, as Viscount of Turenne in 1143.

When the Viscount had agreed to this, Stephen, immediately armed with faith, 'like a bold lion' (Prv 28.1), marched into the armed battle-lines on his own authority as well as that of the Viscount. He separated the close battle-lines and compelled all to return to their own places. Then he went to the forenamed William. When he had learned for certain that the falcon was not then with him, he immediately made his way to the man who had had the bird entrusted to him, even though the harshness of winter and the length of the journey hindered him. For in the cause of peace, nothing seemed hard or difficult to him, since he was prepared even to die so that his homeland might not be destroyed.

When Stephen had finally arrived at the castle in which he was staying, that man saw him and immediately understood what he wanted and why he had come so quickly. Hence, he was exceedingly angry. Not only did he do nothing for him, but also in fact he ordered him, not without insults, to be kept outside the gates.

Stephen bore this patiently. Still fasting, as night was already falling, he and the brothers who were accompanying him turned toward the hut of a certain pauper not far from this same town. That pauper had a wife and children who were still young. Stephen was moved with pity for the children, who were so naked that they had almost none of their limbs covered. When he was now about to leave in the morning, he secretly took off his tunic and left it there, with no one else aware of it, as if he had forgotten it. But when the brothers saw that he was affected by the cold and that his shoulders were shaking, they asked him if he had all his tunics. Then, unwilling to make the fact known, and taking care not to lie, he said, 'I cannot escape this bitter cold with all the tunics that I have!'

Although the brothers were hoping that they would now return home, Stephen directed his course toward the aforementioned town. His companions were debating what they would do, especially with the man who had driven them away from himself so insultingly. Stephen responded to them in prophetic words: 'Let us go now in the name of the Lord, since the man will not be today as he was yesterday.'

Arriving again at the castle, they found all open, which had been closed to them a short time ago. Moreover, that man who had driven them out, seeing that the servant of God came to him again, leaped up immediately from his bed and ran to him just as he was, with bare feet and almost his whole body bare, in the courtyard full of snow. He prostrated himself at Stephen's feet and begged pardon for the insult to him. When he had obtained this, he then delivered the stolen falcon into the hands of the servant of God. He walked with him a little distance and sent him away happy. So the holy man entrusted the falcon he had received to a certain brother to carry, and thus he began his return home happy. It was a marvel to see that the peace of the whole province depended on a single bird. Thus, the falcon was brought to the castle at Turenne. As soon as it was released, it flew into the court of the Viscount. When it was returned, the falcon restored the peace that it had removed when it was taken away. So the peace begun long ago was perfected, and that whole land was fully liberated from destruction and devastation.

40. There was a very religious brother named Aimeric who was accustomed to accompany the saint. Stephen sent him on a journey for certain business. When the brother had spent a considerable part of the day riding, he wanted to spare his beast. As was his habit, he dismounted, to make his journey on foot for a while. Then, when the beast on which he was riding realized that it was free, suddenly it fled (as is the habit of mules), and began to run through the plains and through trackless places. The servant boy had all he could do to block the mule's way. The brother was running as best he could along the road. When each of them accomplished nothing, as the mule was getting farther away, the brother called back the servant boy. He feared that the mule, agitated by his running, might flee even more and then could not be caught.

And so, despairing of it, especially since no one came in sight and that mule did not stop running, he turned toward it and said: 'I adjure you, by the virtue of obedience and the merits of our father, that you go no farther, and you wait for me, as I am very tired.' At these words, the mule, although it was very far off, stood still and, with its head turned toward the brother, remained immobile, not even turning its head in another direction, until the brother arrived and took it by the bridle. Then Aimeric turned to the servant boy and said: 'How good is the virtue of obedience, which even dumb animals respect!'

41. When another brother wanted to draw wine, he opened a cask and placed a pot beneath it; then he allowed the wine to flow into it (as has been written about a certain person in the *Life of Saint Columbanus*).[44] While he was doing this, suddenly another brother came up, calling him on behalf of the abbot. Fervent in obedience, the brother proceeded in haste, with the wine left behind, to Father Stephen, still carrying in his hand the tap by which the wine was held back. When the abbot had enjoined upon him the things that were wanted, the brother recalled the task that he had abandoned. In haste he returned to the cask, expecting that all the wine had flowed out of it. Yet, when he returned, he found the barrel full beyond what was customary, in fact, more so, although the wine in it was still flowing out in such a way that not even a single drop had fallen on the ground. No one could doubt that this was done through the power of the saint and the obedience of the brother. The one in charge of the wine was called Gerald, 'a faithful and wise man' (Mt 24:45) from whose own truthful telling we know that this happened so.

42. In the village of Pleaux,[45] where the holy man had served in the office of priest, two women lived together in one house. One of them was a leper, the other was a paralytic who for many years had been unable to rise from her bed or to move herself. Indeed, the blessed man loved them very much (as one reads about Martha and Mary), so that he never went to that village without visiting them before he left there. This was not undeserved; like Mary, the one who could not do anything used to recline constantly at the feet of Jesus; the other, running about everywhere like Martha, used to obtain whatever alms she could for herself and her companion. In fact, she served Christ diligently in this.

It happened that on a journey the holy man came to the same village out of necessity. When he was preparing himself to celebrate mass, a messenger came to the priests, saying that the paralytic woman, whom a fever had assailed some time ago, was asking for the last sacrament; she was already near the end. Hearing this, Stephen told the priests that he would gladly give communion to

44. PL 87:1026.

45. See 1.1; 3.30.

this woman after mass was finished. After he had done this devoutly at the request of the priests, he then left that village. When he had proceeded a short distance, the aforementioned woman was so suddenly cured, not only of her fever, but even of her paralysis, that she rose from her bed on that very day and went to church. And she remained in good condition in this life for many years. I believe that the holy man wanted her recovery to be deferred until he had departed from the village so that he might escape the applause of those praising him.

43. Once, when the saint went to the chapter at Cîteaux, two boys beset by sickness were brought to him. While one of them was sleeping in a field, with his mouth open, a serpent entered his belly and tormented him with great, unending pains. The other boy was suffering because he never ate with anyone present. Indeed, he did not know how to ask, so that he could eat. His parents sent him to a remote place alone, so that there, like some wild beast, he might take food, not food that was desired, but that was needed. In his appearance, dress, speech and movement, he seemed to be a lunatic, so that whoever merely looked at him would be sure at a glance that he was insane.

Those two were set before the man of God in one grange, but at different times. Although Stephen refused for a long time to receive that one who had the serpent, finally, compelled by his brother monks, he ordered him to stand apart. Then, after he had prayed for him, Stephen blessed water that had been exorcised and sprinkled with salt and gave it to him to drink. When he swallowed it, the serpent was killed and expelled into the latrine, carrying with it all the pain from the suffering boy's body.

When the lunatic was brought by his parents, he was cured by prayer alone and the laying on of hands, so that then and afterward he would eat with others present and watching, and in all his actions he displayed no insanity ever again.

44. One of the holy virgins, who was still a young girl, had lost her sight due to the excessive force of a sickness, so that when it was necessary, she was guided by the hands of others. Finally, in fact, the eyes which were blinded suddenly swelled up and began to jut out in such a way that they seemed to be torn from their sockets.

She was tormented with such great pain from this that the other sisters were moved to tears, as much with regard for her age as for her suffering. However, it happened that the man of God came to the window, according to custom, to visit the sisters. When his arrival was made known, the sisters brought the aforementioned girl into his presence and placed her next to the window. When he asked them what they wanted of him concerning this child, they carefully recounted to him the whole course of her infirmity. They also begged that he place his hands over her eyes, believing that if he did this, God would grant health to her.

Then the man of God asked the girl whether she believed that she would receive her sight through the imposition of his hand. When he asked her for the third time, she responded for the third time: 'I believe.' Then immediately putting his hand through the window, he said a prayer and made the sign of the cross over her eyes and her whole head; he touched her, blessed her, and commanded her to depart in good health. Then she, who had been carried there by the hands of others, arose by herself. When she reached the door of the cloister, her eyes were opened, and her pain was immediately banished, along with the swelling.

The sisters, observing that she saw clearly and that no traces of the past sickness remained in her, wept then all the more for joy, and they glorified God no less for the saint's power than for the girl's health.

45. Also, it happened that a certain dreadful illness, which the physicians declared incurable, seized boys whom the man of God was educating in the divine laws, as with Samuel and Daniel. (They were instructed in the riches of wisdom and afterward stood upright in the sight of God). Indeed, their necks and throat openings were puffed up and swollen so much that they seemed equal to heads in their enormous thickness. And when these boys were in despair, the holy father came to visit them, although he was ignorant of their suffering. Seeing them affected by so cruel a disease, he was exceedingly grieved, even to tears. He prayed long and hard to the Lord for them. Finally, he had them brought to him in private. Having first applied the medicine of his prayers, he touched the neck, throat and also the other diseased places on each one. He made the sign of the cross over them, his eyes uplifted to heaven, with

the invocation of the name of Christ and the salutary impression of the holy cross upon them. Why delay longer? He so completely restored them to health that even on the third day no traces of the past sickness remained in them.

46. Another of the boys already placed in the novitiate was so beset with certain tumors and sores around his neck, along with swelling in the throat and jaws, that he could not lie down or sleep. At last, he could not turn his head to either side or take food. Tormented by violent pain, he did not know what to do, since he himself could not rest, nor did he allow others to have rest. But when the holy father was visiting him and his comrades in the usual way, he observed his pain and bitter suffering, and he took him aside. Praying with his eyes raised to heaven in his customary manner, Stephen traced all the places of the sickness with his health-giving touch, so that immediately, on that very day, the boy took food, and on the following night, and thereafter, he slept sufficiently.

47. And since this discussion is about children, it should not seem absurd if we set forth some examples of their simplicity, so that from this it might be known how innocently they were raised, and how they were strangers to all knowledge of worldly experience.

A certain boy was raised by his mother in the monastery of women. When he now passed the limit of five years (for no male beyond that age was permitted to remain there), he was compelled to leave there and was sent to the residence for boys at the abovementioned cell.

But when he was still on the journey, he was asked by the brother who was taking him how the women, among whom he had been reared, conducted themselves. He responded that he had never seen women, for he thought that those about whom he was asked were not women, but sisters. He knew that they were always called so. However, wanting to test whether he had answered this simply or figuratively, the brother asked him again: 'Then, would you really like to see women?' He responded, 'I would like to.' Looking off in the distance, the brother saw she-goats feeding, and he said to the boy: 'See, those are women.' Hearing this, the boy did not believe otherwise than he heard. Arriving among the boys of his same age, he boasted that, among other things, he had seen women feeding in a field. Indeed, while the more innocent boys marveled, the others who mocked were in fact more aware of the facts, but not for that more fortunate.

48. Also, a boy from another cell was sent by his prior to bring back fresh hay from a meadow. When the servants had loaded his ass, it travelled through a long gully as they were returning. Its burden was stripped away by the adjacent banks on both sides, and the ass ran away and returned home without the boy knowing it. However, the boy stood next to the hay, striking it repeatedly and, as it were, threatening it, and he would not leave the place until the brothers who had set out to find him could, with difficulty, persuade him that the ass had already returned and the hay could not move without someone carrying it.

49. This was, then, the holy simplicity of those children. This was the purity of their innocence, by which they more truly approached divine knowledge and angelic purity, because they possessed none of the impure knowledge of this world.

However, as soon as the children of our time have begun to speak, there is almost nothing that they do not know about the world, so that if you hear them talking, you might think that they are people of the market place. One must not believe that they are thus fit for divine matters, who have dedicated the beginning of their life to worldly studies, just as those about whom we have spoken were not so dull in divine matters as they appeared foolish in human affairs. For of such persons the Apostle said: 'Be little ones in malice, so that you might be perfect in understanding' (1 Cor 14:20). And again: 'I wish you to be simple in evil, but wise in good' (Rom 16:19).

For instance, when a certain wise and very holy boy among them was lying ill and about to die, Stephen, their common father, was standing near him, along with the reverend prior and certain other holy brothers. The boy was not yet finally breathing his last, and while the others were discussing spiritual studies among themselves, a dispute arose concerning the excellence of the Psalms. As they exalted that excellence with praises and many commendations, one among them put forth the view that no curse was contained in the Psalms, but that all of them abounded in divine blessings. Then that venerable boy, with his breath recovered (although he was thought to be almost lifeless) said: 'It is not so, it is not so, my Lords, but a great curse is contained in the Psalms!' All of them were at once struck with astonishment. Then the holy father, together with the prior, said to him: 'And where is that curse, son?' He answered them: 'Cursed are those who turn away from your commandments' (Ps 118.21). They were amazed; they marveled at this response, so pure, so suitable, so certain and ready. They blushed with shame, while giving thanks that they had been defeated, especially by an innocent and almost lifeless boy, one whom they thought could no longer notice or speak.

But in all these examples, Stephen must be acknowledged. He, after God, must be glorified, who sired such sons in Christ and instructed them in the study of wisdom. In them, the image of his virtue shines as if in a mirror, so that with the prophet he could say: 'Behold, I and my children, whom God has given to me' (Is 8:18).

50. I confess that I have never seen such great beauty gleam on the face of anyone, although Stephen's face was ordinary, modest, even furrowed with wrinkles. His hair was growing thin on account of his abstinence, just as dry earth brings forth small crops of plants. And although all the reasons for which the dignity of the human countenance is wont to be praised were lacking to him, yet he shone so brightly from an inner light, that there was never enough of looking at his face. Because of this, many people looked at him curiously. They diligently observed all the gestures of his body, and what or how he spoke, since he edified those who watched him not only by speaking, but also by doing anything, even in passing. Indeed, certain secular noblemen and experienced persons persistently affirmed that, beyond those things which pertain to religious life, they had never seen a man so urbane, so provident, so prudent, so upright and prepared for everything, that nothing was lacking to him of those things through which the cultivation of the human condition is adorned or the glory of the interior life is increased.

Whenever a situation offered itself or an occasion permitted, and he smiled a little with his lips compressed, then his holy shoulders shook, like doves, so that you would think that you had never seen anything simpler. You would believe also that nothing was more frightful, so that you would then fear him no less than if you saw him angry. But if at that time he turned the rays of his eyes upon you, you would think that your whole being was penetrated, so that the very hidden recesses of your heart seemed in some measure exposed to him, and there was nothing which was concealed from his gaze. Hence, scarcely anyone dared to laugh with him, nor did anyone fear him less when he was smiling than when he was angry. Thus it is that blessed Job said of himself: 'If ever I laughed at them' (that is, the household servants), 'they did not believe me, and the light of my countenance did not fall upon the earth' (Job 29:24). Truly, the light of Stephen's countenance did not fall upon the earth, since he never relaxed the reins of his gladness without a worthy and rational reason.

Neither was that arrogance, but prudent simplicity, which the Lord commended in the gospel, saying: 'Be prudent as serpents and simple as doves' (Mt 10:16). In fact, like a prudent man, Stephen wisely provided for all things, and like a simple man, he believed all things. He spurned nothing; he hoped all things, loved all things, endured all things (see 1 Cor 13:7).

51. Furthermore, although he was lovingly feared by all the brothers, and loved with fear, he by no means exalted himself insolently over them on that account, as many do. He governed them not so much out of authority as out of charity, or rather he served them, fulfilling that which is written in the gospel, as Christ commanded: 'Whoever is greater among you, let him be as the lesser, and whoever is superior, let him be as a servant' (Lk 22:26). Wherefore, a certain wise man forewarned, saying: 'Have they made you a prince? Do not be exalted, but be among them as one of them' (Si 32:1).

Now if, for the love of God, he wished to give anything beyond what was customary when those in charge of this were absent, it was taken, as it were, by stealth, not because he feared them, but since he did not want to scandalize them. Neither did he take pains that they not know this, but that they not see it, since, according to the common proverb, 'What the eye does not see does not grieve the heart.' For there are some who cannot look with equanimity at what they wish to be given away from their own possessions. Hence, that saint dispensed many things with those in charge both present and absent. With them absent, he did it in the manner mentioned above; with them present, he did it by asking rather than ordering. He did it with careful and wondrous circumspection, so that he would not grieve those in charge or deny necessary goods to those asking for them. And although no one ever dared to speak against him in this matter, in fact they very often found fault with the reasoning by which the saint dispensed what was his according to the authorization of another, and not according to his own judgment. He used to respond that he claimed none of the monastery's possessions as his own, and therefore he ought to give nothing from those common possessions without common assent.

Moreover, he preserved this respect not only for his provosts and those in charge, but also for the other servants, when blame was lacking, when the sanctity of justice and integrity of life abounded in them, and when, finally, they were obedient in all things and rebellious in none. But if he found them blameworthy or puffed up with a certain insolence, he did not spare them, but immediately threatened their backs dreadfully, as a stern master and angry lord. Not only did he exact those punishments from the lesser brothers, but also he began first with the greater ones, so that those who were raised higher by the dignity of their teaching were in no way immune from correction. It was a wonder to see a man who yesterday determined everything, like a mighty consul, one who managed everything, today cast down to earth (as his faults demanded), afflicted with whips, subjected to rebukes, delivered up for his grievous faults. And when he had utterly overthrown him, as I have said, and lowered him right to the ground, after a little while, when his feelings had quieted down, he restored him to his former favor. He entrusted everything, as before, to his management and judgment, so that he honored him in his accustomed manner and feared him, as it were, and did or ordered nothing without his counsel. And in this, indeed, he imitated the zeal of a wise physician toward those subject to him.

First he severely cut out the destructive tumors, then kindly soothed those wounds and refreshed them, so that smiling prosperity would not wickedly make them haughty, nor impending adversity afflict them beyond measure, until they knew that they would not be spared in any way because of their great honors, nor would anything of their former favor be diminished because of the punishments inflicted on them. But also, Stephen provided no less for the lower ones in this respect. Certainly he did not administer the chalice of whips and tribulations to them before he did so to those greater ones, so that in no way did they think they should not endure what they saw threatening all equally.

52. When he was about to go on a journey, after a general blessing of the brothers, he used to commend himself also to the prayers of the sick. He left them in sorrow and tears, particularly if he were going far away. There is joy when wicked lords are going away and sadness when they return. On the other hand, good lords leave sorrow after them when they go away, which they turn to gladness when they have finally returned. Thus, everything was downcast when he set out, and everything was joyful inside and out when he returned, so that, as the saying goes, the very walls seemed to give thanks at his coming and, in some way, to be cheerful.

Moreover, he took with him persons upright and respected in his sight, so that he might have their counsel at hand, and his own meager and modest person might appear poorer in comparison with them. But when they were well along on their journey, they would ask shepherds or any children who their abbot was. Leaving behind the others whom dignity of countenance commended, all eagerly ran to him. With prophetic voices, as I might call them, they proclaimed that he was the abbot, that he was the father and teacher of all, and from him they hoped for alms. They did not do so without effect, nor did they request them in vain.

53. Therefore, when he came to a grange or any place under his jurisdiction, who could report how he went about everywhere, how he made the rounds, how he left nothing unseen, since the care of everything belonged to him? Scarcely had he dismounted from his horse, when in the next moment he put on his scapular. He went around diligently through all the places or dwellings of the monastery or grange, and if he found anything unsuitable in them, after the brothers were summoned and rebuked, he ordered the negligence he had discovered to be corrected immediately.

Indeed, if anything then had to be done, he took up a hoe or any tool and began the task, or completed what had been begun already, and he summoned others to work. If at that time grains were being threshed, he hastened immediately to the threshing-floor and threshed there long and hard with the companions who had come with him.

Why should I speak about Stephen or his companions, when he did not allow even the mules on which they came to be at rest from work, lest they might receive their fodder while idle and without toil? But also he was not slow to visit the brothers who toiled at a distance or remained in the pastures. Inquiring solicitously how each one conducted himself in his position or his work, he either aided or instructed them in each instance as was necessary. In fact, nothing of rural management was unknown to him, and there was no kind of skill or any administration in which he could not teach or amend or improve something. And although the brothers, according to their different states of health or nature, took their places in diverse labors inside and outside, both far and near, yet he went, fittingly, to see them. In fact, he sternly rebuked the negligent, strengthened the doubtful, comforted the faint-hearted, consoled the mournful, soothed the sorrowful, refreshed the weary and invited the reluctant ones to rest. Then sometimes he recalled the zealous and most disposed to toil from their excessive effort, and sometimes he challenged them with pleasant words to work more. For although vainglory and negligence are contrary to each other, and both are vices, he preferred, as far as the lessening of evil, to free something from vainglory rather than by negligence to incur that prophetic curse, that is: 'Cursed is he who does the work of God in a negligent way' (Jer 48:10). Thus, he certainly proceeded against all negligence and laziness, especially in the young men, since he claimed that nothing among the vices, except criminal acts, was more grievous.

If, while walking through a portico or in some place, he saw vegetables or legumes dropped through carelessness and scattered on the ground, he bent over right away and gathered them up bit by bit, however small they were. And after he summoned those through whose fault they had fallen, he rebuked them harshly for their negligence.

But if he had brought guests with him, or by chance they arrived when he was present, he went into the kitchen, in the granges just as in the abbey, and with great care attended to what or how much ought to be set before them, or what could be left over for the poor. He did this so that they might not prepare either too little or too much and, in either case, appear either greedy or wasteful.

But if he had such great concern about external and lesser matters, so that nothing might be lost negligently or unnecessarily, how great a diligence do you think he could expend on those things that pertain to uprightness of morals and salvation of souls? For when Stephen was present, who would presume to lift a hand or a foot unbecomingly, to raise his eyes impudently, to say uncouth words or to employ vain gestures, much less to pour forth base words or to open his mouth in coarse laughter?

54. Thus, one can easily understand the great severity with which Stephen would punish all serious offenses, when he judged lesser and lighter faults so strictly, although he often corrected certain transgressions by fear alone, with no punishment preceding or following. This will be clearly apparent from the following example.

While he was making his customary rounds of the workshops after compline on a certain Saturday, he found the bakers in the bakery after their weekly work was finished. They were cheerful, and with certain sticks of wood that they had taken up like spears, they were fighting among themselves. He observed this through an opening. Since they did not see him at all, he made a sound in his throat so that he would not be undetected by them, and he passed by. But he left them in such great fear that one of them immediately made himself ready to flee so as not to endure the violence of the trial to come, but he was hardly and with great difficulty held back by his fellow-brother.

However, each came the next day to chapter. Not awaiting an accusation, each sought pardon of his own accord. But when they stood silent awaiting judgment and were asked by the saint what reason they had, they answered only this: 'You know.' As if he were displeased, Stephen ordered them to sit down. Indeed, why was it that he did not condemn them more, except that he knew how much fear he had instilled in them on the previous night? He was unwilling to add pain upon pain for them, as many do, who, the more their subjects are afraid, the more harshly they threaten them, not because they are more guilty, but since they are less to be feared.

55. Another brother, one of the pre-eminent ones, had been severely chastised in the chapter meeting. Afterward, when he was sitting alone outside, dejected and full of bitterness, the holy man saw him

and wished to heal him. He began to pass by in front of him on purpose. Although reluctant, that brother rose up and proceeded with him, for he did not dare not to follow when the holy man was passing by in his presence. The saint turned to him and said: 'Perhaps you are following me so that we might make peace.' When the brother responded: 'By no means. Far be it from me. I have not thought of it,' Stephen then grasped his neck and embraced him closely and kissed him. The brother's heart changed to such great delight that he immediately fell to the ground and embraced the saint's feet. With tears, he begged forgiveness for the fact that he had been angry toward him.

56. But also, when a certain monk wanted to leave the monastery with permission, and he was troublesome to the saint of God daily on account of that permission (which was not granted him), he begged forgiveness for this in the chapter meeting one day. But since the holy man did not want to accede to him but could not break his perverse intention, finally, as if overcome by weariness, he said to him: 'If you truly wish to go, first pay what you owe.' When the monk asked, 'What is that?' he said: 'Prepare yourself for discipline.' When he had done this, Stephen had him severely scourged, so that there was no one who was not trembling with fear. When the monk had risen, the saint said to him: 'Now you can leave, if it pleases you.' Indeed, although it might be thought that he was then more moved and more incited to depart, he responded in this way: 'Lord, I shall not go away from here or forsake you for all the days of my life. For every temptation has been so completely eradicated that I want nothing, ever, less than to leave.' Who could doubt that in that hour the devil had been driven out of him and thrust away, as if he had been scourged in that monk?

Thus did the holy man know how to smite and to heal, to lead to the depths and to lead back, to kill, in a certain way, and to give life. Some, indeed, he corrected with pleasant words, others with reproaches, others with gladness, others with harshness, others with kindness, others even with scourges, and he lead them back to the narrow path of life.

57. But let us return to our purpose. Of all the things that were done in his presence, he was the judge and the witness. He either

made a judgment immediately, if it could not be deferred, or later at an opportune time. For this reason, before he departed from a place to which he had come, he held a chapter meeting with the assembled brothers according to the rule. Presiding in this chapter, he examined faults so strictly that there was no one so bold and so presumptuous concerning his own merits or friendship with him who was not shaking all over with fear when he entered the aforementioned chapter meeting.

Moreover, Stephen always observed this earnestness of administration with equal justice in all the places founded by him, so that either while he was present or when he was expected to arrive, he was always and everywhere feared by all.

If Stephen had at any time grievously saddened anyone through excessive correction, he did not rest until he had assuaged the man's spirit with soothing words or, perhaps, with favors, or even with kisses of friendship, so that the man rejoiced that he had been made sad for his own good and had merited so great a favor of his holy father on account of this. Yet, Stephen did not grant this favor equally to all, but to those whom he knew it would benefit, since there are some men who can be corrected by whippings, but they cannot be persuaded by words or flatteries (like the hardest flint, which can indeed be broken by hammers, but cannot be chiseled). For it is written: 'Strike the obstinate man with a stick, since a fool is not corrected with words.'[46]

58. Stephen so instructed all the brothers by his teaching and examples that by the merit of their remarkable way of life they were unlike not only other men or any other religious, but even those graced by the same order and habit. For even if they were riding through a public place or proceeding on any other path, it soon became manifestly clear where they were from, since their habit as well as their gait made them known very readily. None of them ever took up a journey unprepared or without a worthy and rational reason. Not one of them was accustomed to eat in strange places or to stay in them. No one was accustomed to walk along the streets or highways, but they passed through the middle of a village or city

46. RB 2.28; Kardong, 46, 48, citing Prv 23:14.

with their heads covered and with discipline, or they went to their intended place by a path leading there outside the city. In fact, at that time they were not accustomed to enter villages unless orders or an inevitable necessity compelled them. If by chance they said anything to anyone, they weighed their words with such great circumspection that no one could catch them or find fault with them in their speech. For since they were shown to be disciples of so great a teacher, this was taken as a very sure proof that they would be found without reproach in all things.

When a certain noble matron was sitting at the window of her house, with many other people, she looked out and saw far off two brothers in religious habit riding along. When the others asked among themselves in their uncertainty from what house or order the brothers were who had come into view, the aforementioned matron asserted without delay that they were not monks of Obazine, although she had not yet seen their faces. In a short time this was proven true, for they came closer and confirmed by their own testimony that the matron was speaking truly. Indeed, she had seen that they were riding in a disorderly way and not proceeding in a religious manner, and so she did not think that such disciples could come from the school of so great a teacher.

59. Indeed, who could ever watch Stephen speaking, standing, walking or doing any other thing and not draw from that some lesson? And that we might recall some of the smallest things: he wanted no one to spit indecorously or without restraint; he wanted no one to speak or to laugh with his teeth exposed; he wanted no one to walk or to eat noisily. He also did not want anyone to sit down unless his cowl was drawn to the side, lest the cloth be torn more quickly in the place where one sits, and also so that if some deterioration should occur below the back of the one sitting, it might appear not at the back, but less shamefully elsewhere.

When he was present, either in church or any other place, wherever there was a gathering, certainly no one dared to yawn or to smile inappropriately, or to speak in an undisciplined manner, or to show any sign of negligence or levity. No one presumed to mutter about poverty, or to resist or contradict superiors when they gave orders.

60. Stephen also zealously saw to it that ministers at the altar were properly vested. He carefully arranged their vestments himself, lest they should assist at divine services while unsightly and improperly attired and give scandal, and not edification, to those who saw them.

Truly, he himself appeared so suitably attired in his holy robes that the vestments seemed in some measure just as if they were innate to him, so that no one would discern, unless he knew, that Stephen was wearing a cowl underneath.

And now when it came to performing the sacred rites, he lifted his heart, face and eyes toward God. Also, with his hands spread apart a little, near him, in the manner of a cross (not as certain ones do, with their hands stretched out in the air as if they were going to fly!), he remained fixed thus upon God until he was ready to make the sign of the cross over the sacred mysteries. When he returned again to himself, he did not emit a cough or sighs or groans, but to those divine eyes he offered a pure heart and an ardent spirit, a spirit drenched with tears. For just as the burning sun immerses itself in the ocean so that it might arise from there more brightly, so did his fervent spirit, drenched with the rain of tears, arise more purely before the eyes of God.

Then, when mass was finished, he suitably arranged the holy altar with linen cloths so that none of it remained uncovered because nothing stood out in an unsightly manner from under the linen cloth. He left all the altar cloths level above, all hanging down equally below, well ordered on all sides and cleansed of dust. And all around the altar, when he went away, nothing unsightly or unsuitable remained. The vestments which he took off, although servers stood ready to assist him on either side, he folded with his own hands so that by his diligence he might instruct those who were less inclined and might give an example to others, lest anyone engaged in any great occupations at all should refuse to do this.

That blessed man taught these and things similar to these by actions more than by words. We have described them here not so much for his praise as for the instruction of others, so that those who read of them might learn in the smallest actions what they ought to imitate in the greatest.

There are also many other signs of his honor and uprightness that were shown by the example of his manner of life, as if in a mirror. These the unlearned and less devout easily scorn, but devout and learned men embrace them more dearly than gold, and they do not reckon them among the least of things, which offer much honor and utility, even in the greatest matters.

Indeed, to those who read them and hear them, they offer greater instruction for the inducement of virtues than if they read or heard that a hundred or more blind people had been given sight by him, or if just as many deaf and mute persons had been healed. Not that miracles were lacking to the saint; from the few which we have reported, more can be inferred which we have not recounted.

Truly, since many things have now been said about the life and deeds of so great a father, it seems right to make an end here, so that, in turn, the things that remain might have their own preface. Indeed, time urges us on and our plan demands that finally we direct our pen to his death, so that those who have been unwilling or unable to imitate his life might be challenged to better ways by the example of his glorious death.

End of Book Two

Book Three

Here Begins the Preface to Book Three

We have now said enough above, in the two preceding books, concerning the life and deeds of Lord Stephen, first abbot of Obazine, who was first predestined and then presented in his time. We did not think that everything that could be said or written about him should be reported here, but thought that so great a man's way of life, which benefited so many while he lived, should be known to posterity for their edification.

We spoke above in the preface to the second book about the reasons for which we undertook this great work and who ordered us to do so, since if we had composed this on our own authority, it would have been ridiculed more than written, and deserving to have the ears of the public closed to it. For a monk has no authority without the command of a superior. But just as it is temerity to anticipate, so it is contempt to neglect a command. Although we could have excused ourselves from this work in many ways, yet, placing the peril of this matter in the judgment of God and in the help of our holy father Stephen, with the confidence with which we somehow completed two little books, we hope that we shall set forth this third one, of whatever kind it might be. And we do not so much fear offending him on account of our temerity, as we trust in the grace of the saint because of our devotion to him. Just as once Saint Martin, appearing to his own Severus while he was still living, held out to him in his right hand the book which he had written about his life,[47] Stephen came to us, when we had been put

47. Sulpicius Severus, *Letter* 2, ed. Jacques Fontaine, *Vie de Saint Martin*, I, SCh 133:326–27; Hoare, 52.

in distress after his death, and, weighing the labor of this writing on a scale, he raised upward the sinking weights of our sins, and he restored us, rescued from eternal punishments through the mercy of God, to perpetual life.

Not without cause have we thought that blessed Martin should be inserted into this little preface, whose glorious passing we are going to describe in great part in the honorable death of Stephen. For Martin passed from this world not in his own episcopal see, but in a church under his jurisdiction situated far away, after peace had been established among his clergy.[48] Stephen migrated to the Lord not in his own abbey, but in another abbey under his jurisdiction,[49] after an abbot, whom it had long lacked, had been ordained there. Martin died in the middle of the night on a Sunday; Stephen died in the middle of the night on a Sunday. His monks and disciples bewailed Martin; his monks and disciples bewailed Stephen. Countless people bewailed both with public lamentation and cries raised to Heaven. Both were escorted over very long, circuitous ways and buried in fitting tombs after fitting funerals, as was fitting. Hence, I beg, let it trouble no one if we describe Stephen's passing extensively and, so to say, minutely, because, even if it will perhaps be considered undeserving to disdainful people, yet to devout ones and to those who dutifully love the saint, it will not be unwelcome, I believe, howsoever long it might be.

Here the Preface Ends

Here Begins the Third Book

1. And so, when the blessed man was about to pass from this world, one of the abbeys mentioned above had been without its own shepherd for a long time now. He wished to visit this abbey so that he might make lawful arrangements there, even though he realized that the end of his days was near, as is read about Saint Martin. As

48. Sulpicius Severus, *Letter* 3 (SCh 133:336–343; Hoare, 57–59).

49. Bonneaigue.

the time of solemn fasts was approaching, when ashes are accustomed to be given, he proceeded there with certain abbots. While the matter for which they had come was being dealt with, and the monks had not yet agreed to accept one from among those present as abbot, word was sent back to the monastery so that the prior and certain other monks suited for this office might be brought from there. Meanwhile, Lord Stephen had been asked to visit the archpriest of the region, who was sick.[50] He went and returned from there, and immediately incurred sickness in his body. Indeed, a fever invaded his limbs, which were exhausted from fasting. The fatigue of his body and a cold chill spread this fever little by little into his innermost parts.

And when the election was ready to take place the next day, for now those had arrived for whom it had been destined, then Stephen was seized by a severe ailment during the entire night. Yet he did not think that so necessary a work should be put off lest perchance, if he died, it might be entirely thwarted or executed carelessly. But since he could not be present at their chapter meeting, he entrusted this ordination to a certain abbot who surpassed the others in authority, so that the same abbot might establish there as shepherd one whom he had chosen already with the brothers' counsel. This was happily fulfilled immediately, without delay or any objection.

2. Then the holy man began to be more ill, as his sickness became worse. Because of this, he was moved from a common residence to a more independent cell. Also, when the report of his sickness had spread abroad, with messengers running about everywhere, after it reached the ears of the monks at Obazine, all were exceedingly distressed and thrown into confusion beyond belief. For how could the flock, although it was secure, not be troubled when so great a shepherd was dying, since it is written: 'I shall smite the shepherd and the sheep will be scattered?' (Mt 26:31; Mk 14:27). Indeed, now many eagerly went to him, without having sought permission, or rather they ran to gain a final blessing at least, even if then they could not acquire anything else. Like a dutiful father he received them kindly, just as devoted sons, and blessing them individually he comforted them with his most gentle touch.

50. Evidently the archpriest of Saint-Exupéry.

Indeed, the others who remained behind made a great din with their lamentation and wailing as if the end of the world were imminent. Almost all abandoned their work, and here and there they devoted themselves solely to weeping. And, in truth, it seemed in a certain way as if the end of the world were at hand to those who were being deprived of so great a father, since they did not know how they would survive after the death of this man with whom they had lived intimately and agreeably.

You could observe all the corners filled with groans, sighs joined to sighs, and the desolation of the whole place being deplored by all in a general lamentation. Indeed, just as on Good Friday, all devoted themselves to silence, if ever they refrained from tears. There was no customary contact between those who met each other, no greeting, no consoling. If ever the older brothers wished to console the younger ones, they were immediately overcome with weeping and collapsed with them in the same way. A general prayer for his life was a part of all the masses, and publicly, just as privately, nothing else was asked except that the flock might not lose its defender, the forsaken sheep their shepherd, the children their mother, the sons their father, the monks their abbot, the disciples their teacher, the place its protector, the house its rector, and the ship, already almost shattered, its best steersman. For Stephen was all these things to them always, so that he could say with the Apostle: 'I have become all things to all men so that I might save all' (1 Cor 9:22).

Moreover, it afflicted them more harshly, that when they happened to receive news about him which said that he was desperately ill, the next morning another messenger came saying that he was now better, and when they prepared themselves, as it were, for rejoicing, again later a messenger of despair arrived who took away all the hope which they had received concerning him.

For God, who can do all things, who knows all things before they happen and who makes 'all things work toward the good for those who love' Him (Rom 8:28), so saw to it that the shepherd might enjoy a desired rest and the sheep might not be abandoned. Neither was his place forsaken, but rather, through the merit of the good shepherd, it grew strong, with a greater prosperity of possessions than before and a greater number of brothers. For Our Lord also said to His disciples before His passion: 'It is expedient for you that I depart. For if I do not go away, the Paraclete will not come to you. However, if I go away, I shall send Him to you' (Jn 16:7). And we know that after His passion, the disciples and all who believed in Him were made more numerous, and they were made stronger than they had been for the entire time of the Lord's preaching. Indeed, He worked in them, as He had promised before, saying: 'Behold, I am with you all days, even to the consummation of the world' (Mt 28:20). So was that holy father about to become more present and more powerful after his burial for those whom he then left as if they were orphans.

3. And so, when the same blessed man was beset more vehemently by strong fevers, he indeed rejoiced that he was going to the goods that he longed for, but he grieved that he was leaving his followers deserted and, as it were, orphaned. Because of this, with his eyes lifted to Heaven and his hands stretched out to the Lord, he prayed that the Lord might always illuminate and protect the place entrusted to him; that He might be a kind shepherd to the sheep which Stephen had thus far gathered through Him, and that He might guide them by His providence.

All the brothers were standing near him, especially those who had come from his monastery. They were weeping inconsolably and saying: 'Father, why do you abandon us? To whom do you leave us, now deserted? Our poverty was enough for us, so we counted it riches that we saw you as our shepherd and the guide of our souls. And now, after you, what shall we do or to whom shall we flee in our tribulation?'

Then, he consoled them as much as he could and instructed them, ordering them to fear God always, and he absolved them of all evil. He told them that he would be more present to them after death and that he would more diligently provide all their necessities, if they would obtain this for him by their constant prayers: that he might enjoy eternal rest. And when they asked him at least to direct his final commands to the brothers of Obazine whom he was surely leaving as orphans, he enjoined upon them nothing other than to guard firmly the statutes of the holy order which they had received and not to abandon the observance of holy poverty and humility; also, to preserve the strictness of obedience and discipline in every way, and to pray to the Lord for him always.

Indeed, he then promised this to them, which we have never read that anyone promised before: namely, that if only they would beseech God on his behalf so that he might be saved, he would obtain eternal salvation from the Lord, confident of His mercy, for all of them, especially those dying within the monastery. For this reason, while admonishing them, he warned that no one should ever leave the monastery, especially the nuns, who had recently experienced a disruption, so that some of them migrated elsewhere, as if to serve the Lord better. For they had heard (but wrongly, as now appears evident) that all who were there at the time would remain, but none should be admitted thereafter. Hence, in order to continue in existence and supported by many great authorities, they chose another place for themselves. Gerald, the abbot at this time, with the advice of the brothers, had already selected this place for them from common property. It was then filled with all goods, but not so after this. Moreover, how they departed from the monastery, or with what authority, or how they lived in the place assigned to them, or how they returned to their own monastery after many distresses of extreme want, and how they were received mercifully and kindly, just as that prodigal son who foolishly wasted his fortune, is not to be reported here, but rather what we have begun is to be amplified.

4. There was no end of those visiting the servant of God during his illness, although none except religious and those whose devotion drew them there were admitted. Some, in fact very many, brought candles for use at his holy funeral, and all wept for him just as for the protector and provider of the entire country.

The time for shaving had passed, but he had not been allowed to be shaven because of his illness. Now when death was approaching, he ordered that he be shaven without delay, so that he might torment his sick body more, and so that, as he was about to go to the Lord directly, he might appear before Him freshly tonsured. We do not doubt that this was done according to divine will so that we might at least have relics of his hair. Indeed, all the hairs were collected and carefully preserved, and afterward they were beneficial for many infirmities.

When he was now clearly drawing near death, at his request he was anointed with holy oil and fortified by the reception of holy communion. Then, after a little while, the sounding-board was struck. All gathered from all sides and began to say the litanies with much weeping in his presence. Indeed, he caused these to be repeated frequently, and, though dying, he chanted with them as best he could. Now, when he had become completely weakened, a certain monk took hold of his right hand and made the sign of the cross over the monastery and all the brothers, while Stephen exerted himself as much as he could and, with difficulty, weakly uttered the words of benediction with lips that were growing cold. And thus, while blessing and praying, that holy soul was freed from the flesh.

5. And so, our venerable Father Stephen went to the Lord on the eighth of March, with Heaven rejoicing and earth weeping; Heaven for a fellow-citizen gained and earth for a shepherd lost. He passed away around midnight on the second Sunday of Lent in the year 1159 from the Lord's incarnation. His body, arranged in the customary way and clothed in priestly vestments, was waked in the church for the rest of the night, with all the brothers, along with certain abbots who had come there, standing before him devoutly and keeping vigils solemnly by the light of candles. But when morning came and masses had been said in the usual way, they began to discuss how his body might be brought to the monastery of Obazine.

In fact, since it was a two-day journey between the monasteries, certain ones, looking ahead, advised that strong animals be sought which might easily bear him over the space of so great a journey. Indeed, others, and in particular the abbot of the place, spoke against this, asserting that it was unbecoming for a holy body and formerly the dwelling- place of the Holy Spirit to be carried on the backs of unreasoning beasts of burden. They said that they would never lack men who would eagerly carry him, if only they themselves bore him from the monastery properly and with honor.

Since this opinion pleased all, they set out immediately amidst sublime chanting. The abbots, monks and the rest of the brothers went before and after the mortal clay of his holy body, which they carried. They were accompanied by a very great throng of clerics, together with a multitude of laymen who were glad that they had gathered from diverse places for the funeral procession of so great a father.

Since that monastery was situated in a somewhat steep place, as soon as they came to the higher and more-level ground, immediately all the shepherds of that region, boys as well as girls, left their flocks behind and ran together with the greatest haste to the funeral of the saint, and passing quickly under the bier, they crossed over to the other side. When they had done this, they returned in the same way to be sanctified again, and they proceeded quickly along with the crowds that were walking. Seeing this, the others were taught by the example of the children. Impelling themselves eagerly, they pushed the saint's bier with a violent impulse and returned again. They could not do this in vain and without the reward of their faith. By passing under the bier in this way, many were released from diverse infirmities. It has seemed too burdensome and difficult to relate here their names or the number of persons or the varieties of diseases.

Truly, since there were many towns, many villages along that whole journey, all their inhabitants, as if keeping holy the Lord's Day, ran together from all sides to so glorious a spectacle, and they mingled with the crowd of those walking along. In all the churches and monasteries where they were going to pass by, all the bells were sounding with such an unexpected din that it was thought that they were not struck by a human hand, but divinely shaken.

Priests with stoles, clerics with white vestments, and monks properly equipped with crosses and censers were proceeding for a long distance to meet the holy body. There was no opportunity for absolving anyone or performing any office, so great was the noise of the bells, and the uproar and clamor of the wailing crowds.

Indeed, the entire land was resounding with lamentation. Some, who had known him better, were weeping over the loss to their homeland, and others for the miracle, when they saw that a man of such small body was so glorified that he was more illustrious than the whole earth; he seemed greater than the world and higher than the sky itself.

Not only were men bewailing him, but also beasts. For I have heard from those who saw it that the beast on which he used to sit poured forth many tears for three days before his death and just as many after his death. The beast was indicating beforehand what would happen, and afterward it was showing what had now taken place.

What should I say about his glorious body, when people were contending so fiercely for items of small value? On account of this there was no easy way to carry him, since defenders on all sides were threatening people with sticks because they were rushing forward rudely and trying to carry off something from the relics of the saint. However, it was no small consolation to have touched the tips of his fingers or his bier. Then what the abbot and others had said became perfectly clear, namely that there would never be lacking those who would eagerly carry the saint's body. Indeed, so that they might know with what great ardor people sought to gain his relics: a certain one of the magnates promised a mark of silver if anyone would bring him a shoe-lace from the saint's shoe.

Many people also took off their own shoes willingly and purposely, and proceeded thus with the saint over rocks and very sharp stones; they returned with blood and wounds on their feet.

This faith among the men should not be marveled at, since women also strove with such great devotion. Indeed, the most noble matrons, having abandoned their bedchambers and set aside the timidity of their female sex, were hurrying along here and there with the men. They ran eagerly to the saint's burial. Those who were not able to march before on account of their delicate nature now proceeded unhesitatingly through swamps and certain difficult places, not even having a care for their costly clothes, but dragging all their elegance through the mud, while they considered as relics whatever they could show that had been torn or stained at the funeral of the saint. But they also took hold of the saint's bier like the men and carried it more vigorously than the men over long distances of the journey.

A viscountess, the lady of that land,[51] did this. Although she was limited in her activities by severe, incurable ailments in her private parts, she attained such great virtue then and thereafter that she persevered in a most healthy condition even to this day. This woman sought with the most intense prayers that they would spend the night with the holy corpse in one of her churches until she could invite that whole land to the funeral rites and furnish all their expenses along the way. She could not obtain this because the brothers went to the nearest grange,[52] which was situated mid-way on the journey, to spend the night; they feared that they might sustain some violence from the woman.

51. The wife of Archambaud, viscount of Comborn.

52. Probably Veyrières.

However, she did not delay in fulfilling what was left for her, namely, she sent bread or whatever was necessary for people or pack animals to the place where they travelled. For this purpose only sixty fish were brought; of these, the individual fish sufficed for no fewer than two hundred men. Moreover, of wine they had only one small cask of the kind that an ass is accustomed to carry double. After this was poured into a drinking vessel, through the power of the saint it was enough that it provided drink sufficiently for five hundred men and more through the whole night, and more wine remained for the next day.

In fact, his body was not placed in the dwellings of the brothers, but in a very large exterior house that they had so that more people might be received and access would not be forbidden to the devout women. Of course, this house was entirely wooden and covered with straw. Indeed, in honor of the saint and for the repose of those who came there, it was strewn below with the same straw up to the knees. It contained such a great number of burning candles that it appeared to those looking on from outside as if it were a huge pyre.

I consider it more wondrous than all wonders that amidst so great an abundance of straw, amidst so many men sleeping and half-awake, the fire could harm nothing. For even those who were awake were occupied with the sacred rites around the holy body; the rest were all around half-awake or entirely asleep.

Then, when the night was now just beginning, all the clerics, dressed in albs and with many wearing silk copes, solemnly carried out the first vigils. After these were finished, the others who had remained and those who had then arrived from different places (as they did not cease to arrive through the whole night) prepared themselves for other vigils. Thus, with alternating vigils through the entire night, the holy rites did not cease, so that from the voices of the clerics chanting psalms, just as from the brilliance of the gleaming lights, the very night took on the clarity and dignity of the day, as it is written: 'Since the shadows will not be darkened by you and the night will be made light as day' (Ps 138:12).

6. Arising in the morning, they took up the saint's body and hastened as quickly as possible to the monastery at Obazine. However,

they were expected at the monastery at Tulle because the abbot[53] and monks there had insisted that the body should be placed in their church for a time. And when they approached there, with the bells then sounding, all the monks were solemnly vested, and they processed a long distance to meet the holy body with crosses and censers and with all the people. They had agreed (as later became clear) that they would forcibly detain the body in their church or would take some part of it for relics. Foreseeing this, after the absolution was given, the brothers immediately raised it onto their shoulders and turned around. They went back by the way they had come.

7. At Obazine, the passing of the blessed man did not become known until early Monday morning. Then mass was said immediately after prime. Then all, from the least to the greatest, processed up to two miles to meet their holy father with weeping and wailing and with the cross preceding them. They chanted psalms throughout the whole journey, as best they could in such a disaster. Indeed, they had decided that they would not return, except with the saint's corpse. Although some of the brothers coming from the saint's entourage drove them away and forced them to go back, saying that he would come at length, they could never keep them from the journey they had begun.

When, now weary, they had reached the level ground of a certain promontory, with their eyes uplifted they suddenly saw the preparations of the holy funeral go forth from that monastery (Tulle) with a vast crowd and proceed as quickly as possible toward them. Also, a multitude of noblemen had come there with countless others of each sex and age. Many of them brought new candles, and with their lamps lighted, they awaited the arrival of the saint with the monks and with all the people.

And behold, when he appeared, when he was at hand, when he could be touched, so great a cry arose suddenly that it was thought not only that the earth, but also the sky was shaken in some measure. I confess that I have never heard so great and so terrible an outcry, such a great lamentation, so great a clamor, and, finally, so

53. Gerard d'Escorailles.

great a simultaneous outpouring of tears. Indeed, who could have such a heart of iron that he could restrain himself from weeping when he saw so many sons around their most-beloved father, lamenting and embracing the remains of the deceased with vain and empty hopes? For even those who arrived on horses let go of the reins and fell to the ground, and watering it with their tears, they poured forth unbearable lamentation.

Now among the brothers there was no order, no discipline, no moderation. They assaulted the saint not only with their hands, but also with their teeth. Like madmen, they impatiently bit the bier itself, and unless defenders had stood in their way, striking and repelling the monks no less than the crowds, they would have done no less than tear it entirely apart with their bites. And since the saint was completely covered with priestly vestments, only his hand was exposed for all to kiss. Yet this was still so warm and pliant that it differed in no way from the hands of any living person. These were the ways they brought the saint's body, snatched away rather than lifted up, hurrying with all the people to the monastery at Obazine.

8. And so, when we had arrived together with him at the monastery, Abbot Gerald, the venerable lord recalled at length above, who had already arrived, was waiting dressed in holy vestments, with the few who had stayed behind and with many others who had gathered outside. Seeing the bier at hand and the saint lying on it whom he had always been accustomed to observe standing firmly in the house or in the Lord's work, he suddenly fainted as he made ready to absolve him, and fell forward over the bier as if he were dead. Then the grief of all was renewed and, as if they had done nothing before, they sent forth voices of outcry and wailing no less than on that mountain. The human spirit has this nature, that, although it has been sated with grief and tears, after it has seen others weeping, it cannot keep itself from weeping; its tears do not cease when the reasons for tears do not cease. Finally, the abbot recovered, but he was scarcely able to utter the words of absolution. He absolved the blessed man, insofar as it was in his power to do so.

Since the new monastery was located beyond the boundaries, they stood watch over the revered body until vespers, on account of the people who were waiting, and especially the women. Then, when night was already falling, the body was carried to the church with the singing of psalms and with great honor. There it was watched with unceasing rites for that whole night and the following day and the next night until Wednesday. As long as the body was in the church, the customary order could not be kept, so great was the coming and going of crowds bringing offerings, kissing the hand and the bier, and passing frequently under it, while before the saint they placed their complaints and implored his aid as if he were still living.

But while those were leaving, others were entering, and after them others and still others, so that there was no respite from the throng of those coming in and going out. But if anyone had tried to prevent them, I believe that they would have violently broken down all barriers and caused serious destruction.

Many sick among the brothers of the monastery and the flowing crowd were cured: some from paralysis, others from swelling, others from headache and the onset of diverse fevers, or even from mental aberration. The names or number of these persons who were cured there either while sleeping or passing under the bier, or while it was kept outside or throughout the entire journey, could not be collected so that they could be written down, either because of the vast multitude or because there was no one who had a care for such matters, especially since there was not anyone then who had decided to describe his life or thought about it.

Thus, for two days the saint was kept under watch, not because of the expectation of the people, but on account of the preparation of his tomb, and so that certain abbots who lived far away might at least come to the burial, as they did. For then, all were present.

9. And so on Wednesday of the second week in Lent, after a mass for all had been said and absolution had been solemnly given by all the abbots who had come from different places or orders (for the bishop was not in that area then), the body of the blessed man was brought into the chapter-house to be buried and was placed in a stone coffin.

Along with the bands of brothers and multitudes of monks, there were present many thousands of people who filled all the spaces inside and outside. They were so crowded together throughout the cloister and next to the chapter house that they obscured all the brightness of daylight, except what was produced by candles. With their mournful cries they drowned out the voices of those chanting psalms. And so, as soon as the saint was buried thus, the litter for the corpse was torn apart and broken up into little pieces, with individuals seizing parts for themselves as each one could and obstinately fighting among themselves for them. Indeed, the bier itself, cut up with saws and hacked into small parts with iron tools, was carried off. People even bound the small bits that fell from the teeth of the saw in little pieces of cloth and took them away with them. So great was the faith and devotion of the people that nothing which had touched the saint's body was thought to be without benefit.

10. After these events transpired, all the people went away. The monks gathered around the tomb and chanted psalms through the entire day until vespers, as is the custom on Good Friday. But the candles also remained there, burning through that whole day and night, so that even to this day, during all the nights, the light of oil or candle or both at the same time is never lacking there. None of these is at the expense of the monastery. They are all provided from outside, both from those who rush devoutly and frequently to the tomb and from those who experience many cures there. But even those who are cured in their own homes through invocation of the saint send their candles there or bring candles there themselves, both before their cure and after, first when asking, afterward when returning thanks.

Not only do people pray for people, but also for beasts or herds that are sick. For these also they send candles, so that what is written might be fulfilled: 'Lord, you will save men and beasts' (Ps 35:7). Not even for these are they known to implore in vain, for sick beasts are immediately cured and the healthy ones do not fall sick thereafter.

But also in the time of the barbarian persecution, when their hostile savagery devastated everything all around, certain people fled to him and brought back his protection with them. Neither did they experience a loss of possessions or captivity, although all the rest lost all their goods at once. After their possessions were destroyed, many became themselves captives of the enemy. Some were even placed in chains and dungeons, so that their feet were bound in very tight stocks. The saint appeared as soon as he was invoked, ordering them to rise and take off the stocks by which they were held captive, and it happened right away that the wood fell apart as if it were rotten. And when they were now free, they began to object, saying: 'Lord, how shall we get out of here, since everything is locked and guards are observing on every side?' Then he led them to a certain rear gate, which could hardly be cut down with axes and iron tools, but now was easily opened with a slight push of the hand, so that he might lead them through the midst of the troops of those who had captured them. And none of them even asked where he was going, nor did anyone presume to hold them back.

This was what happened in every respect to one of our brothers who died recently. It was the principal cause of his conversion. Although he was not the only one set free in this way, as is confirmed by the testimony of many people, yet of the persons whom the power of the saint freed in this manner we do not recall their identities, nor have we learned so clearly from their mouths the truth of what happened. However, when we come to this subject, we shall describe very clearly the liberation of certain ones, so that from these will be understood the many others whom we have heard were set free in a similar manner, yet whom we do not recall.

Now we must report about those things that were observed concerning him after his passing, and how he often appeared to certain ones, and by appearing gave them good health.

11. When a certain brother was possessed by excessive grief after Stephen's death, and he was stupefied by that sorrow, the blessed man stood before him in a vision and said to him: 'Why is it, Brother, that you are depressed by so great a sorrow?' To him the brother responded: 'We are sad and violently afflicted, Lord, because you were willing to abandon us so quickly, although you were able still to live long for us and to govern your monastery prosperously and happily.' The saint said to him: 'And so, do I not seem to you to be the abbot, just as you were always accustomed to see me?' The brother said to him: 'If you are truly our abbot, how is it that we now see another in your place?' Then, with a pleasant countenance, as if he were smiling, the saint responded to him thus: 'I have not forsaken you nor do I abandon you on account of this abbot, but wherever he goes, I shall remain with you always.'

12. Lord Robert was then abbot of Frenade. After his third ordination as abbot, he presided over our monastery. When the burial of our most holy father had been completed, the abbot was seated at table in the refectory with the brothers, as is accustomed to happen at such an event. Overcome by weariness and sorrow, he was dozing off. Suddenly, two of our brothers who had died some years before appeared to him. One was a priest, the other a deacon. They were well-known acquaintances of ours once, holy and religious men. When they asked with cheerful faces the reasons for his sadness, and with tears he described the death of the holy man and their common bereavement, they said to him: 'Lord, you should know that as great as is the sadness among you over his departure, so great is the happiness everywhere among us over his presence.' After these words were spoken, he awoke and could not see them anymore.

In fact, after the same abbot had returned to his own monastery, while he was sitting in church and watching over a certain deceased monk with the brothers, between the delays in preparing the tomb and his sadness for a lost loved one, he was overcome by sleep. He saw the aforementioned brother standing before him crying out and saying: 'Lord Father, have mercy on me and help me as much as you can!' The abbot said to him: 'What is it? Why are you suffering, and what do you want from me?' He responded, 'I was in the presence of our common father, Lord Stephen. Other brothers of ours flee to him, but he refused to receive me because I did not keep his precepts. He said that I should go to my abbot and he might help me.' Then the abbot awoke in fear, and that brother did not appear to him thereafter. Therefore, it is evident that this brother had acted negligently in his order and had been rebuked by the saint, but he was not forgotten, because he sought blessings from his abbot and his soul was released from punishments and torments.

13. A certain illustrious and powerful knight came to the monastery of Obazine at a time long after the passing of the holy man. He was seized by a certain sickness there and died after two months. Since he was the lord of many lands, he had fought many battles to defend them, and he had committed many wicked deeds. Indeed, he loved the blessed man and all the brothers very much, and he had enriched them with lands in his dominion. On account of this

he was brought to a good confession and a good end, as far as we believe and could know.

However, during the very night on which he died, a certain priest from his land, although he did not know anything at all about what was going on concerning him (in fact, he was situated far away), was suddenly transported in ecstasy, and he saw that man being led away, captured by demons. In the place through which he was being led there was on one side a magnificent, lofty wall whose end was not visible. In the middle it had a gate through which the sweetest voices of people singing psalms poured forth to the outside. And when they drew near the place, the man began to ask those who were dragging him to let him go a little so that he might listen to those aforementioned mellifluous voices. He did not obtain this wish at all, but suddenly he was torn away from the demons by the divine will. He fled to the aforementioned gate and found it open. Moreover, seeing the holy Mother of God and Queen of virgins standing inside with the saints, he fell forward on the ground and began to beseech her to have pity on him and to free him from the captivity of the demons through her mercy. To him she responded: 'O Man, I cannot help you, because you invaded, despoiled and violated many churches of my Son's and mine. You also slaughtered many men and did many other wicked deeds.' Then Lord Stephen, who was standing on the side, threw himself down at her knees and besought her, saying: 'My Lady, did you not promise me that you would lead all who die in my house into the joy of your Son?' With a kind and happy countenance she responded to him: 'Know for certain, my dearest son, that I shall surely fulfil whatever promise I have made to you.' After these words were spoken, the priest was recalled from his ecstasy. He could not know fully what had then been done concerning that man. It is clear enough that the man had been handed over to the demons so that he might know whom he had served by living wickedly, and then through the saint's intercession he had been set free by the mother of mercy that he might recognize how much Stephen could obtain through the mercy of God and His mother for those whom he especially loved.

14. A certain lay-brother, but one who was simple and naive, loved the holy man exceedingly and was loved by him in a special way. When this brother arose for vigils before the others on a certain

Sunday and was passing by the monks' cloister, as was his custom, he heard the voices of monks chanting psalms as if they were in a procession. Among these, there resounded more clearly and strongly the voice of the man of God, as if he were leading the procession. And since that same cloister was barred shut, because it was night-time, he hurried to the church so that there he might more conveniently hear the voices of those chanting psalms and he might see, if he could, the man of God standing in his own place. But when he entered the church, those voices became silent and could not be heard anymore.

Hence it is clear both from the previous vision and from what this brother certainly heard, that the man of God never neglects this place, and that he chants the offices of divine praise for us in church and in the cloister, even though we are sleeping.

15. A certain strong, young brother was in charge of the teams of oxen. Because of lifting a load, or some other reason, he suffered a rupture. It became heavy, or to speak more clearly, herniated. And since this weight protruded above his groin and increased more and more from day to day, that brother began to have difficulty walking, and he grew sick at heart. He was ashamed that the thing stuck out, and he could not conceal it because of its size. Since such an injury could not be cured without incision, which was formerly forbidden in our order, he was more anxious about it, both because the illness weighed upon him and because there was no hope of healing it. Therefore, destitute of human help, he had recourse to divine aid. Often he fell prostrate before his tomb and incessantly prayed to holy father Stephen to assist him in so great an affliction with a salutary remedy. Thus, on a certain night the holy man appeared to him and began to ask, as if he did not know, why the brother was besetting him with so many cries and why he remained so sad. When the brother explained all his suffering to him, he received from him such consolation as this: 'Do not be too sad over this injury,' he said, 'for in the near future you will be cured by God.'

While he was keeping watch, the brother observed that no remedy had come to him. Yet, since he had been worthy to see the man of God, he was very happy for this consolation. Indeed, not a long time afterward, the saint appeared to him again in the same way as before and asked him how he was. The brother truly gave thanks for his visitation and responded that so far he had not been helped. Then the saint, in keeping with the divine will, completely cured the protruding tumor pressing upon it with his healing touch and, as it were, pushed it back into itself, and he said to him: 'Arise and do not be idle any longer, but strive to carry out promptly the work enjoined upon you.' At this word, he was instantly stirred. He arose and discovered, when he touched the place of his infirmity, that it was so flat outside and so sound inside that it was as if he had never suffered such an injury.

I recently heard this from the mouth of our abbot himself: that the brother, who for a long time was pale and looked like one about to die, now is strong and active; he carries out his work very vigorously.

16. Stephen also appeared sometimes to the nuns who were sick, especially when one of them lay near death. Recently a certain nun told me about when one of the sisters was near death and all were standing around her in the usual way. Since she was still alive after the litanies and psalms had been recited, they all returned to their own beds. When the one who told this was taking off her shoes and was ready to lie down, she was still concerned for that sister. Suddenly, the holy man stood before her bed and said to her: 'Arise as quickly as possible, because that sister is now dying.' When he had said this, the sounding board was heard and, when the others had assembled and were praying, that sister died in peace.

17. Also, at another time, when night was already falling, one of the sick nuns was entrusted to certain sisters to be watched over in expectation of her death. But since they did not believe that she would die that night, gradually they gave up the watch, and all positioned themselves for sleeping around her bed. But around midnight, the holy father, full of care, appeared to a certain one in the dormitory (I know not whether she was sleeping or awake) and ordered her to get up. Since she was sluggish and delaying, he began to pull off her covers and said to her: 'Get up quickly. Light a candle and spread ashes, because that sister is going to die directly.' Then she was stirred. She arose, and when she saw that she was surrounded by darkness, she said: 'And how can I light a candle, Lord, since

the lamp in the dormitory is now out and I do not know where to find fire.' He said to her: 'Go to the kitchen and there you will find it well enough.' She proceeded to the kitchen, but she found no fire there except one little spark that was so small that it could not withstand the force of a slight breeze. Although she did not dare to blow on it at all, lest she might extinguish it entirely, suddenly a copious flame arose, as if from straw set on fire. From this she lit the candle, not without wonder. Then she ran to the infirmary and found that sister already at the point of death and her caretakers sleeping around her. After they were awakened, she immediately strewed the ashes with them, as she had been ordered, and blessed them, and placed that sister upon them. She struck the sounding-board, and at this sound all were assembled; after they had prayed enough, that sister breathed forth her spirit.

18. Some sisters, who were negligently remaining behind in the infirmary, he compelled to go to church, especially if they were to receive the sacred mysteries. But if they could not rise from bed, he showed how or with what assistance they might be brought there, just as recently he instructed a certain one on this matter sufficiently through a vision. He did not want to give up any occasion to come to them, especially those at the point of death, so that they might recognize that he had not set aside after death the care that he had for them while he was alive. He even cured certain ones, who were plagued by very serious illnesses, of their excessive weakness by appearing to them or by touching them, so that those who could not even lie still before or who disturbed the others with their loud cries, suddenly arose from bed. This is clearly shown in the following example.

When a certain sister whom I knew well, but her name escapes me, was walking in the middle of the house, wood falling from the ceiling above struck her and seriously injured her leg. Knocked to the ground by this accident, she was almost unconscious. Running to her from all sides and putting her in a blanket, the sisters carried her with difficulty to the infirmary. After a little while, she came to herself again. When she realized that she was suffering very grievously, she began to scream endlessly, which the extreme pain forced her to do. Amid those very screams she often cried out to Lord Stephen and with a loud voice implored him to help her.

Near midnight, when the sisters were sleeping around her, she could not sleep because of the extreme pain. Without delay, Father Stephen suddenly appeared, and a young man wearing a monk's habit followed him. Stephen took hold of the leg that was in pain. When he began to pull it with one hand near the foot and the other on the upper part, he inflicted so much pain on her that all the sisters around her were awakened by the loud cry she raised. When the sisters ran to her from all sides, the holy man disappeared. The saint whom she was able to see and feel before, when she was infirm, could no longer be seen. However, she motioned to the sisters with her hand (since it was not the time for talking) that they should go away and allow her to rest a little, since she was now doing well. Then, when the sisters assembled at dawn, she related to them how the saint had cured her that night when he pressed on her pain. And so, after a little while, she rose up, cured, from her bed. She showed no evidence of the past fracture.

19. A certain Sister Eustorgia was so gravely ill that she could not rise from her bed or even turn herself to either side without assistance. One day around vespers, when she was suffering with extreme pain, another sister happened to be passing by her bed. With her hands stretched out and with tears in her eyes, she implored that sister to help her a little for God's sake, so that she might relieve her sick body somewhat by changing sides. However, that sister was moved by bitterness because she had worked all day waiting on other sisters. Among other shameful words which she then hurled at her, she even cursed herself, saying: 'May my hand and foot wither if I bring you aid now!' Saying these words, she passed by.

And so, on the following night, when that sister arose from bed after sleep and wanted to go somewhere, and had already proceeded a little distance, as she was then very healthy and unimpaired in all her limbs, suddenly she sensed that her foot was weighed down. When she grasped the frame of a little bed (which she had then reached by chance) with her hand, so that at least by leaning on it she could continue, immediately the same malady took possession of her hand and rendered it useless. Then, after she fell to the floor, she dragged herself over the ground as best she could with the one hand and foot which were left to her, so that the sisters running to her aid and pitying her misfortune brought her with difficulty to the infirmary and placed her on a little couch that had been prepared. Then, after a little while, they all returned to their own beds.

Perceiving that she had been left alone, with her eyes raised upward, she groaned to the Lord, and with great sorrow in her heart she called upon the Lord and holy Father Stephen to assist her in the very great distress into which she had been put. While she lay awake and in prayer, the holy father immediately appeared. Looking upon her with a stern countenance, he said: 'Wretched sister, this has happened to you just as you deserve. For you should know that this has come about because yesterday you shunned that sister who was beseeching you, and you refused to help her. Moreover, you bound yourself by a wicked curse. Hence, this has justly taken hold of you according to what you deserve. And unless we had interceded for you, you would not be suffering such afflictions, but you would have died a sudden death. But it is also fitting that you know this, because as long as you live, you will never be without this suffering. Hence, do not hesitate to speak on our behalf to the other sisters, so that warned by your example they will not despise their sick sisters, but will serve them according to their own ability, lest even worse should befall them.' Saying these words, he was taken away from her sight.

When morning came, the sisters returned to visit the sick one. They tried to console her and assured her of remedies to restore her health. She responded: 'In no way will it be as you say, for it has been determined otherwise by the Lord God.' Then she related to them how she had seen Lord Stephen that night, and what he had said to her, and what he had ordered to be told to the others. And so it happened that Sister Eustorgia passed from this life first, and then that sister followed, with no other coming between.

Since we said above that many people were set free from prisons and chains through Stephen's patronage, and we promised to return to some of them, let us now carry out what we promised.

20. There was a certain layman who lived beyond the river Dordogne. He loved the man of God as a close friend, and he in turn was loved with no small affection by Stephen and the brothers because of the devotion of his faith and the favors frequently done by him. After Stephen's death, this man was seized by evildoers. He was put in chains and shackles, and because of the wealth that he was believed to have, he was kept under strict guard.

When this was reported to our brothers, they were exceedingly troubled. On their own and through friends they began to entreat those who held him prisoner to accept their plea and release to them their confrere, whom they held unjustly. They could accomplish nothing, but the captors became even harsher. In fact, when the captured man saw that he could be aided by no one, he approached with prayers (not feet) his former friend, now truly his patron, Lord Stephen. With many groans, he prayed that Stephen might free him by his prayers if he had influence with God. Then, overcome by sleep because of his great weariness and sadness, he saw standing before him the same beneficent father, as if he were reproving him and saying: 'Why do you sit here when the needs of your house are neglected and your household is going to ruin?' To him that man responded: 'Lord, do you not see how I am held here tightly-bound and shackled and cannot break out?' Repeating his words to him, the saint said: 'Go in safety. Do not hesitate, because those chains which you fear will not harm you.' At this word, the man awoke immediately. When he tried to rise, all the chains suddenly fell from his hands and feet. He attempted again to stand up, but he fell on account of his numbness, for his shins had been damaged by the shackles. But, standing up later, he considered what to do, since he feared very much to go forth because the guards and those who had captured him were watching on all sides; almost all were standing outside in the open. Yet faith in his patron won out, so that through the midst of his guards and captors, since no other way was open, he returned a free man to his own home. No one asked him where he was going, nor was he held back.

21. The son of this man was recently captured in a similar way. Bound hand and foot, he was put in a small cask that was open on one end. After he had been placed inside, it was tightly closed as if wine were being kept in it, not a man. Placed in such great straits, he was already despairing of his life. At last he remembered Lord Stephen, about whom he had heard much, but he had never seen him. He immediately had recourse to his help, praying with many cries and sighs that just as the saint had once rescued his father from chains, so now he might hasten quickly to set him free. While he turned these things over in his mind amidst tears, suddenly he was freed of all chains, except that he was still enclosed within the cask.

When his friends and relatives arrived to visit and to ransom him, he was led outside. When the guards saw him free, they were extremely agitated. They bound him with even stronger chains and thrust him again into the cask in such a way that between the top of the cask and a beam of the house they placed planks of wood pressing strongly against the top, so that no strong blow could move them. However, their malice was no benefit to them at all. For as soon as that man implored the assistance of his faithful liberator, all his bonds were suddenly loosened a second time, although he still did not see his liberator in all these events. Then, he stretched out his hands and lightly touched the top of the cask. All the planks that had been piled upon it suddenly fell to the ground. The cask itself was split into pieces so that, freed from the shattered barrel, he leaped out, just as if he were a chick leaping from a broken egg. And, (lest we delay), thanks to such speedy assistance, he departed a free man just as his father had once done, with his enemies present and looking on, so that when he had passed by, they only marveled and said: 'Isn't this the man whom we were guarding after he had been bound so carefully? How is it that we have now permitted him to go away, right before our eyes as we are stationed here? Truly, since divine power has set him free, we have no strength against him.'

Therefore, paying his vows to his liberator, this devout man went to Stephen's tomb on the feast day of Saint Mary's nativity. When asked, he explained to us, who were assembled in chapter for the observance of so great a day, how he had been set free. And he gained for himself as many faithful witnesses of his liberation as he had hearers.

22. Another man, a certain peasant, was captured in the same region by two brothers who were leaders of bandits, for this purpose only, that he might redeem himself by a payment of money. One of them led the man bound before him, or rather drove him, while the other followed after them. Both were accompanied by a large troop of bandits.

And so, while he grieved that he was bound and being led away, he lamented in such a way that he was more tormented on account of fear and expectation of things to come than by those which he was suffering at the present time. Indeed, he saw that there would be no hope for him of escaping, just as if a sheep were held captive among wolves. Finally, after he regained a little hope, he immediately had recourse to God's help. He recalled Lord Stephen because of the example of the two men described above whom he had heard were liberated. Since he could not and dared not invoke him with his voice, he called upon Stephen with all his heart to aid him in the great danger in which he had been placed. And although he expressed this in sighs more than in words, immediately the chains fell from his hands as if someone had suddenly released him. When he thus, in a wondrous manner, had gained confidence that he could get away, he started to depart from the way in another direction, as if he were being led by someone, so that free and unhindered he returned to his own home without anyone questioning him or following after him. Released in this manner from captivity, he gave a gift of thanks to his rescuer, having as witnesses of his salvation even those who had captured him and dared not pursue him as he walked away.

23. Recently, a certain man came to the saint's sepulcher. After he said a prayer and placed a candle there, he had departed from the place. I took him aside and asked who he was and where he came from and for what reason he had sought out the saint's tomb. Then he said: 'I and four others were taken captive in the castle of Gagnac, which is beyond the Dordogne. The feet of all of us were bound very tightly together to one beam. When we had tasted no food or bread at all for four days in this dungeon, I was oppressed by hunger and grief at the same time. I began to pray from the depths of my heart to holy father Stephen, about whom I had heard many things, to free us from these chains through his merits and prayers. And while I was turning over this matter in my mind, I was transported as if into ecstasy. Neither fully awake nor completely asleep, I saw a certain most venerable man in religious habit enter the prison, accompanied by one monk of youthful age. When he had asked me how I was and what I was requesting from him with such great lamentation, I said to him: 'Lord, you see in how much affliction and calamity we are held. Hence we pray that you have pity on us and help us if you can'. Then he said: 'If you want to be set free along with your companions, seize quickly the wooden nail with which the stocks are held tight and it will soon be loosened. Then rising immediately, go forth with these others. Proceed any-

where, and you can be kept safe'. At this word I awoke right away, and he vanished from my sight. Immediately, I seized the nail and drew it out with a slight movement. Soon that beam was as loose as if it had never been tightened. I arose and gently roused my companions, warning them to get up cautiously lest perchance anyone should wake up. It was around midnight. We feared not less, but more, when we were free than before when we were bound, because the guards were sleeping inside in front of the door. We could not pass by except through their midst, and the door itself was purposely shut so firmly that it could not be opened without a loud noise'. Finally, hurling their hearts into peril, as the saying goes, and strengthening their spirits with confidence and trust in him who had already set them free, they passed by the guards and went out through the open door without anyone hearing or sensing them. And so, they spent the remaining interval of night in making their journey. Just at twilight, they arrived at Château-Neuf, which was almost two miles away, and there they were safe.

24. A certain man wanted to go from his own home to another town situated far away. He carried with him some coins. After he passed through a grove that he had entered, he came to a wide stretch of field. When he raised his eyes, he saw at a distance some bandits who were accustomed to watch the roads and paths. They would drag strangers or those whom they met on the way and captured to secluded places and force them with torture to pay ransom, or even murder them. Thus, trembling at this sight and almost beside himself for fear, the man did not know what to do. He dared not go back, lest they should pursue him, nor proceed as before, lest he be captured. He was not afraid now for the money, which he considered lost, but more for himself, lest he be abducted alive, or killed if he resisted.

And so, destitute of all other hope, he had recourse to divine aid and to that holy father by whom he had heard that many men were liberated. From the depths of his heart he began to pray that Stephen might swiftly help him now that he was placed in such great peril, and that the saint might obtain through his prayers before God that he might not be captured.

The sky was so serene that no cloud was visible in the atmosphere. When the man had prayed for these things with all his heart, a certain slight mist arose from the ground. It spread so great a fog between that man and the bandits that they could not see him nor could he see them thereafter. He continued safely on the road by which he was going with all fear of harm removed. Now let us relate how Stephen assisted certain people in the matter of lost possessions.

25. A certain brother lost some coins that had been entrusted to him in such a way that he did not doubt that someone had stolen them. Although he did not dare to accuse anyone of this by name, there were two youths among those who were being taught there who, because of their faults, were particularly indicated as perpetrators of this theft or as knowing about it. However, they denied this with such great obstinacy and with such frightful oaths that no one could even have suspicion about them.

Therefore, the brother who had lost the coins was destitute of all hope in his investigation. He had recourse to the merits of the holy father, offering a candle at his tomb and praying with confidence that Stephen might obtain for him definite proof from the Lord about this matter and that the perpetrators of the theft might be detected. Instantly, one of the aforementioned youths was seized by a fever and brought to the point of death. While he anxiously sought someone to whom he might confess the secrets of his heart, he became mute before anyone arrived. Then God had mercy on him. He regained the use of his speech around midnight and confessed to the priest now standing before him that his companion had stolen the coins that were being sought, and he knew of it. When he had told these things and accepted his penance, he expired not many hours later. When they came to the other youth, who had been discovered through the testimony of his now-deceased companion, he was unwilling to confess, but denied the theft even more obstinately. Immediately, he was seized by a very powerful fever. When he feared to die in the same way, he confessed with his own mouth that he had stolen not only the coins about which he was accused, but very many others as well. However, he did not die then, for shortly afterward he was restored to health.

Thus the holy man judged fittingly about both, so that the first one who had perhaps sinned less was snatched from this life immediately, lest while living he might be changed for the worse.

The second youth was saved for penance, lest dying he might be snatched away to eternal punishments for these and other thefts.

26. There was a certain priest at the church of Saint Hilaire,[54] which is situated within sight of our monastery at a distance of about one mile. Once, while he was having breakfast around the sixth hour, a thief entered the church. With certain devices he secretly opened the church coffer and then, after almost two hundred coins were removed along with certain other things, he fled in secret, with no one knowing about it.

After his meal, the priest happened to enter the church. When he discovered that the coffer had been broken into and the coins stolen, he was filled with such great grief and sadness that he almost lost his mind, for he could find no indication of who had done this. At last, he returned to his senses. On the advice of friends, he sought out our monastery so that he might obtain from our holy father Stephen some relief in this great calamity. Then, having lit a candle, taking off his shoes he prostrated himself at his tomb. He entrusted his complaints to the saint with such great lamentation and such deep sighs that he could certainly not have been more afflicted by the most grievous sins.

Then, after he had gained a measure of confidence, he went outside. We comforted him accordingly, as was necessary in such a disaster. After a span of two or three hours, a messenger sent from the church came to him in great haste and reported that the thief had been arrested with the coins and the other things that he had stolen. When the priest heard this, he leaped with such great joy that we cannot describe it. By reason of this, what the prophet said seemed to be fulfilled in him: 'According to the multitude of sorrows in my heart, your consolations have gladdened my soul' (Ps 93:19). And when he inquired diligently 'in what hour the thief' (Mt 24:43) had been discovered, he found that it was the very same one in which he had faithfully sought out the patronage of the saint.

27. A certain head of a household had two oxen which he held very dear, both for the sake of agriculture and also because they

54. Saint-Hilaire-Peyroux.

were outstanding in size and strength. However, it happened that a pestilence among the animals devastated that entire region far and wide, so that all the peasants' barnyards were left almost empty of animals. Moreover, when one day the aforementioned man saw those oxen of his staggering, he was afraid that they might die in his farmyard. He ordered his wife to drive them a distance away so that they might not infect the animals which had not yet incurred the sickness. To him the wife responded: 'By no means should we do this, Lord, but rather let us make statues of them and cover them with wax and send them to holy father Stephen. If he wishes, he can save those oxen and keep the others safe from all danger.'

The counsel of his prudent wife pleased the husband. Then, he took the measure of the oxen with ropes from the front and back. Covering them with wax, he sent them to the monastery to be burned at the saint's tomb. When this had been done, not only were those oxen suddenly made well, but also the rest of the animals remained unharmed thereafter, just as the faithful wife had promised.

28. After a few years, when the animals had been replaced throughout that land, a certain knight, one of those who are wont to engage in taking plunder, had lost many possessions at the games that they call 'The Greater Games.' Seeking to restore the losses he had suffered by numerous plunderings and ravaging everything all around, he even led away captive with him those oxen along with much booty. When the man mentioned above returned to his house around evening, he learned that his oxen had been captured. Then he fell to the ground, crying and shouting with a great clamor: 'Ah me, Lord Stephen, our father, how have I lost my oxen that you saved before and which I entrusted to your faithful protection? But you who could save them from dying, how is it that now you have been unwilling to save them from being stolen? Surely, if you do not restore them to me, I shall never again pay the customary vows for them.' For in fact he used to send those waxen-statues every year.

When he had said these words, behold, those oxen suddenly ran away from the midst of the plunder and took turns driving themselves with very great swiftness without anyone urging them on. They returned home as if they were impelled by many men threatening them from behind. None of those robbers could hold them back or pursue them. There is no doubt that they were led back by the power of that one whose intercession had been implored concerning them.

29. Afterward, when the same man was violently afflicted by a quartan fever, and the physician who was called wanted to give him a potion to drive out the sickness, his wife did not agree. She said to her husband: 'Lord, it is not right that you, who were long ago aided by the power of a saint, should now receive worldly medicine. But rather, go with faith to his tomb and he will grant the health you desire as you pray to him.'

Hearing this, that man agreed with this wise counsel. On a day when the onslaught of the fever was approaching, he went with some other men to the monastery, which was almost two miles away. In the midst of the journey, when he was passing near the house in which stones were cut and brothers stayed, he was suddenly seized by the fever. He lay on the ground and began to be so grievously distressed that it was thought he would die immediately. Then, after the brothers were called to his aid, he was carried just like a corpse by his companions and those brothers to their house, and placed on a small bed. When his companions had departed and he remained in agony, suddenly he saw Lord Stephen dressed in holy vestments coming to him, along with certain white monks. When the saint stood together with his comrades at the bed where the man was lying down, he sprinkled him with blessed water and recited those prayers that are accustomed to be said over the sick. He restored him so completely to health that the man continued to be very healthy from then on. Directly, the man of God disappeared. After the brothers were summoned, the man reported fully what had happened to him. Then, after he eagerly took food, which he had abhorred for many days, he, who had been brought there half-alive, went away in good health. This I heard myself from the mouth of that man.

30. Peter, a priest at Pleaux,[55] was a man renowned for integrity and noble birth. He incurred a pain in his eyes which, increasing little by little, invaded his whole head and then his entire body. And so, despairing of life, he remembered Lord Stephen, who was formerly

55. See 1.1; 3.30.

his pupil and dear friend. He gave a candle to a boy and sent him off, instructing him to go quickly to the saint's tomb and there to implore God's mercy for his health, through the merits of the saint. So this was done. At that very hour his master recovered from his malady, so that at the first light of morning the priest arose from his bed, went to the church, and took part in the celebration of masses for it was the feast of the Purification, which is called 'The Meeting of the Lord.'[56]

But since the priest neglected to go to render thanks, the renewed pain, of which he had just been cured, afflicted his eyes until he sought out the saint's tomb himself. And so, after some days, he returned to his own place happy and healthy.

31. A certain woman who lived beyond the Dordogne, a widow, lost the sight in her eyes and remained blind for a whole year. However, she heard about the powers of Lord Stephen. Since she could not go to him, from her own house, as was written,[57] she prayed to the Lord with constant prayers that through the loving and enduring merits of that saint she might recover the needed sight, which she had justly lost through her own wicked deserts. When she begged for this faithfully for two days, she recovered the sight in her eyes, so that she saw everything clearly.[58]

Knowing that no woman ever entered his monastery, and because a journey of such length was dangerous for her, she directed her servant-boy to travel to the place bearing a candle in his hand. On the very vigil of the Purification, this boy came to the tomb of the saint together with the servant-boy of the priest named above, whom he met along the way. He placed there what he had brought, that is a light for light, and thanks for health. And so it happened that on the next day when all were gathered in the chapter meeting, the prayer of each was reported: of the one asking that his master might obtain his health; of the other rendering the thanks for his mistress for the cure she had received.

56. *'Ypapanti Domini'*, the meeting of Jesus with the aged Simeon.

57. Ex 16:29.

58. Mk 8:25.

32. A certain widow who lived in the territory of Turenne castle once entrusted herself and her possessions to Lord Stephen. She had nothing on which to live except what she acquired by working with her own hands.

However, while one of the sergeants of the viscount was exacting kitchen-dues from the individual dwellings, he came to the widow to demand them. She said that she was taking nothing from the land for which she might be obligated to pay anything, nor did she have any provisions beyond what she had gathered by gleaning during the past summer or collecting ears of corn in the fields of others. When that same tax-collector took this little bit which had been stored away in a sack, along with a few hens, that widow resisted as much as she could, partly by pleading with tears, partly by threatening, so that he would not unjustly take away her sustenance and leave her to live in hunger, perhaps to perish. He not only disdained to listen to her, but beyond that, he kicked her. He went back the way he had come with those things he had carried off.

Then the poor woman fell to the ground. With her hands uplifted to Heaven, she cried out with mournful words to God, the Judge of widows, and to holy father Stephen, that if she could not obtain anything else, at least she might get revenge on that malefactor as a consolation. Her prayer was heard without delay. For soon a violent pain in the head assailed that unjust man while he was still on his journey, along with a very powerful fever and delirium, so that his head and his whole body were swelling up. He barely reached the next dwelling. From there he was supported and carried to his own house. After the space of not many hours, he expired, without viaticum and without any remedy for his salvation.

33. Also, another widow lived in a certain place next to our property. She had one little pig that was running about on her farm. It used to run in the brothers' crops, which were enclosed by no fence. When the ears of corn had begun to sprout, the little pig was frequently driven out. When it sensed that it was free, it ran back there again, so that the aforementioned woman could do almost nothing but constantly watch it and keep it out of the fields of other people. And when she was thinking of selling it so that it would not do constant damage . . . [the text breaks off at this point in the manuscripts and resumes at Chapter 34].

34. We have added another miracle that happened in that house at Obazine in the same year in which the holy father departed from this wretched world to eternal bliss.

There was a certain large house constructed of cheap wood near the new monastery, that is, near the church which was then being built, but far removed from the other houses. It happened that after the death of the man of God, it caught fire because, apart from the quality of the wood from which it was constructed, the house contained in it kindling-wood and many tools.

And when all the brothers came running from all sides to extinguish the blaze, they saw that the whole house was engulfed by fire inside and outside. Since they could not save it, they were stunned and stood off to the side. They grieved much for the loss of the house and of the things that were kept in it. The entire new building had then been covered on account of the approaching winter.

Meanwhile, a wind arising from the north had turned that whole conflagration with fury toward part of the new monastery, so much that the ends of the flames, with their leaping sparks, were reaching the highest parts of the roofs that were hanging down. Then, after a cry was raised, all left the house forsaken, which they could not save and immediately rushed to the new monastery and tried to uncover the part near the fire. Then, with all hearing him, one of the brothers, calling to mind Lord Stephen (for he had died that year), said: 'O holy father Stephen, how is it that you do not aid your house in so great a danger? For behold, the fire will consume everything which we provided to cover it, unless you assist us quickly, and the fire will turn the white walls black.'

While he was shouting so, the other brothers were invoking the name of the saint with loud cries. A wind from the south soon stirred itself and drove the north wind back, along with the roaring of the flames. The fire almost consumed the brothers who were standing secure on that side, and it left the house of God untouched.

We have composed these books on the life and deeds or miracles of the blessed man, although in an unskilled manner, as a testimony to his virtues. We passed over many of those things we heard or knew, so that an extended narration might not cause weariness in readers or listeners. At last, therefore, it is pleasing to make an end here, not because we have written here all the things which could deservedly be reported about him, for this would be impossible, but because we believe that these can suffice even for the most avid readers.

For all of these, we implore the mercy of God, through the merits of the saint, so that we might be able to imitate, according to our capacity, at least a small number of those great things which we have told, although unworthily, about him. Following in the footsteps of so great a father, may we be able to attain the eternal joys of Heaven, with him as our leader and guide. Amen.